Victims of Sexual Aggression:

Treatment of Children, Women, and Men

Victims of Sexual Aggression:

Treatment of Children, Women, and Men

Edited by

Irving R. Stuart, Ph.D.
Joanne G. Greer, Ph.D.

VNR VAN NOSTRAND REINHOLD COMPANY
NEW YORK CINCINNATI TORONTO LONDON MELBOURNE

Manufactured in the United States of America

Published by Van Nostrand Reinhold Company Inc.
135 West 50th Street
New York, New York 10020

Van Nostrand Reinhold Company Limited
Molly Millars Lane
Wokingham, Berkshire RG11 2PY, England

Van Nostrand Reinhold
480 Latrobe Street
Melbourne, Victoria 3000, Australia

Macmillan of Canada
Division of Gage Publishing Limited
164 Commander Boulevard
Agincourt, Ontario M1S 3C7, Canada

15 14 13 12 11 10 9 8 7 6 5 4 3 2 1

Library of Congress Cataloging in Publication Data
Main entry under title:

Victims of sexual aggression.

    Includes index.
    1. Rape victims—Care and treat—Addresses, essays,
lectures. 2. Incest victims—Care and treatment—
Addresses, essays, lectures. 3. Sexually abused children
—Care and treatment—Addresses, essays, lectures.
I. Stuart, Irving R. II. Greer, Joanne G. [DNLM:
1. Sex offenses. 2. Crisis intervention. WM 401
V642]
RC560.R36V53 1984   616.89   83-10264
ISBN 0-442-28087-4

List of Contributors

Christine Adams-Tucker, M.D.
Child Psychiatrist
Louisville, Kentucky

Paul L. Adams, M.D.
Kempner Professor of Child Psychiatry
University of Texas Medical Branch
Galveston, Texas

Ebrahim Amanat, M.D.
Clinical Assistant Professor of Psychiatry
St. Louis University Medical School
Medical Director, Child Center
  of Our Lady of Grace
St. Louis, Missouri

Judith V. Becker, Ph.D.
Associate Professor of Psychiatry
Columbia University College of
  Physicians and Surgeons
Research Scientist New York State
  Psychiatric Institute
New York City, New York

Lucy Berliner, M.S.W.
Social Worker
Sexual Assault Center
Harborview Medical Center
Seattle, Washington

Patty Carnavale, M.S.W.
Mental Health Therapist
Sarpy County Clinic
Eastern Nebraska Community Office
  of Mental Health
Belleview, Nebraska

Donald J. Cotton, Ph.D.
Clinical Psychologist
Kern County Mental Health
  Department of Forensic Service
Bakersfield, California

Elise Ernst, M.S.W.
Social Worker
Sexual Assault Center
Harborview Medical Center
Seattle, Washington

Paul M. Fine, M.D.
Associate Professor of Psychiatry
  and Pediatrics and Director
Division of Child and Adolescent
  Psychiatry
Creighton University School of Medicine
Omaha, Nebraska

A. Nicholas Groth, Ph.D.
Director, Sex Offender Program
Connecticut Correctional Institution
  —Somers
Somers, Connecticut

Dorothy J. Hicks, M.D.
Director, Rape Treatment Center
Jackson Memorial Hospital
Miami, Florida
Professor, Department of Obstetrics
  and Gynecology
University of Miami School of Medicine
Miami, Florida

Karen A. Holmes, A.C.S.W., Ph.D.
Assistant Professor, Graduate School of
  Social Work
University of Houston Central Campus
Houston, Texas

Arthur Kaufman, M.D.
Director, Division of Family Medicine
Department of Family, Community and
  Emergency Medicine
University of New Mexico School of
  Medicine
Albuquerque, New Mexico

William R. Miller, Ph.D.
Director of Clinical Services
Director of Research
Assistant Professor of Psychology in
    Psychiatry
Marriage Council of Philadelphia, Inc.
Philadelphia, Pennsylvania
Private Practice
Devon, Pennsylvania

Denise M. Moon, B.S.
Social Worker
Rape Treatment Center
Jackson Memorial Hospital
Miami, Florida

Carol C. Nadelson, M.D.
Professor and Vice Chairman
Department of Psychiatry
Tufts University School of Medicine
Director of Training and Education
Department of Psychiatry
New England Medical Center, Inc.
Boston, Massachusetts

Malkah T. Notman, M.D.
Clinical Professor of Psychiatry
Tufts University School of Medicine
Director of Psychotherapy
New England Medical Center, Inc.
Boston, Massachusetts

Carl M. Rogers, Ph.D.
Associate Director
Division of Child Protection
Children's Hospital

National Medical Center
Washington, D.C.

Edward L. Rowan, M.D.
Department of Psychiatry
Dartmouth Medical School
Hanover, New Hampshire

Judith B. Rowan, Ph.D.
Private Practice
Hanover, New Hampshire

Mimi H. Silbert, Ph.D.
President, Delancey Street
    Foundation, Inc.
San Francisco, California
President, Community Mediation Boards
San Francisco, California

Linda J. Skinner, Ph.D.
Instructor of Psychiatry
Columbia University College of
    Physicians and Surgeons
Research Scientist
New York State Psychiatric Institute
New York City, New York

Tremaine Terry, M.S.W.
Senior Social Worker
Division of Child Protection
Children's Hospital National Medical
    Center
Washington, D.C.

Ann Marie Williams, Ph.D.
Private Practice
Philadelphia, Pennsylvania

Preface

This book is not designed to increase the sensitivity of the reader to the extent of the problem of sexual abuse and its increasing number of victims. The surge in such cases has alerted professionals in the mental health services to clients who have had such experiences. Age is no deterrent to such attacks; the very young as well as the elderly are victims. An exchange of information from those practicing their skills and training in the service of alleviating the trauma is made available in this book.

The goal is to inform practitioners in the mental health services of the variety of current approaches, some truly innovative, others reflecting the relative unsophistication of the population they serve. Programs being conducted in teaching hospitals attached to medical schools contrast with privately funded, simple community efforts on the neighborhood level. Treatment is provided along the lines of traditional therapies, as well as interesting eclectic applications of some of the more innovative ones. The description of the variety of procedures also expands upon our knowledge of some clients who most often have been ignored in the literature. There are chapters on treatment of children; male victims outside, as well as inside, of correctional institutions; prostitutes victimized by their "johns"; older females; husbands and wives who are trying to resume a relationship after an attack.

The emphasis is upon practicality and those techniques which have valid application to individual and group experience. Not only immediate manifestions of traumatic residuals, but long-range convert ones as well, including assessment procedures and restorative individual and group therapy via behavior modification and insightful techniques, are extensively reviewed.

Accordingly, this book has been divided into three major portions. Each examines the problem from a number of viewpoints and considered influential factors.

Section I, Professional Considerations, explores psychodynamic considerations through the disciplines of psychology and psychiatry, and clinical social work. There are chapters on the psychodynamics of the sexual assault experience; the clinical social worker as an advocate for the client; and developmental variations in rape trauma syndrome.

Section II, Children as Victims: From Six to Sixteen, revolves around the special problems presented by child victims and concentrates upon the complexity of the delicate handling that this developmental level demands. There are chapters on treatment of such children; crisis intervention with the male child victim; and group work with preadolescents.

Section III, Adult Victims of Sexual Assault, includes chapters on prevention and treatment of sexual assault in correctional institutions; rape of men in the community; the special problems of the elderly assault victim; marital and sexual dysfunction following rape; behavioral treatment of sexual dysfunctions following such assaults; the special considerations required by assaulted college students; and victimized prostitutes.

We are indebted to our editor, Ms. Susan Munger, for her encouragement, patience, and support in organizing this volume. We also appreciate the cooperation exhibited by our contributors in the face of repeated requests for changes and additions to their chapters. All deserve our thanks.

I.R.S.
White Plains, New York

J.G.G.
Silver Springs, Maryland

Contents

Victims of Sexual Aggression:

Treatment of Children, Women, and Men

Section I
Professional Considerations

The psychological processes underlying the rape experience are most frequently of greater importance in their long-standing effects than is the physical hurt. The three chapters constituting Section I review the concerns of the various disciplines that most often are responsible for the victim and her well-being.

In Chapter 1, Dr. Carol C. Nadelson and Dr. Malkah T. Notman delve into the problems of a variety of developmental groups in evaluating the effects of rape. They do not neglect the influence of significant others in alleviating its effects. This chapter is a practical exposition of contemporary views of the emotional problems facing rape victims.

In Chapter 2, Dr. Karen A. Holmes takes the position of the social worker as advocate as well as therapist for such victims in assuring that they receive all the services they deserve, legal as well as psychological. This chapter is a practical model of the desired working relationship between social worker, psychiatrist, and representative of the law.

In Chapter 3, Dr. Ebrahim Amanat expands upon rape trauma syndrome theory and illustrates its application within his clinical practice in a medical setting. Assessing children as well as adult victims as to their temperamental styles, with associated reaction patterns, he makes recommendations for suitable therapeutic approaches for each. This chapter is a valuable ordering of such reaction variables and recommended approaches.

1
Psychodynamics of Sexual Assault Experiences

Carol C. Nadelson, M.D.
Malkah T. Notman, M.D.

ABSTRACT

Sexual assault is a traumatic experience with both short- and long-term conse-
quences for the victim. The authors trace the development of psychoanalytic
theory regarding concepts of response to external trauma and relate these to
sexual assault as an ego disruptive experience with implications for self-esteem.
They describe the phases of response to rape as a stressful life event and elucidate
the psychodynamic issues evoked, including guilt and self-blame. Specific
life-stage considerations are delineated, including the impact of sexual abuse in
the single young woman, the divorced or separated woman, and the middle-aged
woman. The implications for therapy are explored in terms of the reestablish-
ment of a sense of control and return to function. The authors indicate the need
for immediate counseling as well as the potential need for long-term therapy
with some victims. The authors also describe the repercussions of sexual abuse
in subsequent symptoms including anxiety, depression, and phobic responses.

The experiences that can be considered rape range from a surprise attack with
threats of death or mutilation to an insistence on sexual intercourse in a social or
family interaction where sexual contact was unexpected or not agreed upon;
thus incest can be considered a form of rape. Consent is crucial to the definition
of rape (Notman and Nadelson, 1976). This is a frequently misinterpreted issue
since one must consider who can give informed consent and under what circumstances. For example, can a child consent to sexual interaction with a parent
(Nadelson and Rosenfeld, 1980)? Further, there is an assumption that certain
social communications imply agreement to a sexual relationship when that may
not be the intent. Although men, women, and children are raped, the largest
number of rape victims are women. This chapter will focus on understanding
rape as a physical and psychological stress for women.

Burgess and Holmstrom (1974) have divided rape victims into three groups:
(1) victims of forcible completed or attempted rape, (2) victims who were an

accessory due to their inability to consent, and (3) victims of sexually stressful situations where the encounter went beyond the expectations and ability of the victim to exercise control. Despite the different circumstances, the intrapsychic experiences of rape victims share common features.

The rape victim has usually had an overwhelmingly frightening experience in which she fears for her life and through the sex act pays for it. Generally this experience engenders a sense of helplessness, intensifies conflicts about dependence and independence, and stimulates self-criticism, shame, and guilt. Difficulty handling anger and aggression, and persistent feelings of vulnerability are also very common repercussions. These are integrated and coped with by the individual victim in ways that depend on her age and life situation, the circumstances of the rape, ethnic background, specific personality attributes, and the responses of those people whom she encounters, particularly in the acute period after the rape. Availability of support is crucial to the eventual outcome (Notman and Nadelson, 1976).

Rape can be viewed as a crisis situation in which a traumatic external event breaks the balance between internal ego adaptation and the environment (Notman and Nadelson, 1976). Since it is an interaction between an extreme environmental stimulus and the adaptive capacity of the victim, it is similar to other situations described in the literature on stress, which includes studies of victims of community disasters (Lindemann, 1944; Tyhurst, 1951), war (Glover, 1941; Glover, 1942; Radi, 1942; Schmideberg, 1942), surgical procedures (Janis, 1958; Deutsch, 1942), etc. The unexpected nature of the catastrophe and the resources of the victim in coping with an experience that she views as life threatening are critical factors in rape, as in other crisis situations (Notman and Nadelson, 1976).

PSYCHOLOGICAL RESPONSE TO EXTERNAL TRAUMA

A traumatic event is defined as one that provokes stress beyond the resources of the individual to cope with and is thus experienced as overwhelming. The extent and nature of the psychological impact of such an external distressing event has been debated for many years (Nadelson and Notman, 1979). Freud (1920) stated: "Such an event as an external trauma is bound to provoke a disturbance on a large scale in the functioning of the organism's energy and to set in motion every possible defensive mechanism." The individual attempts to master the experience in a variety of ways, often involving repitition of the event or portions of it. Freud understood the dreams of those who had experienced severe trauma as attempts at mastery. Sometimes these dreams revived early childhood psychically traumatic memories and were thus an exception to this proposition that dreams were wish fulfillments.

Theoretical psychoanalytic emphasis, however, continued to focus on neurotic anxiety responses, and was less specifically concerned with external trauma itself until the extensive investigations of war neuroses of the 1940s brought this issue into focus when maladaptive responses were reported (Grinker and Spiegel, 1945; Kardiner and Spiegel, 1941; Rado, 1942). The concept of trauma had originally applied only to childhood experiences; it was extended to include stress experienced by adults. Furst (1967) described mechanisms used by individuals that were protective against further exposure to trauma but were psychologically costly and resulted in loss of self-esteem. Kardiner and Spiegel (1941) stated: "as soon as fear is directed inward, in the form of questioning the individual's resources to cope with external danger or toward the group in the form of questioning its ability to be a protective extension of the individual, then a new and more serious danger situation is created."

During this same time period Deutsch (1942) and Sutherland and Orbach (1953) observed the impact of illness and surgery on patients. They noted that many of the patients they studied manifested little overt concern about dying, but expressed more concern about disruption of their daily patterns of living. They considered these reactions aspects of normal adaptation under fear-provoking circumstances, rather than evidence of pathological denial or symptoms of neurotic disorders. Fenichel (1945) suggested that differences in reactions to external events depended on differences in individual defensive patterns. Greenson 1949) emphasized that an extremely stressful event causes the victim to feel helpless and to resort to extreme defenses, including denial. Identification with the aggressor has also been seen as a means of attempting to gain control of the frightening experience. Wolfenstein (1957) discussed variations in reaction related to sociocultural factors.

Engel (1963) further described the threatening components of trauma. He classified these into several groups: (1) the loss or threat of loss of an object, body part, status, plans, or way of life, ideals, etc.; (2) injury or threat of injury with infliction of pain or mutilation that is actual or threatened; and (3) frustration of drives. He emphasized the interrelationship between prior experiences and response and also stressed the importance of individual variability. Strain and Grossman (1975) have emphasized the importance of the individual's guilt and fear of retaliation, the reactivation of separation anxiety, and the threat to narcissistic integrity as determinants of responses.

Janis (1954), in his early work on surgical patients, stated that the guilt that is often seen after trauma is related to the aggressive impulses that emerge. A decrease in self-esteem may occur because aggressive impulses are mobilized and experienced by the victim as violations of superego requirements (Deutsch, 1942; Grinker and Spiegel, 1945; Strain and Grossman, 1975). Furthermore, Janis (1958) believed that threats that could not be influenced by the individual's own behavior were unconsciously perceived in the same way as childhood threats of parental punishment for bad behavior, resulting in attempts to control anger and aggression in order to ensure that there was no further provocation.

This may in part explain the lack of overt expression of anger in so many rape victims, and the overwhelming experience of shame and guilt.

Janis (1958) also described the exacerbation of past anxiety symptoms that may occur in those experiencing great stress. Optimistic fantasies about compensatory satisfaction in the future may be used to attenuate anxiety. These fantasies derive from those which functioned as effective reassurances in childhood threat situations. If there is a substantial degree of victimization, however, there is a disappointment in parental figures or those in authority who would be expected to be protective.

The special developmental influences on the expression of aggression in women also bear on the responses of rape victims (Nadelson et al., 1982a). Because there are more stringent restrictions on the expression of aggression in women than for men, women have difficulty acknowledging and accepting their own aggression, or responding actively to those who are hostile in attacking them. This clearly has special implications for the rape victim. In addition, the rape victim is often blamed for the crime; she is considered provocative, insufficiently cautious, or in other ways responsible. Thus the terrifying and traumatic nature of the experience is not acknowledged.

In general, stresses that involve a threat of body damage may reactivate early memories of physical danger that had previously been repressed. Past feelings of helplessness or lack of control are evoked, and regression may occur (Furst, 1967). Freud (1920) stated that powerful external factors can arouse, in anyone, the weak and helpless child that is ordinarily covered by the mask of conventional adult behavior.

Titchener and Kapp (1976) present recent evidence that symptomatic reactions to catastrophes "are not those of individuals with weak egos," but that a disaster may reawaken anxieties in most people, so that "all of us are susceptible to traumatic neuroses." From their work with survivors of the Buffalo Creek disaster they also reported that they were able to be effective therapeutically by helping the victims link past and "previously worked through childhood anxieties with the overwhelming anxieties aroused by the disaster."

These descriptions are all applicable to the rape victim, who experiences a threat of death or serious injury, is fearful of retaliation, and feels helpless. She often suppresses aggression and feels guilty whatever her course of action. This guilt is reinforced by social criticism of her for having been raped, and she can be disappointed in people in authority, such as police, who often do not support her or give credence to her story (Nadelson and Notman, 1979).

The preservation or loss of self-esteem is an important component of the reaction to stress. Jacobsen (1975) states:

Normally, the rise and fall of self-esteem develops in response to actual experiences, such as success or failure, and the intensity and direction corresponds to the nature and extent of the provocation. The more that irrational factors and unconscious conflicts come into play, the more abnormally will self-esteem be altered in its level of intensity and its affective and ideational expression.

She also says that "self-esteem depends on the extent to which the individual can live up to the goals and standards of his ego ideal." Glover (1941) and Schmideberg (1942), in describing responses to war threats, felt that the outstanding mediating factors were the individual's self-attitudes and the loss of previously effective self-assessments that had strengthened that person's sense of invulnerability. Thus, the individual's positive or negative view of his or her ability to cope may change the course of the resolution of that trauma and the future capacity to respond to trauma. A successful response enhances self-esteem, an ineffective one leaves a damaged self-esteem. As noted, since the rape victim is usually blamed for and sometimes accused of provoking the rape, her self-esteem is damaged.

THE RAPE STRESS

The profound impact of rape is best understood when it is seen as a violent crime against the person, and not as a specifically sexual encounter. Bard and Ellison (1974) emphasize the significance of the personal violation for the rape victim. When an individual is robbed, it is experienced as a violation of the self because home and possessions are symbolic extensions of the self. Stress is intensified when armed robbery occurs because of the coercive deprivation of independence and autonomy, in which the victim surrenders his or her controls under the threat. When actual injury occurs in a physical assault, there is concrete evidence of the forced surrender of autonomy. Rape is the ultimate violation of the self, short of homicide, with an invasion of the inner and most private space of the individual as well as loss of autonomy and control (Nadelson, Notman and Hilberman, 1980).

PHASES OF RESPONSE TO STRESS

Descriptions of stress reactions (Janis, 1958) have elucidated four stages which vary in intensity and duration. Four major phases of stress response have been described (Weiss and Payson, 1967). These are also applicable to rape. These stages are: (1) an anticipatory or threat phase; (2) a danger-impact phase; (3) a post-impact or recoil phase; and (4) a stage of rescue and recovery.

   1. In the anticipatory or threat phase a degree of anxiety facilitates recognition of potentially dangerous situations. The threat or anticipatory phase occurs when perception of a situation of possible danger occurs and is likely to arouse fear. Denial takes place when the threat of danger seems remote (Wolfenstein, 1957). Most people protect themselves with a combination of defenses that maintain an illusion of their invulnerability, and at the same time maintain

enough reality perception to afford protection from real danger. In a situation where a potential stress is a planned event, for example, elective surgery, an individual can protect his or her ego integrity by strengthening those defenses that will ward off feelings of helplessness. The sense of invulnerability is important because it can cause the individual to become skeptical about impending danger. In this way it may prevent appropriate perception of potential threats. This is particularly relevant for the rape victim who, as we have noted, is often accused of not having exercised sufficient caution.

Engel (1963) comments on the incapacity of the unprepared ego to cope with severe stress, and states that anxiety is lowered when preparation is possible. For rape victims who have no opportunity to anticipate the assault, resulting anxiety is therefore greater. For those rape victims whose assailant is known to them, the change from the original relationship is unanticipated and unprepared for, and a sense of betrayal results, as well as mistrust of relationships.

2. The danger-impact phase occurs with the recognition that chances of escape depend upon the individual or those who are in a position to help. There is a strong tendency to feel that one is alone at the center of a disaster (Wolfenstein, 1957). A person sharing the experience with a group is less prone to self-blame afterwards than is the victim of a solitary traumatic event. Since the rape victim is generally alone, she does not have this group support; in fact, the opposite usually is true. Varying degrees of disintegration may occur in a previously well adapted person, depending on the degree of trauma and the adaptive capacity of the individual. During this phase major physiological reactions may occur, including vasomotor and sensorial shifts. Tyhurst (1951) reported on the extremes of reaction in victims of fires and floods. He described that 12% to 25% of those people he studied were "cool and collected" during the acute situation, 10% to 25% showed "inappropriate" responses with "states of confusion, paralyzing anxiety, inability to move out of bed, hysterical crying or screaming." The majority of the victims showed variable but less extreme responses; they were "stunned and bewildered," and demonstrated restricted attention and other fear responses such as automatic or stereotyped behavior.

3. The post-impact or recoil phase occurs when the person perceives the losses that were sustained. The response in this period is unpredictable and may vary with different stresses and times, depending on their meaning to the individual. In this recoil phase emotional expression, self-awareness, memory, and behavioral control are gradually regained in the context of possibly limited perspective and increased dependency feelings. In this phase the individual perceives his or her own adaptive and maladaptive responses and may question his or her reactions. A positive or negative view of one's ability to cope may affect the course of resolution of this trauma and future stress capacity. Self-esteem may be enhanced or damaged during this phase.

Group support enables the victim to feel less isolated and helpless. Obviously a victim who is alone (i.e., the rape victim) can only hope for support later, and may be disappointed by the failure of the group, including family, friends, and the community, to validate her experience.

4. The fourth stage is that of rescue and recovery, with a gradual return to activity and responsiveness (Wolfenstein, 1957). During this phase human contacts are important to the outcome. Thus social variables are important determinants of the eventual response. At this time, the loss of self-reassuring mechanisms that had fostered a sense of invulnerability may result in a decrease in self-esteem. The victim then blames herself for lack of perception or attention to danger.

As noted above, the neuroses reported during World War II stimulated study in this area (Kardiner and Spiegel, 1941). Maladaptive responses were reported, and the response to the "gross stress" of combat was seen as possibly leading to "traumatophobia," where the individual develops mechanisms that are protective against further exposure to trauma but prevent reintegration. Grinker and Spiegel (1945) include war neurosis in a larger group of traumata which involve loss of pride and self-esteem.

Burgess and Holmstrom's (1974) description of the specific "rape trauma syndrome" focuses on rape and separates the post-rape response into two stages: (1) an acute disorganizational phase with behavioral, somatic, and psychological manifestations; and (2) a long-term reorganizational phase with variable components depending on the ego strengths, social networks, and specific experiences of the victim. They stress the violent, life-threatening aspects of the crime. In addition, they comment on two types of victim response. They describe "the expressed style" in which the victim is emotional and visibly upset, in contrast with the "controlled style" in which denial and reaction formation seem to be the most prominent defenses. They describe feelings of shock and disbelief in many victims as part of this initial phase and they comment on the prevalence of guilt and self-blame. While they report considerable individual variation in the reorganizational phase, the overall patterns of response appear to be similar to those reported in the other types of stress reactions we have discussed. In the immediate phase of acute response the victim's life-style and functioning are disrupted by the rape; in the next phase a long-term process of recovery and restitution occurs. Sutherland and Scherl (1970) describe an early period of outward adjustment as part of the rape response in victims they studied, with an apparent temporary resolution of the immediate anxiety-provoking issues during which the victim often returns to her usual life patterns and attempts to behave as if all is well. Denial of the reality of what has happened and suppression of affect are prominent. This is followed by the integration and resolution phase in which the victim integrates the experience with her self-image and attempts to restore her sense of competence.

PSYCHODYNAMIC ISSUES

Rape constitutes a stress to which all women are vulnerable. It evokes previous sexual and aggressive conflicts, fantasies, and experiences. In addition, the real helplessness of the victim reinforces feelings of powerlessness and vulnerability deriving from early in life. Restitution is interfered with by lack of support, and condemnation reinforces guilt and lowers self-esteem (Notman and Nadelson, 1976).

While unconscious masochistic and sexual fantasies are universally present, the existence of these fantasies cannot be construed to mean that an individual provokes a rape. Similarly, although unconscious murderous wishes and aggressive fantasies are also universally present, they do not actually bring about deaths and disasters, nor accusations of provocation.

The effect on the victim is complex and usually profound. Conscious and unconscious aggressive and sometimes sexual fantasies can be evoked in the rape victim. These fantasies can produce considerable guilt, which may be especially problematic for women who have had conscious rape fantasies at any time. Helene Deutsch (1944) considered rape fantasies as variants of masochistic sexual fantasies. She believed that they reduced the guilt produced by forbidden sexual pleasure. Thus within fantasy the woman surrenders passively; she is freed from the responsibility for her sexual wishes. It is important to emphasize that these fantasies do not in any way correspond to the violence and humiliation of an actual rape (Nadelson and Notman, 1979). Furthermore, the rapist is not the object of the fantasy.

Other aspects of the response to rape have implications for restitution from this crisis. Despite varying circumstances and different degrees of surprise, violence, and degradation, guilt and shame are almost always experienced. They are related to the societal perception of the rape as a demeaning sexual act for which the victim is held responsible. Since taboos against the expression of sexuality in women continue to persist, a victim in a sexual crime may be accused of complicity. Furthermore, since women are expected to exert impulse control in sexual encounters, the rape victim's sense of failure in setting limits, impossible though they may have been, contributes to her guilt. Concerns about the degree of activity or passivity that might have prevented the attack are frequently expressed. The assumption is made that she should have, or could have, handled it better; perhaps that her unconscious wishes prevented more appropriate assessment and more adaptive behavior (Notman and Nadelson, 1976). Other violent crimes without a sexual component do not carry quite the same stigma. As we have discussed earlier, confusion results from conflicting expectations as to the appropriate response. Passivity and compliance are internalized as "appropriate" feminine behavior. However, compliance in this circumstance may be interpreted as inadequate resistance and therefore construed as willing participation.

DEVELOPMENTAL CONSIDERATIONS

We have considered some general features of the response to rape. Let us focus briefly on some of the determinants related to age and life stage (Notman and Nadelson, 1976).

1. The Single Young Woman

The single woman between the ages of 17 and 24 is the most frequently reported rape victim. She is vulnerable often by virtue of being alone and inexperienced. Her relationships with men have frequently been limited to the trusted, caring figures of her childhood, or the young man she dated in high school, so she enters the world with little sophistication in some of the nuances of human interaction and may easily be involved in an unwelcome sexual encounter. In this age group the frequency with which the rape victim reports prior knowledge of the rapist is important and is often the reason for her refusal to prosecute. She may have been raped by a date, an old friend, or even an ex-husband. Often she responds with shame or guilt, reproaching herself because she should have "known better" or been more active in preventing the rape, or because she does not fully recognize her right to refuse sexual intercourse she does not want.

Feelings of shame and guilt are prevalent regardless of the circumstances. The ability for the woman to work out her feelings and her sense of vulnerability may color her relationships with men. This is especially true for the very young woman who may have had her first sexual experience in the context of violence and degradation.

For a young woman the experience of rape may revive concerns about separation and independence. Her sense of adequacy is challenged when she asks, "Can I really take care of myself?" and parents, friends, and relatives respond with an offer to involve themselves in taking care of her again. Although it may be a supportive and reassuring gesture, it may also foster regression, and prevent mastery of the stress and conflict evoked by the experience. Families often respond by becoming overprotective. This also can foster regression.

Another problem for the younger rape victim involves the gynecological examination which may be perceived, especially by an inexperienced or severely traumatized woman, as similar to a rape. While she is concerned about the intactness and integrity of her body, and wants the reassurance she can obtain from an examination, she may still have difficulty with necessary procedures.

The woman whose first sexual experience is rape may confuse the sexual and the violent components, especially if the experience confirms early fantasies and expectations. A woman who experiences orgasm is even more likely to suffer from severe guilt and self-reproach and may cut herself off from her sexuality.

2. The Divorced or Separated Woman

The divorced or separated woman is in a particularly difficult position because she is more likely to be blamed and not believed. Her life-style, her morality, and her character are frequently called into question. Her sexual availability makes her seem more approachable sexually. She may experience the rape as a confirmation of her feelings of inadequacy and is likely to feel enormous guilt, leading also to failure to report the crime. Her ability to function independently is called into question. If she has children she may become concerned about her ability to protect and care for them. Certainly others are likely to raise questions about her adequacy as a mother.

The woman with children must deal with the problem of what to tell them, how to tell them and when to tell them. If the event is known in the community, then its implications for her and her children may be difficult to manage. It is not possible to deal with these problems without careful assessment of each situation. However, the anxiety related to these concerns is considerable and may lead to inappropriate behavior in an attempt to avoid facing the issues.

3. The Middle-Aged Woman

For the "middle-aged" woman the issues of control, independence, and dependency are particularly important. She is often in a period of critical reassessment of her life and she may be experiencing menopause. She may feel useless in relation to her grown-up or already absent family or her competitive relationship with adolescent daughters. Husbands in their own midlife crises are often less responsive and supportive to her sexual and emotional needs. At this point of sensitivity the overwhelming experience of life-threatening and autonomy-shaking rape is particularly damaging. The self-devaluation, the feelings of worthlessness, dirtiness, and shame can be particularly acute in a female already sensitive to her sexual adequacy and physical attractiveness.

SOCIALIZATION AND THE THERAPEUTIC PROCESS

Therapeutic intervention in a crisis must address itself to helping the victim return to the previous level of adaptation. This does not mean "forgetting" about the experience, but it involves an integration of her individual dynamics and coping patterns, the symbolic significance of experience, and the life-stage concerns evoked by the trauma and the ability to work them through as far as possible. It may need to include an initial period of support with restitution of functioning as the primary goal and a later period of counseling or reevaluation. Although therapeutic principles are similar to those for other types of crisis, particular considerations are related to the specific nature of the rape trauma.

Feelings and conflicts about sexuality are aroused because of the nature of the event. The victim may find it difficult to obtain help because to do so she must reveal herself and reexperience her humiliation. Many rape and incest victims are reluctant to expose themselves to further violation, so they remain secretive and do not seek help. The victim may perceive any medical or psychiatric intervention as intrusive and therefore equivalent to another rape.

A particularly important aim of therapy is to facilitate the reestablishment of a sense of control. Since helplessness, feelings of vulnerability, fear, deception, and humiliation are so prominent, in order to be effective the therapeutic encounter must increase the victim's capacity to gain and maintain control. It is important to help her restore her self-esteem, and to support her sense of competence. Regression must be prevented in the immediate posttraumatic period, and therapeutic efforts should be directed toward developing mastery.

Another issue of the immediate crisis period is the effect of the rape on the victim's relationships. The ability of those in her environment to support her will determine, in part, the extent to which continued therapeutic help becomes necessary and the outcome of the experience. In contrast with most personal crises, where the counselor or therapist reinforces the importance of sharing feelings about the experience with those who are significant in the person's life, no firm guidelines exist about communicating the event of the sexual abuse because of the real possibility that such a revelation may disrupt relationships. Thus a husband may perceive the rape as a deception by his wife, and the parents of an adolescent may project their own sense of guilt and become angry with the victim. Likewise, the incest victim is often not believed, or may actually precipitate the disruption of the family.

Family and friends must be sensitized to the meaning of the rape so that they are able to give support to the victim. Since the rape may intensify preexisting conflicts in relationships, these may be increased. If the victim chooses not to tell close friends or family members, guilt or estrangement may occur. If she is able to talk about the experience, mastery is facilitated. However, a friend or family member who is initially willing to listen may find the repetitive reworking of the experience difficult to tolerate and may need to be warned to expect this.

Since the victim feels isolated, alienated, ashamed, and guilty, the initial response to her by professionals, friends, and family is particularly important. Group and family support enables the victim to feel less isolated and helpless. Where possible, the therapist may be helpful in bringing about actual changes in the responses of people to the victim, and help the victim herself to be able to take a more active position. Some victims have sought mastery by helping other victims. The therapist thus has multiple functions and must deal with both intrapsychic issues and environmental realities.

COUNSELING CONSIDERATIONS

In assessing what resources should be offered to rape victims in the acute phase, her previous adjustment, including stress tolerance, available adaptive resources, and environmental supports are important to consider. In addition, issues that are specific to her life stage must be considered.

There is a problem in recommending further therapy or counseling. Women who have been raped are often reluctant to be labeled as patients in the usual sense. The idea of being seen as psychologically "sick" may intensify lowered self-esteem. The victim needs reassurance about the way in which she handled the rape, and about her efforts to cope following it. She must be offered the opportunity for constructive catharsis with a caring and empathic person who does not label her as a "patient."

An additional therapeutic goal, if possible, is to utilize the crisis experience for some further growth. The trauma may be too great for this. However, at times genuine gains may be made. For instance, reactions of significant people may enable the victim to assess her relationships more realistically. The experience may leave her open to intervention, and thus to help which reaches to other areas of her life. At times changes in defensive patterns occur which are more adaptive.

It is useful to differentiate short-term crisis goals from long-term issues that require referral for psychotherapy. Those individuals requiring therapy are more likely to be people who have difficulty resolving crises. Indications of this may be a history of deterioration of relationships in the past, phobic reactions, sexual problems, anxiety and depression, or previous instability (of jobs or living situations). In some cases the nature of the rape itself may have been more traumatic to the victim because it involved more violence, it may have been prolonged, or it may have been a group rape. It may also have been more closely related to underlying conflicts and previously stressful experiences, or the individual may have been undergoing an intercurrent life stress, for example, divorce.

Although crisis-oriented therapy is aimed at restoration of the previous level of functioning, long-term effects of rape also occur and are not always apparent superficially. Long-standing depression or recurrent depressive reactions may follow a rape. The victim may also have difficulty with current and future sexual relationships. She may remain mistrustful of men and conflicted about sexuality (Nadelson et al., 1982b). Her sexual partner may respond to this defensively, angrily, or critically, further contributing to the difficulty. Failure in this relationship then accentuates her sense of being helpless, damaged, and incompetent. The therapist can help by predicting and preparing for these longer-term effects. Counseling for the partner is helpful to enable him to understand his own motivations for his response. Criticizing or blaming the victim, denial of the degree of her distress, may be protecting him against awareness of his own vulnerability.

Since, as we know, the tendency to repetition in fantasy is a response that characterizes people's attempts to master a trauma, the rape victim may have recurrent nightmares and phobic responses and reexperience the rape in fantasy. On occasion some women unconsciously place themselves in a vulnerable position again. This can be understood, in part, as an attempt to master by repetition. The therapist must be aware of this possibility.

Therapy of the rape victim thus includes components of short-term crisis-oriented therapy with the additional necessity of working with the impact of the external reality and its implications. The therapist must be able to see the complex interaction of all these factors. A focus on one with consequent neglect of the others is unlikely to facilitate resolution in a way that promotes long-term gains.

If the victim chooses to prosecute, support at every step of the process is very important. Some attention to long-term effects is important. It is difficult to predict the long-term needs of the rape victim, since the working out of the trauma proceeds in many different ways. Some of the issues that seem to reemerge and may be present emotionally at a later date are:

1. Mistrust of men with consequent avoidance or hesitation
2. A variety of sexual disturbances
3. Phobic reactions (e.g., inability to walk on the street where the rape occurred)
4. Anxiety and depression often precipitated by seemingly unrelated events that may in some small details bring back the original trauma (e.g., an acute anxiety attack when followed down the street)

Sometimes this leads to behavior that could be puzzling if it were not for the rape. For example, a young woman who was otherwise independent and resourceful found it difficult to make property arrangements during a divorce. She insisted on staying in a house that was otherwise too large for her needs, and inconvenient. In exploring the issue with her therapist, she told of a rape five years previously that she had mentioned to no one, which left her too frightened to think of moving back to the city from the suburbs.

A systematic study of long-term consequences and treatment implications is clearly indicated especially in view of the increasing understanding of rape as a stress and the growing feeling that one is permitted to discuss it and to bring to light past unreported experiences in a climate of acceptance and empathy. It is important to view rape as a stress situation that tests the capacity of the individual, and that must be met with support and understanding rather than further victimization by questioning the credibility and character of the victim.

An understanding of the psychodynamic and developmental issues for the rape victim will facilitate appropriate intervention. The woman in this situation needs help with both short- and long-term issues. Initially, she needs support and reassurance about her intactness, her femininity, and her relationships. She may be sensitive, volatile, and somewhat disorganized. She may attempt to expiate her guilt by being compliant or by suppressing negative or angry feelings. She may even accept blame. At times she may displace her anger onto those who are attempting to help, for example, friends, doctors, or the police. It is important that she have the opportunity for constructive catharsis with a person she views as caring and empathetic. The counselor's patience as well as that of friends and family may be tested by the victim's repetitive cathartic attempts expressed as telling and retelling the story.

The counselor may need to be available frequently for the more overtly upset rape victim. The more subdued victim may need to be encouraged to communicate and should be offered the opportunity for contact with a counselor in the future.

Each woman presents special considerations and requires the acknowledgment and support of the counselor in verbalizing and working through the complex problems she confronts.

REFERENCES

Bard, M., and Ellison, K. 1974. Crisis intervention and investigation of forcible rape. *The Police Chief,* May.

Burgess, A. W., and Holmstrom, L. L. 1974. Rape trauma syndrome. *Am. J. Psychiatry,* **131**(9):981–986.

Deutsch, H. 1942. Some psychoanalytic observations in surgery. *Psychosom. Med.,* 4:105–115.

Deutsch, H. 1944. *Psychology of Women.* New York: Grune & Stratton.

Engel, G. 1963. *Psychological Development in Health and Disease.* Philadelphia: Saunders.

Fenichel, O. 1945. *The Psychoanalytic Theory of Neurosis.* New York: Norton.

Freud, S. 1920. Beyond the pleasure principle. In J. Strachey, ed., *Standard Edition,* vol. 18, pp. 7–64. London: Hogarth Press, 1955.

Furst, S. S. 1967. Psychic trauma: A survey. In S. S. Furst, ed., *Psychic Trauma.* New York: Basic Books.

Glover, E. 1941. Notes on the psychological effects of war conditions on the civilian population. Part I: The Munich Crisis. *Int. J. Psychoanal.,* **22**:132–146.

Glover, E. 1942. Notes on the psychological effects of war conditions on the civilian population. Part III: The Blitz. *Int. J. Psychoanal.,* **23**:17–37.

Greenson, R. 1949. The psychology of apathy. *Psychoanal. Q.,* **18**:290–303.

Grinker, R., and Spiegel, J. 1945. *Men Under Stress.* Philadelphia: Blakiston.

Jacobson, E. 1975. The regulation of self-esteem. In E. J. Anthony and T. Benedek, eds., *Depression and Human Existence.* Boston: Little, Brown.

Janis, I. 1954. Problems of theory in the analysis of stress behavior. *J. Social Issues,* **10**:12–25.

Janis, J. 1958. *Psychological Stress.* New York: Wiley.

Kardiner, A., and Spiegel, H. 1941. *War Stress and Neurotic Illness.* New York: P. B. Hoeber.

Lindemann, E. 1944. Symptomatology and management of acute grief. *Am. J. Psychiatry,* 101:141-146.

Nadelson, C. C., and Notman, M. T. 1979. Psychoanalytic considerations of the response to rape. *Int. Rev. Psychoanal.,* 6(1):97-103.

Nadelson, C. C., and Rosenfeld, A. 1980. Sexual misuse of children. In D. H. Schetky and E. P. Benedek, eds., *Child Psychiatry and the Law,* pp. 89-106. New York: Brunner/Mazel.

Nadelson, C. C., Notman, M. T., and Hilberman, E. C. 1980. The rape experience. In W. J. Curran, A. L. McGarry, C. S. Petty, eds., *Modern Legal Medicine, Psychiatry and Forensic Science.* Philadelphia: F. A. Davis Co.

Nadelson, C. C., Notman, M. T., Miller, J. B., and Zilbach, J. 1982a. Aggression in women: Conceptual issues and clinical implications. In M. T. Notman and C. C. Nadelson, eds., *The Woman Patient. Vol. 3: Aggression, Adaptations, and Psychotherapy,* pp. 17-28. New York: Plenum.

Nadelson, C. C., Notman, M. T., Zackson, H., and Gornick, J. 1982b. A follow-up study of rape victims. *Am. J. Psychiatry,* 139(10):1266-1270.

Notman, M. T., and Nadelson, C. C. 1976. The rape victim: Psychodynamic considerations. *Am. J. Psychiatry,* 133(4):408-413.

Radi, S. 1942. Pathodynamics and treatment of traumatic war neurosis (traumatophobia). *Psychosom. Med.,* 4:362-369.

Schmideberg, M. 1942. Some observations on individual reactions to air raids. *Int. J. Psychoanal.,* 23:146-176.

Strain, J., and Grossman, S. 1975. *Psychological Care of the Medically Ill.* New York: Appleton-Century-Crofts.

Sutherland, A. M., and Orbach, C. E. 1953. Psychological impact of cancer and cancer surgery; depressive reactions associated with surgery for cancer. *Cancer,* 6:958-962.

Sutherland, S., and Scherl, D. 1970. Patterns of response among victims of rape. *Am. J. Orthopsychiatry,* 40:503-511.

Titchener, J., and Kapp, T. 1976. Family and character change at Buffalo Creek. *Am. J. Psychiatry,* 133:295-299.

Tyhurst, J. S. 1951. Individual reactions to community disaster: The habitual history of psychiatric phenomena. *Am. J. Psychiatry,* 107:764-769.

Weiss, R. J., and Payson, H. E. 1967. Gross stress reaction. In A. M. Friedman and H. I. Kaplan, eds., *Comprehensive Textbook of Psychiatry.* Baltimore: Williams & Wilkins.

Wolfenstein, M. 1957. *Disaster Glencoe.* New York: Free Press.

2
Working For and With Rape Victims: Crisis Intervention and Advocacy*1

Karen A. Holmes, ACSW, Ph.D.

ABSTRACT

Although much has been written in recent years about the plight of the rape victim, relatively little is explicit enough to provide prescriptive guidelines for mental health professionals who work with rape victims. Further, most of the treatment-oriented literature to date addresses only direct intervention with the individual victim, an approach that this author believes to be too limited to have a significant impact on a problem of this scope and magnitude. In this chapter, a dualistic practice model is presented wherein two social work strategies, crisis intervention and advocacy, are combined to more fully address the needs of potential as well as actual rape victims. The rationale for the dualistic model is presented, the two strategies are examined within a social work context, and step-by-step implementation of the model is described based on practice experience with rape victims. In addition, based on research findings from a study in which this author was involved, treatment implications for racial-ethnic minority victims are discussed, as are implications regarding the current rape-as-crisis conceptualization. Although the author views crisis intervention as the most logical and helpful approach in working with rape victims, particularly when combined with the advocacy strategy, there is little doubt that it (like most, if not all treatment models) is a class- and culture-bound model that has inherent risks for black and Mexican American victims. These risks are identified and guidelines for practitioners are provided for the effective use of crisis intervention and advocacy as the dualistic practice model.

There are probably few areas in human service delivery where the need for continued humanization in conjunction with development of expanded services is so apparent as in helping victims of rape. The legal definition of rape — with some variations across state and criminal law — is the sexual penetration of a

---

[1] This chapter is an expansion of "Services for Victims of Rape: A Dualistic Model," which appeared in *Social Casework*, January 1981, Family Service Association of America, publisher.

woman by a man, who is not her husband, without the woman's consent.[2] Given that the issue of rape has received increasing attention in recent years and given the push for positive changes in relation to service delivery to victims, it is clear that both the working definition(s) and the responses to rape are much more problematic than the legal definition would suggest. This chapter outlines an expanded practice model for helping rape victims, with specific attention given to treatment implications regarding black and Mexican American victims.[3]

Based on the concept of dualism, this model uses two social work strategies: crisis intervention and advocacy. Two basic premises should be acknowledged initially: (1) Although most interventive efforts with rape victims have been directed toward the individual via the crisis intervention strategy, the advocacy strategy must also be consciously implemented to effect institutional change aimed at helping *all* rape victims; and (2) although a relatively small number of social workers are directly responsible for service delivery to rape victims, there are undoubtedly a significant number of "hidden victims" among practitioners' case loads in a variety of settings. It is probably safe to suggest that rape victims, like victims/survivors of incest and battering, are well represented among clients seeking help for a variety of presenting problems such as marital difficulties, sexual dysfunction, or depression. Additionally, although the expanded model presented here was developed in relation to a specific client group, it need not be limited only to practice with rape victims. It is hoped that presentation of this model will generate thoughtful response on two fronts: First, that social workers and other mental health professionals will incorporate relevant aspects of the model into their existing repertoire of skills, and second, that educators will appreciate the need for specific curriculum content on the crisis intervention and advocacy strategies, as well as content on treatment issues regarding racial-ethnic minorities.

THE RATIONALE FOR DUALISTIC STRATEGIES

The concept of dualism has long-standing historical roots within the social work profession (Hamilton, 1947; Bisno, 1952; Friedlander, 1958). As the term implies, interventive efforts must be directed not only toward a given client

---

[2] In recent years, some states have adopted statutes with provisions for husband-wife rape, variations in the degree of assailant force and victim resistance, and additional categories such as rape with an instrument.

[3] The specific identification of Mexican American is used here because the author's practice experience has been in Texas where the term is used to denote a blending of the two cultures. The exact extent to which the discussion of Mexican American victims in this chapter can be generalized to other Hispanic groups (for example, Puerto Ricans or Cubans) is not known.

system (e.g., the individual, the family, or the community), but also toward effecting change in the larger society or toward its social systems. Evidence of the importance of dualism to social workers is found in the profession's first Code of Ethics where it states: "I regard as my primary obligation the welfare of the individual or group served, which includes action for improving social conditions."[4] If this philosophical-ethical stance is extended to work with rape victims, a dualistic model naturally evolves. First, an interventive strategy is needed to provide the framework for direct services to each victim, and second, a strategy is needed to effect change in those systems that contribute to the existence of rape as a social fact and that may impinge upon the subsequent social functioning of all rape victims. Although the quote from the Code of Ethics would suggest that all social work practice maintains a dualistic focus, this may be more an ideal than an accurate reflection of reality. Because of personal preference, variations in worker "style," and/or the use of track systems in most graduate schools of social work (i.e., having students choose between a track emphasizing direct practice, interpersonal helping, and casework/group work *or* a track emphasizing social policy/planning, administration, and community organization), it is perhaps more realistic to acknowledge that social workers, by and large, practice basically on one end of a continuum or the other, but only infrequently combine efforts to effect change on both micro (individual) and mezzo or macro (community, society) levels. This is less a criticism than an observation acknowledging that interventive efforts are often somewhat dichotomized by target systems, but they need not remain so.

The specific rationale for selecting the two particular strategies used in developing the dualistic model is straightforward. Despite the rapidly expanding body of literature about rape and rape victims, knowledge gaps still remain; however, most of the literature on victims and their needs reflects the assumption that rape is a crisis experience or that it precipitates a crisis response from the victim (Sutherland and Scherl, 1972; Burgess and Holmstrom, 1974a, b; McCombie, 1976). Apparently this assumption has served as the basis for using the crisis intervention strategy with rape victims; clearly the proliferation of rape crisis centers throughout the country would seem to support this. Beyond this assumption, however, it appears that crisis intervention is pragmatically congruent with the presenting problem of rape victimization; that is, practice experience suggests, as do research findings from victim studies, that immediate, directive intervention which focuses on providing concrete information, exploring alternatives regarding decision making, and giving support and realistic reassurance are helpful, viable techniques in working with rape victims (Burgess and Holmstrom, 1974b; Williams and Holmes, 1981). And, as will be noted in

---

[4] "Code of Ethics" adopted by the Delegate Assembly of the National Association of Social workers on October 13, 1960, and amended April 11, 1967.

the overview of crisis intervention, these are among the techniques of this strategy.

The inclusion of the advocacy strategy in the dualistic model emanates from both a philosophical and a pragmatic, action-oriented framework. If one accepts the view that rape is essentially an act of power and/or violence rather than sex (a view first and most often espoused by feminist writers such as Griffin, 1971, and Brownmiller, 1975), then one also views rape as symptomatic of a stratified (unequal) system of power relationships between males and females in° this society. Therefore, the advocacy strategy is used in an attempt to protect the rights of rape victims (e.g., to receive adequate services from formal service-delivery systems, to be treated fairly and nonjudgmentally) and to combat sexist attitudes and stereotypes that serve to maintain the status quo vis-à-vis male-female inequality. While there are, no doubt, some practitioners who would not consider advocacy to be a form of therapy or treatment, this is true only from a very narrowly or traditionally defined perspective of micro intervention. As will be shown as the model is presented, the advocacy strategy can help to enhance the social functioning of rape victims in a variety of ways. Finally, while each strategy used independently can result in positive change for the individual victim and within a facet of a system, use of the dualistic practice model should help to produce greater overall change in less time.

AN OVERVIEW OF CRISIS INTERVENTION

Crisis theory is perhaps best viewed as a synthesis of knowledge and concepts drawn from several theoretical and practice areas. Briefly, these include the fusion of crisis concepts and brief treatment concepts originating in the community mental health movement, plus influences from stress theory, learning theory, personality theory, systems theory, and the public health model (Rapoport, 1970, p. 268). Several crisis theorists have proposed definitions of the crisis concept; however, in developing the dualistic model, the definition offered by Gerald Caplan is used: ". . . crises are the short periods of psychological upset which occur from time to time as a person wrestles with problems which are temporarily beyond his capacity" (1974, pp. 200-201). From this framework come six characteristics of the crisis state, each of which serves as a sort of guiding principle to crisis intervention practice.[5]

1. All persons seek to maintain equilibrium or a steady pattern of functioning in their lives. Although each person may define his or her indi-

---

[5]The various summaries of the model presented in this chapter have been synthesized by this author from the works of others. See, for example, Rapoport, 1965; Pasewark and Albers, 1972; Caplan, 1974; and Golan, 1978.

vidual pattern of functioning somewhat differently, there is a striving to maintain balance.

2. When someone is in crisis, his or her equilibrium is upset and this often manifests itself in behavioral and emotional disruption. For example, the person in crisis may experience uncharacteristic problems at work or in interpersonal relationships, or may experience unpredictable changes in mood or affective functioning.

3. A crisis or state of crisis is neither a pathological experience nor an illness. This characteristic dictates divergence from a more traditional treatment model that might require a diagnosis-treatment-cure sequence, and by its nonpathology orientation there is a tone of optimism; that is, the individual's behavior in a crisis is seen as a realistic response to current reality rather than a deviation from normalcy.

4. Crises are temporary and time limited; it is not possible to remain in an active state of crisis indefinitely. Therefore, crises are acute rather than chronic; resolution of the active crisis will occur in that equilibrium of some sort will be established, generally within six to eight weeks.

5. Individuals tend to be more amenable to help when in a state of active crisis, in which case a minimal effort is likely to produce a maximal effect.

6. Success in effectively handling a current crisis helps the individual cope more successfully with future crises; this is true to the extent that existing coping mechanisms are strengthened or that new coping skills are learned in the process of crisis resolution.

Goals and Techniques of Crisis Intervention

The primary goals of crisis intervention can be summarized as follows: to reduce the immediate impact of the crisis event or crisis state (i.e., to relieve symptoms), to understand the relevant precipitating event(s) or factor(s), and to use the crisis situation to help the individual not only to regain control and a sense of mastery over the current situation, but also to strengthen the capacity for more effective future coping. At the very least, it is hoped that the individual's precrisis level of functioning will be restored as a result of effective intervention. Clearly, there is an emphasis on the here and now. This, in turn, dictates that the crisis interventionist take an active, directive, and supportive role as opposed to a more traditional role of neutral moderator or quasi-passive reflector. A crisis situation is not the time for nondirective, insight-oriented reflection from the worker; rather, basic intervention skills are crucially important. For example, the crisis interventionist must be highly skilled at establishing rapport and communicating at a level the client can understand. In addition, the ability to observe carefully and to assess the client's behavioral and affective functioning is extremely important. Working with people in crisis simply does not afford the luxury of time to slowly build rapport or to work through the subtleties of various communication styles. The importance of these skills cannot be overemphasized. Unfortunately, brief descriptions are often deceptive because they leave the impression that these are easily mastered skills since they are basic to all therapeutic intervention. However, the reality of intervention in emotionally charged, time-limited crisis situations demands a greater degree of skill than would otherwise be required.

The range of specific crisis intervention techniques encompasses the following:

1. Anticipatory guidance and rehearsal for reality are two interrelated techniques that reinforce the educational component of crisis work. They are designed to help the client first anticipate, then prepare and learn to cope more effectively with, problematic situations that are likely to occur.
2. Advice giving, although a definite taboo in some interventive strategies, may be appropriate depending on the specific circumstances of the crisis situation.
3. Realistic reassurance is used to provide emotional support and a sense of optimism in relation to the crisis and its resolution.
4. Clarification and selective interpretation are used to focus attention on the immediate alternatives for action. In particular, partialization may be especially helpful. This refers to breaking the totality of the situation into manageable parts so that alternatives, decisions, and specific tasks can be identified, explored, and prioritized jointly by the worker and the client.
5. Identification and mobilization of existing support systems, including the involvement of community resources as well as significant others, helps to move the client into a supportive atmosphere where collective action can be initiated directed toward immediate problem resolution.
6. Throughout the process, emphasis is placed on the capacity to predict and control in order to enhance coping skills and facilitate mastery of the immediate situation; the distant past rarely, if ever, is a focus in crisis intervention work.

A final point that should be stressed is that crisis intervention is not simply a truncated version of more traditional interventive strategies. Rather, it is an independent strategy with several distinct advantages: It offers immediate and direct help in a time-limited framework; it can be adopted and implemented by service-delivery persons with a broad range of educational and experiential backgrounds; and it has wide applicability in terms of practice setting and target of intervention.

AN OVERVIEW OF ADVOCACY

The dictionary offers two definitions of the term *advocate*. First, an advocate is "one that pleads the cause of another"; this is essentially the meaning given to the legal advocate or lawyer. The second definition is "one who argues for, defends, maintains, or recommends a cause or proposal." The latter is the broader of the two definitions, and incorporates the political connotation by which the interests of an entire group may be represented. Although perhaps not wholeheartedly supported by all members of the profession, social work's commitment to an advocacy role or function is amply documented in the literature (Grosser, 1965; Thursz, 1966; Brager, 1968; Ad Hoc Committee, 1969; Richan, 1973; Tropman et al., 1977; Kutchins and Kutchins, 1978). In particular, the social activism of the sixties spawned renewed concern for widespread social injustice, including such national issues as poverty, racism, and sexual inequality; in response, an Ad Hoc Committee on Advocacy was established by the National Association of Social Workers in 1968.[6] And, in a paper presented at the 1967 National Conference on Social Welfare, Scott Briar argued convincingly for "an expanded conception of social casework," involving a revitalization of the social broker and advocacy functions which he saw as having been sacrificed to the therapeutic function. Reflecting on earlier views of the caseworker's function, Briar (1967, p. 28) stated: "The caseworker was to be his client's supporter, his adviser, his champion, and if need be, his representative in his dealings with the court, the police, the social agency, and the other organizations that affected his well-being."

Although the literature reflects a distinction between *case* advocacy — action taken on behalf of a specific client — and *class* advocacy — action taken to effect change in policies, practices, or laws affecting *all* persons in a specific group or class — the two are highly interrelated (Ad Hoc Committee, 1969, p. 19). For example, to argue successfully on behalf of a particular rape victim that the county pay for expenses incurred in collecting medical evidence so the case can be prosecuted may set a precedent that can ultimately be established as the policy regarding payment in all subsequent cases. In other words, class advocacy may be viewed as an extension of case advocacy: The precedent-setting individual case serves as the basis for new policy. However, the caveat of all social work

---

[6] The Ad Hoc Committee on Advocacy was established by the NASW Task Force on the Urban Crisis and Public Welfare Problems which itself had been established by the Board of Directors in 1968 to coordinate and redirect NASW's program to make it more responsive to current national crises.

intervention must be kept in mind: The client has the right of self-determination. If, in the above example, the victim did not wish to file charges, did not wish to pursue prosecution or to seek medical attention, that must be her prerogative; a particular victim-client must not be held responsible for the practitioner-advocate's desire to effect change or improve services for future victims-clients. As stated by Kutchins and Kutchins (1978, p. 39), "The social worker as an advocate cannot weigh competing claims, cannot sacrifice his client's interests for any cause. . . . The advocate can only represent his client's interests as the client defines them." Returning to the dualistic model, if one is willing to concede that rape victims, individually or as a group, are "subject to discrimination, other forms of injustice and indignity, or simply bureaucratic bungling" (Richan, 1973, p. 220), then the advocacy strategy has a place in the practitioner's repetoire; however, the decision to implement this strategy must neither compromise the wishes, nor be at the expense, of an individual victim-client.

Functions of the Advocate

The basic function of the advocate is to make sure that the system is responsive to the needs of those it is supposed to serve and, specifically, to ensure that service consumers receive all the benefits to which they are entitled. The tactics or techniques of the advocate are often flexible, depending on the situation; they may range from partisan tactics where there is little, if any, room allowed for modification of one's position, to tactics of accommodation where cooperation is often both appropriate and desirable. In order to use the advocacy strategy effectively, advocates must master several knowledge and skill areas. Not only must they have knowledge of service-delivery systems, organizational dynamics, and institutional change strategies, but they must have a thorough understanding of the policies, regulations, and appeal procedures of the agencies and systems that they will confront. Equally crucial, however, are skills in organization, data gathering, environmental manipulation, and public relations (the last specifically including effective use of the media).

However, there are two significant dilemmas that tend to arise for social workers vis-à-vis the advocacy strategy. The first is what might loosely be termed the element of *style*. Although professional education (particularly in social work) has tended generally to support a consensus orientation, the advocacy strategy — by definition — dictates an adversary or conflict orientation which requires a more aggressive worker style than is typically found in the more traditional repertoire of interventive strategies. For many human service workers the "combative stance" is neither comfortable nor natural, and it may, for some, create discomfort by challenging a certain world view of the relative "goodness" of all persons (Ad Hoc Committee, 1969). There are few greater disillusionments, particularly for social work students and new practitioners, than the discovery that not all persons share a behavioral commitment to integrity, honesty, and social justice. The second dilemma centers on the need for knowledge of the law, especially in relation to civil rights and in terms of understanding how the legal-judicial system actually operates. Although some social work educators recognize the importance of pragmatic legal knowledge for practitioners, curricula of schools of social work are crowded and simply may not have room for courses pertaining to the law. Unless curriculum changes occur, the result will likely be a graduate with a deficient background for the effective practice of advocacy.

IMPLEMENTATION OF THE DUALISTIC MODEL

The service-delivery program with which the author worked as a coordinator, training consultant, and counselor-advocate for more than three years is typical of many rape crisis programs across the country. Its primary objective is to provide around-the-clock, in-person counseling to rape victims at the emergency room of the county hospital. Much of the thinking that led to the development of the dualistic model has been based on the author's experience with this program; this has included not only firsthand encounters with rape victims, but also encounters with the network of formal service-delivery systems with which victims interact. These systems include medical (emergency room staff and physicians from the medical examiner's office), law enforcement (police officers, detectives, and deputy sheriffs), legal (prosecutors from the district attorney's office), and judicial (courtroom personnel, including clerks, bailiffs, justices of the peace, and county and district court judges). Although there are regional variations in the structure of formal service-delivery systems, the implementation of the dualistic model is generalizable since all victims who pursue prosecution must (1) have a medical examination (for the collection of medical evidence), (2) report the offense to law enforcement officials (and subsequently give a formal statement of their complaint), (3) cooperate with the district attorney's office in preparing the case (this may involve appearing at preliminary hearings or examining trials prior to the defendant's indictment), and (4) appear in court for the trial. The following two sections describe the implementation of crisis intervention and advocacy in relation to working with rape victims. Although examples are used to demonstrate certain points, identifying information has been altered to protect the privacy of the individuals involved.

WORKING WITH RAPE VICTIMS: CRISIS INTERVENTION

Typically, the first encounter between the victim and the counselor-advocate occurs at the hospital emergency room, usually within a few hours following the assault. Keeping in mind the characteristics of the crisis state described earlier, the counselor-advocate assumes that whatever behaviors and emotions the victim exhibits are most likely in response to the assault and the circumstances surrounding it. In view of the traditional social work admonition of "start where the client is," the counselor-advocate attempts to assess the victim's needs. Frequently these needs dichotomize around the immediate situation: first, a need for specific information (e.g., when is the doctor coming? What is he or she going to do? What happens next?), and second, a need for emotional support and acceptance in light of what has happened (e.g., the victim may feel "dirty," ashamed, or angry, and she may be wondering whether anyone will be able to accept her nonjudgmentally). Crisis intervention skills are well suited to this type of situation. The counselor-advocate is directive enough to introduce a degree of structure into the interaction, thereby reducing some of the anxiety that the victim may be experiencing in this otherwise unknown, unstructured period of waiting for the medical examiner. Specific information is offered by the counselor-advocate about the physical examination; this is especially important if the victim has never had a pelvic exam. Once questions about medical treatment have been answered, victims frequently ask about police procedures. Some victims have certain preconceived notions about the police (particularly because the mass media have tended to portray law enforcement officers as rude, insensitive skeptics with little regard for rape victims), while others may have already had an encounter with an officer who has made some impression (positive or negative), thus shaping expectations about subsequent interactions with police. If, for whatever reasons, the victim's expectations are negative, she may express considerable apprehension in this regard. The crisis techniques of anticipatory guidance and rehearsal for reality are very appropriate in such situations. That is, as someone knowledgeable about police procedures, the counselor-advocate is able to anticipate and describe the setting, structure, and probable content of the victim-police interaction. The counselor-advocate is able to tell the victim what kinds of questions will be asked by both the reporting officer (if she has not already made an initial report of the offense) and by the detective(s) who will take her statement if she chooses to file formal charges against her assailant.

Following the medical examination and collection of evidence at the hospital, the victim will usually go to the police department and give her formal statement to one or more detectives. The counselor-advocate may accompany the victim to provide support but, depending on departmental policy, may or may not be allowed to be present when the statement is taken. After the victim has completed her statement, her tasks in relation to the processing of the criminal complaint are finished until the police need her to look at "mug shots" or to make an identification of a suspect in a lineup. She does, however, have other tasks to attend to in relation to the rape experience. For example, she may have specific medical problems or concerns about pregnancy or venereal disease, and she may have to contend with the often unpredictable reactions of family, friends, and whoever else may know about the assault. While one can hope that responses from family and friends will be supportive and constructive, realistically, they may be severely damaging to the victim's emotional and perhaps even physical well-being. The support and realistic reassurance of the counselor-advocate continues to play an important role in helping the victim regain a sense of control in relation to what has happened. In particular, it is imperative that the victim know that a fear of being alone, the existence of what might otherwise be labeled paranoid feelings with regard to men, and generalized anxiety are all typical or "normal" responses for someone who has been raped.

The Importance of Follow-up

With the victim's permission, the counselor-advocate continues to keep in touch at agreed-upon intervals for several weeks, or until the victim indicates no further need for services. Unless continued follow-up is stressed, it may become sporadic, sometimes due to reticence on the part of the counselor-advocate (e.g., not wanting to intrude on or bother the victim, preferring instead to have her initiate contact), but often due to a tendency on the victim's part to try to "forget" what happened. How successful a coping mechanism this is for rape victims is unknown, but while "forgetting it happened" may be effective for a time, it probably leaves the victim with some unresolved feelings and questions. It is entirely possible that these unresolved issues may, at some later time, perhaps even years later, show themselves concretely in divorce statistics and in impaired levels of social functioning. Although this has yet to be documented, it is an area that calls for investigation.

There is a more definitive reason for continued follow-up with the victim who pursues prosecution. Although a victim may be coping adequately and may have essentially returned to a pattern of functioning much like that which preceded the rape, it is often disconcerting, if not clearly traumatic, to be subpoenaed to court for the trial, particularly because, for many victims, this is the first indication that a suspect has been arrested and indicted for the rape. When this occurs (and it may happen weeks or months later), it is likely to revive memories of the assault as if it had just happened; victims may not only remember or "relive" the rape in vivid detail, but new feelings of fear and anxiety may develop. In general these feelings are related to seeing the assailant again, having to testify, perhaps being instructed to describe the rape in graphic detail, and being subjected to cross-examination by a defense attorney, all in open court. Even if the victim has significant others with whom she can share her feelings (but especially if she does not), it is still important that the counselor-advocate be available to provide continued emotional support, realistic reassurance, and information related to judicial procedures.

At this time, just as in dealing with the medical and law enforcement systems, the victim may need factual information regarding the legal-judicial system. For example, many victims are disturbed and disillusioned to find that the prosecutor (an assistant district attorney) plans to talk with them only briefly, and that this preparatory meeting may take place only hours (or minutes) before court. Nor are many victims prepared for the frequent courtroom delays or trial postponements that are judicial facts of life, but that may also be tactics used by the defense to discourage the victim from following through with the case. In addition, given that the vast majority of felony cases are plea bargained rather than brought to an actual courtroom trial,[7] the victim needs to know this and she needs to be informed about sentencing options such as probation. (Although many people assume that a felony conviction for rape will result in incarceration, in some cases, the convicted rapist is placed on probation; hence, he remains free in the community under the supervision of probation authorities.) To some extent, the crisis interventionist and advocate roles may seem to overlap at this point because there is only a fine distinction between providing information, being supportive, and ensuring that the victim-client receives all the services to which she is entitled. Although it can certainly be argued that it is the responsibility of the prosecutor to advise the complainant about judicial procedures and local courtroom norms, in this author's experience, this is rarely done — hence, the evolution of the dualistic intervention model.

WORKING FOR RAPE VICTIMS: ADVOCACY

Potentially, the decision to implement the advocacy strategy exists in relation to every encounter with the network of formal service-delivery systems with which victims interact. At the hospital, for example, the counselor-advocate is initially engaged in providing support to the victim, offering information to clarify and partialize the situation so that attention may be focused on immediate concerns and decisions. However, if there is evidence that medical treatment is inadequate or that the emergency room staff or other personnel are degrading or insensitive to the victim's needs, the counselor-advocate may need to shift into an advocacy position on behalf of the victim. This is not to suggest that the counselor-advocate should compromise or in any way jeopardize the victim's situation by being arrogant or intrusive; however, the mere presence of the counselor-advocate in the emergency room can be an incentive for the provision of adequate rather than marginal or inadequate treatment. Based on this author's observations, for example, most cases involving inadequate collection of evidence by the medical

---

[7] Although exact figures on the frequency of plea bargaining efforts are not available, a safe estimate is that approximately 85% of felony cases are administratively plea bargained to disposition rather than judicially disposed by formal trial before a judge or jury. See Arthur Rosett and Donald R. Cressey, *Justice by Consent*. Philadelphia: Lippincott, 1976.

examiner seemed to result more from ignorance or carelessness rather than malicious intent, and often a few tactful but directive suggestions were all that was needed to correct the situation. Still, there are instances where the medical examiner or representatives from other service-delivery systems resent the apparent intrusion of an outsider into "their" domain. Rather than engage in overt, probably unpleasant, conflict where the victim is caught in the middle, the more appropriate and effective approach is for the counselor-advocate to discuss the problem privately with the specific individual involved; if the problem cannot be resolved in this manner, then a formal complaint, in writing, including detailed facts of the situation, should be filed with the individual's immediate supervisor. This should then be followed through until an acceptable response has been received. It is at this point that case advocacy makes the transition to class advocacy; there may be no way to retroactively correct an error of omission in the collection of medical evidence in one particular case, but if the error is not allowed to slide by, if the proper procedure is subsequently clarified and communicated to those who provide the service then the error may not occur for future victims.

Class Advocacy

The advocacy strategy is more commonly implemented on behalf of all (potential as well as actual) rape victims in the sense of class advocacy. In this way there is less risk of jeopardizing a specific case and individual victims do not feel compelled to "fight for a cause" publicly unless they choose to do so. Fortunately, from the advocate's position, there are victims willing to share their experiences in the hope of helping others, and it is their experiences that provide the data necessary to identify problem areas and to document needs in a given community. In relation to identifying problems and documenting needs, one of the inherent difficulties in advocacy on behalf of rape victims is the reality that there are numerous views and connotations of the term rape. To the extent that rape is viewed as multidimensional, there are multiple definitions and conflicting interests represented. For example, to a law enforcement officer, prosecutor, or judge, rape is a crime, a violation of the penal code; to a medical examiner, rape is a vaginal culture; to a mental health professional, rape may be symptomatic of the offender's mental illness; to a feminist, rape is an act of power-dominance-violence; to the general public, there are two kinds of rape — those that are "real" and those where the victim "asked for it."

In view of these somewhat simplified operational definitions, it is also clear that rape is a highly charged issue, and when the emotionalism surrounding rape is coupled with the lack of definitional consensus, the advocate is frequently forced to be somewhat manipulative in order to be effective. Although many social workers are offended at the suggestion that manipulation be used consciously as a practice technique, it would be helpful to move beyond the emotionally loaded connotation of the word and acknowledge, if only tacitly, that manipulation is frequently a part of social work intervention. According to Brill (1978, p. 141), manipulation simply refers to skillful management. The effective use of manipulation would suggest that the advocate recognize these diverse views on rape and select the most effective and appropriate approach vis-à-vis the individual, group, or system at hand. Realistically, this is a commonsense interventive technique.

Given that the basic advocacy function involves making sure that the system(s) is responsive to the needs of rape victims, then ensuring that victims actually receive the services to which they are entitled (and it should be emphasized here that the manner in which services are delivered, that is, how constructively or humanely services are delivered, is at least of equal importance), several objectives emerge. Figure 2-1 shows both the objectives and the methods or techniques of advocacy on behalf of rape victims. In practice, the advocacy strategy is neither as simple nor as straightforward as it appears in the figure. The development of surveys and interview schedules requires considerable time and skill, and even then there is the question of whether full cooperation can be obtained from potential respondents. This may be particularly problematic if representatives of service-delivery systems feel threatened or hostile toward "outsiders," especially if the outsiders are known to have a vested interest that is viewed as challenging the status quo. In this respect public relations skills are needed in order to allay anxieties and elicit cooperation. Assertiveness, purposefulness, and flexibility are needed in order to proceed effectively with the advocacy strategy.

Objectives	Techniques
Identification of relevant-service delivery systems	Community research and data gathering: surveys and personal interviews
Victim needs assessments	Literature reviews; surveys and interviews with victims and rape crisis staff
Evaluation of service-delivery systems	On-site monitoring; surveys and interviews with victims and service deliverers
Public position statement(s)	Development of ad hoc committees; coalition groups; community-based conferences; media coverage
Litigation and legal redress	Class action suit(s)
Policy change(s)	Legislative lobbying; advisory council memberships; media support

Figure 2-1. Objectives and techniques of advocacy on behalf of rape victims.

NEW KNOWLEDGE: PRACTICE IMPLICATIONS

Thus far, the discussion of the dualistic practice model would lead one to believe that all women respond to rape or sexual assault in the same way and that they all share the same needs with respect to intervention. However, recent research (as well as common sense) suggests that this may be a rather simplistic notion. Specifically, research conducted in part by this author investigating the rape-as-crisis conceptualization has raised two significant issues pertinent to this discussion: the variations among different racial-ethnic groups in response to rape, and the viability of the rape-as-crisis conceptualization.

Racial-Ethnic Variations in Response to Rape

In research conducted by Williams and Holmes (1981), data gathered from 61 female rape victims (32 white, 11 black, 18 Mexican American, 14 to 67 years of age) were used to assess the impact of rape from a crisis perspective.[8] Not surprisingly, all victims were negatively affected by the rape experience to some degree. However, what was surprising was that the only variable that reflected significantly different degrees of crisis response was victim race-ethnicity, a variable that has not yet been addressed by crisis theorists. Specifically, Mexican American victims tended to experience the greatest degree of crisis, blacks the least, with whites in between (Williams and Holmes, 1981, pp. 98-99). In "Survival Strategies for Oppressed Minorities," Trader (1977, p. 10) states that "it is important to remember that most, if not all, theories underlying practice are culture-bound." Therefore, with the crisis model (as in most models) there is a risk of operating from certain class- and culture-bound expectations that presume to suggest how rape victims *should* react to their experience and for *how long.* For example, in discussing the crisis intervention model in relation to rape victims, Golan (1978, p. 218) states: "After several weeks of extensive work, most women tend to integrate the experience and place it appropriately in their past." In light of the Williams and Holmes findings, practitioners need to be especially sensitive to such potential racial-ethnic variations in victim responses. Specifically, the practitioner's failure to temper his or her expectations of how victims "should" respond and how soon they "should" get over it, may well result in misunderstanding and, ultimately, in unsuccessful intervention. While black victims may be met with skepticism because they do not appear sufficiently upset by the experience, Mexican American victims may risk being labeled as seriously disturbed because they "overreact" or fail to resolve the experience quickly enough. Both examples represent risks inherent in crisis intervention

---

[8] For a detailed description of this research, including methodology and findings, see Williams and Holmes, 1981.

when the model is oversimplified and used without regard for its inherent class- and culture-bound expectations.

Further, when a presenting problem as controversial and emotionally charged as rape is being dealt with, it is clear that the knowledge, values, and attitudes of the helping person are more crucial than ever. Good intentions, though admirable, are not a guarantee of competent help. Given that each person is a product of his or her socialization and life experience, each of us carries with us certain preconceived notions about rape and about how "real" victims are expected to (or "should") react. To the degree that these subtle, preconceived notions are translated into behavioral expectations, all rape victims are in jeopardy from those who wish only to help. Practitioners must remind themselves that each person, therapist and client alike, enters the helping relationship as a unique composite of values, attitudes, and life experiences. Rape victims from different racial-ethnic groups will bring their identity, shaped both by their unique historical relationship to the dominant (white) society and by contemporary inequality (sexual and racial-ethnic), to bear on the definition of the problem, its meaning, and its resolution. However, as a further word of caution, this is not to suggest that practitioners adopt still another set of rigid expectations based solely on skin color or surname. The point is that while an awareness of racial-ethnic and cultural diversity is a beginning, the knowledge base of practitioners must be expanded to include substantive understanding as well as an appreciation of the *range* of responses to rape associated with race-ethnicty (and class) differences.

Rape as Crisis: A Reconceptualization

Another of the findings from the Williams and Holmes (1981, p. 98) research that bears discussion here relates to the rape-as-crisis conceptualization. Several variables derived from crisis theory (e.g., time since assault, victim's maturational stage, institutional and personal support systems) were tested in relation to victims' crisis responses, but no significant relationships were found. For example, although crisis theory suggests that crises are, by definition, time limited, that disequilibrium last only six to eight weeks, this was not supported by the data. For this group of victims, assaulted from one to 36 months prior to the research interview, the degree of affective and behavioral disequilibrium they experienced did not vary significantly according to time. Although rape does seem to precipitate some degree of crisis response for victims, the resultant disequilibrium may *not* end within a six-to-eight-week period. Rather, victims appear to be left with a variety of disruptive residual crisis effects, or what might be called a *prolonged crisis.* Additional data from this research suggest that public or community attitudes about rape appear to be contributing factors to the victim's experience of rape as a prolonged crisis. Referring to this connection as the "second assault," the authors state that ". . . the rape experience can be more thoroughly understood, not simply as the victim's 'personal trouble,' but as the interplay of both extrinsic and intrinsic forces that, working together, all too often seem to culminate in a 'second assault' " (Williams and Holmes, 1981, p. 170).

Consequently, for those concerned with service delivery and treatment for rape victims, it is clear that attention must be given not only to the victim's significant others, but also to prevailing community attitudes. In other words, victims of rape do not exist in a social vacuum; they interact with and are influenced by the social and community context in which they live. For the practitioner then, assessment of the degree to which the attitudes of others mitigate *or* exacerbate resolution of the rape experience is crucial in understanding (i.e., individualizing) the client's response and, ultimately, in carrying out effective intervention.

Finally, it is important that practitioners begin to examine some of the practice questions raised here in an attempt to determine whether the crisis intervention strategy needs modification in relation to rape victims. In particular, the following beliefs or expectations about the rape-as-crisis conceptualization should be scrutinized carefully: (1) that the rape experience precipitates a kind of unidimensional crisis for all victims, (2) that the rape per se is the only source of stress for victims, and (3) that six to eight weeks is sufficient time for victims to resolve the rape experience. Until practitioners who use the crisis intervention strategy begin to collect their own systematic data, interventive efforts are likely to remain framed in a context of good intentions and intuitive practice wisdom. I believe that our clients deserve more.

THE DUALISTIC MODEL: SOME PARTING THOUGHTS

The dualistic model presented here, the planned combination of crisis intervention and advocacy, holds promise for achieving effective intervention at both the micro (individual) and macro (societal) levels. Despite the questions raised here about the rape-as-crisis conceptualization, the crisis intervention strategy, when used skillfully, probably remains the most viable treatment approach for helping victims of rape in the short run. In the long run, however, it is the advocacy strategy that may have the greater impact, especially when the advocacy role is extended to the macro level of social change with the aim of eradicating rape. If, as feminists contend by their definition of the problem, rape represents predatory sexual inequality, a means of social control whereby women are "kept in their place," then only the restructuring of society and resocialization toward sexual equality can be the advocate's final objective. In the interim, the dualistic model presented here can serve to help victims deal more effectively with the existing realities of rape and can improve and humanize the services that they must have.

REFERENCES

Ad Hoc Committee on Advocacy. 1969. The social worker as advocate: Champion of social victims. *Social Work*, 14:16–22.

Bisno, H. 1952. *The Philosophy of Social Work*. Washington, D.C.: Public Affairs Press.

Brager, G. A. 1968. Advocacy and political behavior. *Social Work*, 13:5–11.

Briar, S. 1967. The current crisis in social casework. *Social Work Practice*. New York: Columbia University Press.

Brill, N. 1978. *Working with People: The Helping Process*. Philadelphia: Lippincott.

Brownmiller, S. 1975. *Against Our Will: Men, Women and Rape*. New York: Simon & Schuster.

Burgess, A. W., and Holmstrom, L. L. 1974a. *Rape: Victims of Crisis*. Bowie, Md.: Robert J. Brady.

Burgess, A. W., and Holmstrom, L. L. 1974b. Crisis and counseling requests of rape victims. *Nursing Research*, 23:196–202.

Caplan, G. 1974. *Support Systems and Community Mental Health*. New York: Behavioral Publications.

Friedlander, W. A. 1958. *Concepts and Methods of Social Work*. Englewood Cliffs, N.J.: Prentice-Hall.

Golan, N. 1978. *Treatment in Crisis Situations*. New York: Free Press.

Griffin, S. 1971. Rape: The all American crime. *Ramparts*, 10:26–35.

Grosser, C. F. 1965. Community development programs serving the urban poor. *Social Work*, 10:15–21.

Hamilton, G. 1947. *Theory and Practice of Social Case Work*. New York: Columbia University Press.

Kutchins, H., and Kutchins, S. 1978. Advocacy and social work. In G. H. Weber and G. McCall, eds., *Social Scientists as Advocates*, pp. 13–48. Beverly Hills, Calif.: Sage.

McCombie, S. 1976. Characteristics of rape victims seen in crisis intervention. *Smith College Studies in Social Work*, 46:137–58.

Pasewark, R. A., and Albers, D. A. 1972. Crisis intervention: Theory in search of a program. *Social Work*, 17:70–77.

Rapoport, L. 1965. The state of crisis: Some theoretical considerations. In H. J. Parad, ed., *Crisis Intervention: Selected Readings*, pp. 22–31. New York: Family Service Association of America.

Rapoport, L. 1970. Crisis intervention as a mode of brief treatment. In R. W. Roberts and R. H. Nee, eds., *Theories of Social Casework*, pp. 267–311. Chicago: University of Chicago Press.

Richan, W. C. 1973. Dilemmas of the social work advocate. *Child Welfare*, 52:220–226.

Sutherland, S. F., and Scherl, D. J. 1972. Crisis intervention with victims of rape. *Social Work*, 17:37–42.

Thursz, D. 1966. Social action as a professional responsibility. *Social Work*, 11:12–21.

Trader, H. P. 1977. Survival strategies for oppressed minorities. *Social Work*, 22:10–13.

Tropman, J. E., Lauffer, A., and Lawrence, W. 1977. A guide to advocacy. In F. M. Cox, J. L. Erlich, J. Rothman, and J. E. Tropman, eds., *Tactics and Techniques of Community Practice*, pp. 199–207. Itasca, Ill.: F. E. Peacock.

Williams, J. E., and Holmes, K. A. 1981. *The Second Assault: Rape and Public Attitudes*. Westport, Conn.: Greenwood Press.

3
Rape Trauma Syndrome: Developmental Variations

Ebrahim Amanat, M.D.

ABSTRACT

Clinical evaluation of a group of 54 victims of sexual assault reveals a variety of significant issues to be considered for therapeutic intervention:

1. *Demographic data reveal the greatest frequency in the age group 14 and 15 years.*
2. *The alarm phase with hypothalamic-pituitary response and hyperemotionalism resembles most other life-threatening traumas.*
3. *During the reorganization phase, there are three distinctly different response patterns correlated to the victim's premorbid personality and developmental background.*
4. *The popular belief systems about the victim's "promiscuity" has much more to do with a combination of temperamental styles of "positive approach" and "intensity" as defined by Stella Chess.*
5. *Complicating factors and appropriate therapeutic interventions for each one of the developmental variations have been enumerated.*

INTRODUCTION

Psychological development and the process of individuation depend upon three major factors:

1. Natural temperamental and hereditary characteristics
2. Environmental influences
3. Chronological influences

Stella Chess (1968, 1969) and her co-workers, in a brilliant longitudinal study of individuality, have identified nine temperamental styles that influence psychological development. None of these temperamental qualities is "good" or "bad" when considered alone, but in the context of environmental expectations, they may lead to favorable or unfavorable outcomes.

Natural "temperaments" reported by Chess include:

1. Activity
2. Intensity of reactions
3. Persistence
4. Sensitivity threshold
5. Distractibility

6. Rhythmicity
7. Quality of mood
8. Approach
   (extroversion-introversion)
9. Adaptability

The author of this chapter has created a temperamental rating scale to evaluate these characteristics during the clinical evaluation.

Child psychologists as well as ethologists have well documented the significance of childhood experiences in later life through the phenomena of imprinting and "critical age" patterns.

Of the many schools of thought in early psychological development, those of Erik Erikson (1959) and Margaret Mahler (1967) have gained momentum in recent decades. Erikson's epigenetic theory focuses on the entire life cycle, passing through successive stages of trust, autonomy, initiative, industry, identity, intimacy, generativity, and integrity. A regressive development in any of these stages may cause personality problems.

Mahler's developmental psychology, on the other hand, focuses on the first three to four years of life and the development of object constancy. According to her, the two major tracks of psychological growth include (1) separation and (2) individuation.

1. The track of separation passes through the following stages:
   a. Presymbiotic isolation along with attraction to gratifying experiences and coenesthetic human contact
   b. Symbiotic bonding and attachment with trust, dependence, clinging behaviors, and confident expectation of safety
   c. Postsymbiotic separation, with autonomy liberation and self-regulation
   d. Rapprochement
2. The track of individuation has its own parallel stages:
   a. Autistic and spontaneous self-stimulation
   b. Imitative, replicative modeling with optimal discrepancy and stranger's anxiety
   c. Mutative linking and connection of parts to differentiate wholes
   d. Integration of wholeness and a sense of constancy-permanence

Major difficulties interrupting the normal progression of these stages may lead to personality makeups identifiable in clinical evaluation. These personality patterns may be differentiated as:

a. Presymbiotic — isolated or autistic
b. Symbiotic — imitative or dependent
c. Postsymbiotic — independent and autonomous

Ann Burgess (Burgess and Holmstrom, 1976, 1979; Burgess and Lazare, 1976) and Linda Holmstrom (Holmstrom and Burgess, 1975a,b), in their intensive research of reactions of adult women rape victims, revealed for the first time the existence of "rape trauma syndrome" and its variations as clinical entities. They alerted clinicians to the possibility of rape even when the patients did not consciously mention it.

Rape trauma syndrome, according to these authors, has an "acute" phase (with physical and emotional symptoms) and a long-term reorganization phase (with life-style changes, etc.). Burgess and Holmstrom have also recognized compounded and silent forms, as well as trauma syndrome in previously assaulted patients and those with unresolved rape trauma.

Adelman, Concetta, and Estalone (1976) have focused on society's blaming of the victims, as well as the women victims' self-blame phenomena. According to these authors, anxiety and fear are two major components of rape trauma syndrome compounding the normal process of grief and mourning. Burgess and Lazare, (1976) have reported on the acute and chronic phases of rape when accompanied by life-threatening assaults and have reviewed the multidimensional aspects of treatment.

Treatment approaches commonly in practice focus not only on the victim's defensive operations, level of stress, support systems, etc., but also on the therapist's motivation, reaction to the victim's feelings towards men, and organizational support. This focus is particularly necessary to avoid burnout in the rape counselors.

During the years between 1974 and 1981, in collaboration with a multidisciplinary team (Greater St. Louis Sexual Abuse Committee, S.A.C.) and the Governor's Task Force for prevention of rape in Missouri, a group of 230 male and female rape victims were evaluated and treated by the author. Fifty-four of these victims were studied for a period of 12 months to evaluate their reaction patterns to rape trauma.

Based on Mahler's developmental psychology, I had hypothesized a variety of reactions to rape trauma according to the premorbid personality and psychological development of the victims. I had also hypothesized that temperamental characteristics would be of great significance in the patient's intensity of reaction, as well as his or her tendency to report or not report the incident.

No less an authority than Eric Berne (1970), in his sarcastic interpretation of the fairy tale "Little Red Riding Hood," has encouraged the popular belief that rape victims "set up themselves and the rapist" for the incident, so that they can complete their "rape" game and shout "Rape!"

My interest in this study was to focus on such personality characteristics which might create the illusion of "set up" or flirtation-teasing in the minds of victims or their friends, relatives, and even clinicians.

POPULATION

Fifty-four rape victims referred from a variety of sources including emergency rooms, victim witness programs, self-help groups, physicians, social workers, and pediatricians were evaluated and treated for a period of 12 months.

Table 3-1 reviews the demographic characteristics of the victims.

METHODOLOGY

A "rape trauma syndrome" checklist (Appendix I) based on the research findings of S.A.C. and a review of the literature was developed and distributed to all

TABLE 3-1A. Demographic Characteristics of Rape Victims

Age	< 5 / 2	6–11 / 11	12–18 / 16	18–30 / 10	> 50 / 2
Ethnic Group		Caucasian / 32		Black / 22	
Metropolitan Area		City / 26		Suburbs / 28	
Economic Group	< $5,000 / 1	$5,000–10,000 / 21		$10,000–20,000 / 29	> $20,000 / 3
Religion		Protestant / 42	Catholic / 9	Other / 3	
Education		Grade School / 19	Junior-Senior High / 25	College / 10	
Occupation	Unemployed / 8	Unskilled Laborer / 6	Skilled Laborer / 22	Other (school) / 18	
History of Trauma or Emotional Problems			Yes / 19	No / 35	

TABLE 3-1B. Demographic Characteristics of Rape Victims.

Former Rape History	Mother 6				
	Self 5				
Developmental Background	Presymbiotic 6	Symbiotic 23	Postsymbiotic 25		
Ego Identity Defenses	Normal 44	Deviation 10			
Complicating Factors	22 Including VD, BD, death, mutilation, surgery, gunshot, depression alcoholism, enuresis, convulsions, sexual attitude changes				
Referral Symptoms	Physical 38	Depression 28	Phobias 48	Anxiety 20	Withdrawal 16
					Life-style change 18
	Anger Response 14	Neurotic Behavior 12	Breakdowns 3	Hypochondriasis 8	
Temperament				Positive Approach 30	Negative Approach 11
	Intense 28	Mild 26	Persistent 19	Active 10	
		Predictable 24			

emergency rooms, rape crisis intervention centers, and local clinics. Initially all patients completed this checklist in collaboration with another clinician or myself and again 4 to 6 weeks after the rape incident. The checklist was also completed at the end of the treatment period for follow-up reasons.

Complete psychiatric, psychological, and temperamental evaluations were carried out on the victims, reviewing their presenting problems; family background; attitudes towards rape, sexuality, aggression, and trauma; developmental background; autonomous ego functions; object relationships; perceptual cognitive and intellectual functioning; speech and vocabulary; fantasies; self-concept; trusting ability; superego development; defense mechanisms; and emotional conflicts. A temperamental rating scale evaluating a variety of behavioral styles, particularly approach, intensity, impulsivity, regularity, activity level, and persistence, which has been independently standardized by the author, was used to evaluate the victims' qualities.

Complicating factors, such as recurrence, severe physical injury, and family reactions, were studied separately. Patients were treated individually and in groups, initially for crisis work and later for regular biweekly counseling sessions. A variety of approaches, particularly psychodrama and group sharing, were utilized for alleviation of symptoms and resolution of emotional conflicts.

Most patients were encouraged to participate in legal action supported by several local groups and legal authorities to enhance and improve social justice in rape trials.

CLINICAL PICTURE

1. Alarm Phase

In accord with all major life-threatening crises, the immediate response of most victims in our group included the following symptoms: hyperawareness, revival of other crisis emotions, hyperemotionalism, specific physical symptoms, sleep disorders, blocking of thoughts, poor concentration, multiple fears of injury or death, and sexual behavior changes.

This *alarm phase* of the trauma syndrome lasts anywhere from a few hours to several weeks. For more intense and sensitive patients the alarm phase lasts longer, at times leading to breakdowns, suicidal ideation, delusional thinking, and hallucinations. Somatic symptoms are also variable in their intensity.

Shirley, a 31-year-old woman who was raped simultaneously with her 12-year-old daughter, was a very intense woman, with great impulsivity and a positive-approach temperament. During the rape incident she had attacked her assailant with a screwdriver, puncturing his lungs, which later led to his arrest and trial.

However, during the alarm phase her intense rage and helplessness in relation to the rape of her daughter, coupled with strong guilt feelings for "not protecting her child adequately," led to a psychotic breakdown requiring hospitalization. In less than two weeks she recovered from her psychosis, starting her long reorganization phase.

Jackie, a 24-year-old woman who was raped by a friend of a colleague during a local festival, was a rather mild-mannered but positive-approach person. Although her life was threatened during the rape incident and she was beaten severely by the assailant, her alarm phase was very short.

The day after the assault she had regained her calmness and only displayed mild boredom, mild mistrust of men, and mild sleep disturbance. She moved to the reorganization phase very quickly, gave up drinking, shared her feelings with some friends, and moved to another state. Follow-up telephone calls, 3 and 12 months later, revealed complete recovery of all symptoms.

TABLE 3-2.   Rape Trauma Syndrome.

---

1. Immediate Alarm Reaction
   (Hypothalmic pituitary response)
   Threat to Autonomy
   Survival challange
   Physical intrusion
   Loss

   ↓ ↓ ↓

   a. Hyperawareness: 86%
   b. Revival of all other crisis memories and affects: 76%
   c. Hyperemotionalism: 86%

•	Anxiety	92%	•	Hate	39%
•	Fear	82%	•	Humiliation	58%
•	Shame	44%	•	Helplessness	72%
•	Guilt	48%	•	Depression	57%
•	Anger	56%			

   d. Specific physical symptoms: 42%

•	Nausea	27%
•	Cough	12%
•	Abdominal pain	18%
•	Muscle spasms	58%
•	Discharge	22%

   e. Sleep-eating disorders: 68%
   f. Blocking of thoughts: 72%
   g. Poor concentration: 72%
   h. Fear of injury-death: 78%
   i. Sexual behavior changes: 78%

Table 3-2 reviews the frequency of symptoms observed during the alarm phase.

2. Reorganization Phase

Depending on the personality structure and psychological development of victims prior to the incident of rape, three distinctly different reaction patterns are observed in this phase. Delayed reactions last anywhere from three to four weeks to several years, according to a variety of elements. Shorter duration of this phase is prevalent among postsymbiotic personalities with less intense temperament and adequate emotional support. Longer duration of reorganization is linked with symbiotic or presymbiotic personalities, intensity and non-adaptability of temperament.

A. Presymbiotic Personalities.   These victims reveal a greater level of isolation, withdrawal, mistrust, and disengagement. These characteristics are intensified during the reorganization period with a high frequency of reliving experiences, somatization, hypoactivity, conservation depression, preoccupation, and fantasy.

TABLE 3-3.   Rape Trauma Syndrome.

2. Delayed Reorganization (resistance) Reaction
(sympathetic-adrenal response)

A. Presymbiotic isolated individuals: 11%
- Mistrust
- Withdrawal
- Fantasy
- Reliving experiences
- Somatization
- Hypoaction
- Conservation of Energy
- Preoccupation
- Irritability

B. Symbiotic dependent individuals: 43%
- Clinging
- Overdependence
- Multiple fears
- Nightmares
- Regression
- Reliving experiences
- Hypochondriasis
- Neediness
- Drinking

C. Post-symbiotic autonomous individuals: 46%
- Hyperkinesis
- Life-style changes
- Intellectualization
- Irritability, agitation
- Compulsive behaviors
- Depression, self-reproach, guilt, shame
- Reliving experiences
- Repression

The reported "silent" form of rape trauma syndrome was most frequent in this group, which constituted 11% of our population. These victims had the hardest time in reporting, applying for help, or pursuing counseling. It seemed as if they wished to suffer their pain alone.

Wythia, a 35-year-old divorcee, was a type of person who would stay home most of the time as a loner. She was not dating at the time since her experiences in marriage were negative and she mistrusted men. Her circle of friends was very small with no really close friends to count on at times of crises. She was a very cautious and withdrawn person who had quit school at eighth grade. Her personality evaluation revealed an overactive, negative-approach, and intense person who avoided risk, was very serious with her work, and displayed self-concept problems.

She was raped by a masked man in her home, under life-threatening circumstances and with forced sodomy. She had a feeling that her assailant had followed her for a while and learned a lot about her predictable life-style. Her delayed reaction to rape, which lasted eight months, included multiple fears, hypoactivity, paranoid delusions, severe withdrawal, occasional visual or auditory hallucinations, startle response, and many somatic symptoms. About three months after the rape incident, due to lack of available emotional support and intense depression, she had a psychotic reaction necessitating hospitalization. During this time she revealed that at age 12 she had been raped, and had kept the incident completely to herself throughout the years. Recently a man with the same name as her childhood aggressor had approached her for dating, reviving all the negative and damaging memories of the past leading to a psychotic adaptation pattern.

B. Symbiotic Personalities. The second type of reaction to rape trauma is developmentally linked with the symbiotic personality structure. These victims are basically trusting but dependent people. Most of them have a significant ally for their dependency needs: a husband, boyfriend, mother, father, friend, or sibling. They feel much more relaxed and comfortable in the presence of this ally. There is a strong sense of bonding-attachment and a depressive reaction when away from the symbiotic pair. During the reorganization phase this group, which constituted 43% of our population, became much more dependent and clinging. They showed regressive tendencies, a strong desire to be taken care by the symbiotic ally, and intense phobic reactions.

The prevalence of hypochondriasis, drug and alcohol use, nightmares, and a great desire to share the details of the assault with the symbiotic ally was striking. It seemed that these victims needed to bring their ally to every little detail of the experience in order to regain equilibrium.

Interestingly enough, in this group the reactions of the symbiotic ally was similar, almost mimicking those of the victim; a great deal of protective empathy and sympathy existed, along with fantasies of killing the rapist.

Grace, a 13-year-old girl who was raped by a good friend of her mother's, was brought to the first interview with chief complaints of restlessness; irritability; multiple fears; depression; annoying of her mother; death wishes; feelings of shame, helplessness, and self-blame; stomachache; and burning and pain with urination. These symptoms lasted for four weeks before the reorganization phase of her trauma syndrome started. Psychiatric evaluation had revealed a symbiotic dependent personality with features of predictability, mild intensity, low persistence, and negative approach.

As a child she was easy to raise and easily persuaded, and had developed a strong bond to her overprotective mother. According to her mother she was a spoiled child, very dependent and clingy to "mom."

Her childhood and school adjustment were reported as uneventful. Her mother presented herself more as a friend or an older sister than an authority figure. They frequently looked at each other to check facial expressions before answering any question. They insisted upon being evaluated and treated together. Often they talked and projected feelings for each other. The patient's mother, who herself had been raped at age 16, identified completely with her daughter, and displayed similar behavior patterns.

Immediately after the rape incident her mother had become far more protective, not allowing her to visit the neighborhood store, etc. Grace had regressed to babyish behaviors, clinging to her mother and sharing with her details of her experiences with men on repeated occasions; she ignored her appearance, became more active and sexually promiscuous with a cousin, and wished to sleep in her parents' bed. Her appetite had decreased, leading occasionally to her mother's feeding her. Often during the next several months Grace would present herself with a finger in her mouth complaining of physical problems that demanded attention from her mother.

C. Postsymbiotic Personalities.   For this group of autonomous, independent, outgoing, and assertive victims, the characteristics of rape trauma syndrome were most striking. Constituting 46% of our population, these victims displayed a very high prevalence of positive approach and intensity of emotions in their temperament.

They were self-confident and trusting in human relations, placing themselves often at risk due to their impulsivity, risk taking, intensity of involvement, and positive approach to unknown or strange situations. Even as young children, *approachers* smile at strangers and go to them with open arms. They like exploring new situations or friendships. They are colorful people, always involved in a multitude of activities and never unnoticed in a group. They like to know immediately how other people feel about them, thus often acting impulsively. Development of delay mechanisms in this group is often inadequate. *Intensers,* on the other hand, feel their feelings very strongly, come on too strong in their reactions, blurt out and need to know that other people are stimulated by their emotions. It seems as if they wish everyone to experience their intensity and difficulty in cooling off. Because of such intensity it is very common for other people, including clinicians, to consider *intensers* "hysterical" or "histrionic." The combination of these two temperamental characteristics often gives the impression of flirtatiousness or provocation, at least at the surface.

Interviewing relatives and friends of our postsymbiotic population revealed a greater prevalence of "blaming" towards these victims and feelings that they had set themselves up.

Judith, a 36-year-old woman who had revealed a postsymbiotic, aggressive, intense, and colorful personality, was scapegoated by her family and singled out by friends as a "difficult" person to get along with. Her family members always felt that she took too many risks and that her approach to men was seductive. She was first raped at age 15, with a tremendous amount of blame from her family members. Due to poor psychiatric management she had never resolved her feelings until the second rape. This time her intensity and impulsive positive approach had again put her at risk.

After the second rape she had a depressive psychotic reaction necessitating hospitalization. The clinician who was treating her diagnosed her as a case of manic-depressive illness in a hysterical personality. He categorically blamed her for "setting herself up" and suggested the use of electric shock before her family transferred her to my care. Apparently the clinical picture of rape trauma syndrome in intense people was unknown to this particular clinician.

Some representative statements made by this group of victims include the following:

"I am simply fascinated by new situations"; "I get involved in a lot of things and at times into jams"; "It is impossible for me to look at things purely objectively"; "Sometimes things dawn upon me giving me feelings of independence"; "I can't stop myself or my curiosity"; "At times I act impulsive. I cannot use my common sense"; "My feelings are quite intense"; "I hurt kind of deep inside;" "It is hard to describe my feelings: when I am afraid I am terrified, when I am in love I am very romantic, once I sent 24 bouquets of roses to a man I loved, completely overwhelming him"; "When I am alone I feel very isolated"; "When I get attracted to a new idea, it is difficult to block it or push it away"; "I never enjoy being a spectator, I want to be a participant"; "I am mystified by new things."

These autonomous, self-assertive, involved, outgoing, sociable, and impulsive victims at times do create an illusion of flirtation. A closer evaluation of their interaction patterns reveals an intensity of emotions, a positive-approach temperament, and a general lack of cautiousness in human endeavors. Feeling tones are very important to them. They can bring subjective reactions to clear focus very easily. They are expressive and give details of the rape incident. They are vivid about the effects of rape trauma under different life situations. Their expressions are intense, such as: "I was overwhelmed," "I felt blue," "I was scared pea green," "I was hysterical," "I was paralyzed," etc.

Under the circumstances, their recollection of details is astounding. Their emotional reactions fuse easily with past experiences, creating an acute sense of crisis and a reexperience of intense pain. These particular victims have no trouble evoking in their listener or counselor an appreciation of the intensity, uniqueness, or magnitude of their misery. Clearly this is a basis for the "over-identification" in rape trauma counselors as reported by Zonderman (1975). In our population more than half of the victims were in this category. Many of the postsymbiotic victims use words of emphasis and exaggeration. Superlative vocabulary and past progressive-tense language is typical. They have had a more frequent exposure to highly charged romantic situations.

This group of victims display a greater level of hyperactivity, life-style change, irritability, reliving experiences, intellectualization, agitation, compulsive behaviors, depression, self-reproach, guilt, shame, and eventually repression. Three victims in this category had psychotic breakdowns requiring long-term treatment.

3. Children's Reactions

More than half the victims in our clinical population were below age 18. This is in line with reports by Hayman and Lanza (1971) who found peak incidences of

TABLE 3-4.   Rape Trauma Syndrome.

3. Children's Reactions	
a. Nonverbal expression	f. Inhibition
b. Physical reactions	g. Clinging
c. Motor activity	h. Sexual fears
d. School phobias	i. Self-blame
e. Learning problems	j. Hiding–masking

rape at age 14 and 15. Children's reactions were essentially similar to those of adults in terms of developmental variations, except for a greater frequency of nonverbal physical reactions, increased motor activity, poor concentration, learning problems, school phobia, clinging, inhibition, sexual fears, self-blame, choking, bruises, pain, itching, withdrawal, preoccupation, apathy, and masked depression (see Table 3-4).

Detection of rape trauma syndrome in children, as in any other situation of sexual abuse, needs careful history taking, complete physical and psychiatric evaluation, and also a very high index of suspicion. Pediatricians and teachers play a very important role in uncovering rape trauma syndrome in children since they are likely to be the first people in contact with them. Coordination of treatment and adequate follow-up services are a very important factor that should be a central part of treatment. Efforts should be directed towards prevention and treatment of VD and other vaginal infections, protection from pregnancy, and emotional treatment. Depending on the psychological situation of the family, and the child's relationship to significant family members, the same varieties of reaction reported for adult victims are observed in children after the rape. In symbiotic personality structures it is extremely important to keep the child and her mother, or the symbiotic ally, in treatment together. Counseling sometimes continues for six months to a year to resolve the intensity of psychological trauma for both the parent and the child.

COMPLICATING FACTORS

Like any other life-threatening trauma, the victim's reactions to rape trauma could be intensified by many complicating elements. In this particular study the most significant complicating factor was the loosening of affective and relational ties. The reaction to the rape trauma of boyfriends, spouses, parents, and close friends is often negative and devastating.

Several of the husbands in our group began to abuse their violated wives immediately after the rape, feeling sure that the women had provoked the rape assault. This reaction led to intense pain and further personality disintegration of the victims. Limited and fixed interest levels, disturbances of social or family roles, diffusion of self-identity, VD, pregnancy, memory disturbance, problems of decision making, limitation of emotional support systems, negative sexual or

TABLE 3-5.   Complicating Factors.

Limited fixed interests
Loosening of affective ties
Disturbances of social-family roles
Diffusion of self-identity
Disturbances of memory and concentration
Disturbances of decision making
Limitation of support systems
Negative former experiences
Cognitive-appraisal problems
Other stress: Illness, life changes, etc.

similar former such experiences (particularly rape), problems of cognitive appraisal and self-concept, all add to the intensity and length of symptoms (see Table 3-5).

PRINCIPLES OF TREATMENT

A variety of therapeutic interventions may be necessary according to the specific needs of victims and their families. We divided our efforts into the categories of crisis intervention and long-term supportive therapy (see Table 3-6).

During the alarm phase we found individual or conjoint intervention to be more beneficial for presymbiotic and symbiotic victims, while group intervention was more effective with postsymbiotic personalities.

Knowledge of general characteristics of the alarm phase, as well as recognition of the need for reliving experiences are very helpful to the victims. Dissemination and sharing of information must be clear and understandable for patients. Many of the victims hinder therapeutic attempts, out of desperation or fear that things will get worse. The therapist needs to remain very active in clarifying and

TABLE 3-6.   Intervention.

1. Crisis Intervention
   - Support: Hospital, medical, legal, police, safety
   - Alliance
   - Complete evaluation of assault
   - Defining reactions
   - Sorting former problems
   - Setting up rituals
   - Focus and reassurance
   - Separating immediate vs. long term reactions
   - Utilizing social network
2. Long-term Counseling:
   - Medical, social, behavioral, or psychological models according to victim's needs—response

sorting various emotions, helping the patient to develop a perspective. Pacing of the patient's hyperemotionalism often happens naturally in counselors, leading to overidentification. Peer group support for the counselors may help decrease such unnecessary reactions, which cause burnout.

Therapists do much better if they keep many options open as treatment progresses, shifting methods as necessary. One of the most helpful attitudes we found during the alarm phase was pacing the victim's representational systems as defined by Bandler and Grinder (1975). We could easily communicate the need for and the value of the alarm phase using appropriate tone of voice and eye movements.

Attention to the patient's pattern of reporting, recalling, and constructive imagery is also very helpful in court hearings. This gives credibility to the history of events.

We found timing of interventions and pacing of the patients' step-by-step responses as used in hypnosis very helpful to all patients, particularly to pre-symbiotic personalities. Encouraging the patients to cry, fidget, be loud or mute, isolated, worried or fearful, etc., was very helpful in giving credence to their natural coping mechanisms. Along with the pacing exercises, mobilization of the patient's support system and comprehensive data collection for therapeutic and legal purposes are essential.

During the reorganization phase we found small groups to be more valuable for presymbiotic victims, while individual counseling was more generally effective for postsymbiotic personalities.

In the case of symbiotic patients, the reaction of the significant ally to the rape trauma must be noticed and treated simultaneously. We encountered such intense emotions as anger (based on a belief that the victim had betrayed the sanctity of the relationship or somehow participated in the rape incident), disgust (based on delusions of contamination and worthlessness), mistrust, rejection, sexual or physical coercion along with projection of blame (the victim had not put out adequate resistance), questioning the victim's judgment, disinterest and inertia, overidentification (too much sympathy and pain, which burdens the relationship), and belief in distorted views of rape.

During the reorganization phase brief therapy methods are usually effective unless there are severe complications. We encourage the victims to become more specific and focused. We assess their complaints carefully, review their coping mechanisms and strengths. We educate them about safety and things to avoid as well as how to enhance their self-expression. After sorting and clarifying new and old problems we help the victims to develop strategies of action. These strategies incorporate their intensity of reactions as well as impulsivity and positive approach. Specific tactics of intervention include encouragement of small changes in handling their problems. Most patients accept small alterations in their responses better than any major change. For example, in a victim whose crying spells or fear reactions continue after several months, we suggest that they continue to cry or be afraid, only move to have these experiences in a different area of their household. We use paradoxical injunction in group or individual therapy, postponing, sharing and floating, rage work, and imagery for mastery or reliving experiences.

We focus on the victims' feelings of pain, fear, helplessness, depression, guilt, etc., and help them to accept these feelings as normal responses to trauma and to express them openly. We encourage the victims to seek social support as much as possible by discussing their temperamental styles and clarifying doubts about flirtation. Patients need assurance that their temperamental styles are not bad or horrible, but that they are at risk for misunderstanding. The victims need to realize their tendency for impulsivity and to learn that being cautious does not mean failing.

They should learn safety precautions and how to hold back. Practicing "delay" for minor situations can gradually increase victims' ability to postpone action. *Intensers* are prone to feelings of helplessness in the face of their strong reactions. Their helplessness often leads to anger, frustration, and temper outbursts with family or friends. They tend to blurt out these feelings strongly to stimulate others, as they wish everyone to know the extent of their pain. It is impossible for them to cool off fast, so they need more time to deal with their feelings. These victims need reassurance by family, friends, and the therapist that they will have adequate time for recovery.

History of previous rapes, and also previous traumatic sexual experiences, should be taken and separated from the emotional reactions to the current rape trauma syndrome. Legal help should be offered with adequate social and therapeutic support. Predictable emotional reactions, such as the "silent rape reaction" or the "pseudo-adjustment" which are so common immediately after the acute phase, should be discussed with patients to educate them to the prevalence of the three types of response during the reorganization period.

REFERENCES

Adleman, Concetta, and Stallone, 1976. Psychological intervention into the crisis of rape. In E. C. Vianao, ed., *Victims and Society*. Washington, D.C.: Visage.

Bandler, R., and Grinder, J. 1975. *Structure of Magic*. Science and Behavior Books.

Berne, E. 1970. *What Do You Say After You Say Hello?* New York: Grove Press.

Burgess, A. W., and Holmstrom, L. L. 1976. Rape trauma syndrome. *Am. J. Psychiatry,* **131**:981–986.

Burgess, A.W., and Holmstrom, L. L. 1979. Adaptive strategies and recovery from rape. *Am. J. Psychiatry,* **136**:1278–1282.

Burgess, A.W., and Lazare, A. 1976. Sexually abused. In A. Burgess, ed., *Community Mental Health Target Populations.* Englewood Cliffs, N.J.: Prentice-Hall.

Chess, S. 1969. *An Introduction to Child Psychiatry.* New York: Grune & Stratton.

Chess, S., Thomas, A., and Birch, H. G. 1968. *Temperament and Behavior Disorders in Children.* New York: NYU Press.

Erikson, E. H. 1959. *Identity and the Life Cycle.* New York: International Universities Press.

Finkelhor, D. 1979. *Sexually Victimized Children.* New York: Free Press.

Hayman, C. R., and Lanza, C. 1971. Sexual assault on women and girls. *Am. J. Obstet. Gynecol.,* 109:480–486.

Holmstrom, L. L., and Burgess, A. W. 1975a. Assessing trauma in the rape victim. *Am. J. Nursing,* 75:1288–1291.

Holmstrom, L. L., and Burgess, A. W. 1975b. Counselling the rape victim. Scientific Proceedings in Summary Form, 128 Annual Meeting of APA, Washington, D.C.

Mahler, M. S. 1967. *On Human Symbiosis and the Vicissitudes of Individuation.* Vol. I. N.Y. International Universities Press.

Mazur, M. A., and Katz, S. 1979. *Understanding the Rape Victim: A Synthesis of Research Findings.* New York: Wiley.

Pepitone, A., Rockwell, B. H., and Frances, S. J. 1979. Patterns of rape and approaches to care. *J. Family Practice,* 6:521–529.

Peters, J. J. 1974. The psychological effects of childhood rape. *World J. Psychosynthesis,* 6(11)1974.

Zonderman, S. 1975. A study of volunteer rape crisis counselors. *Smith College Studies in Social Work.*

APPENDIX

RAPE TRAUMA SYNDROME CHECKLIST

A. Immediate Emergency Reactions (first several days after trauma):

1. Patient cries loudly and continuously
2. Patient is restless and fidgety
3. Patient is irritable and frustrates easily
4. Patient is intensely angry and agitated
5. Patient is uncooperative with medical examination
6. Patient cannot relax or sit still
7. Patient is jittery, jumpy, and tense
8. Patient is loud and noisy
9. Patient laughs loudly or teases staff members
10. Patient blocks her thoughts and shows long pauses
11. Patient cannot concentrate or remember what happened to her
12. Patient insists on being left alone
13. Patient is mute and uncommunicative
14. Patient acts bored and uninterested
15. Patient is lost in her own world
16. Patient feels afraid all over
17. Patient is worried about numerous issues
18. Patient is unhappy, sad, or depressed
19. Patient is mistrustful of staff

20. Patient asks too many questions
21. Patient criticizes the staff and annoys others
22. Patient is afraid of dying
23. Patient is afraid of permanent damage to her body
24. Patient is afraid of losing her mind
25. Patient is afraid of men or people in general
26. Patient is withdrawn
27. Patient expresses intense feelings of

Shame	Revenge
Guilt	Disbelief
Helplessness	Self-blame
Humiliation	Panic
Hatred	

or any other forms of hyperemotionalism.
28. Patient complains of

Soreness	Fatigue
Skeletal muscle tension	Other
Headache	

29. Specific gynecological symptoms:

Burning	Vaginal discharge
Itching	Other

30. Other physical reactions:

G.I.	Skin
G.U.	Other

31. Sexual behavior changes:

Aversion	Inhibition of desire
Dysparunia	Orientation change
Vaginismus	Overinterest
Anorgasmia	Other
Promiscuity	

B. Delayed Reorganization Reactions (consult with the patient and her relatives or friends):

Yes   No

1. Patient has become more mistrustful after the rape
2. Patient has become withdrawn
3. Patient daydreams often
4. Patient remembers and relives the experience repeatedly
5. Patient complains of many somatic problems
6. Patient has become less active in her everyday life
7. Patient shows unusual preoccupation with fears or depressive thoughts
8. Patient has become more irritable
9. Patient has become more clinging and dependent on others
10. Patient has developed multiple fears
11. Patient has had sleep problems since rape

Yes   No

12. Patient has had nightmares since rape
13. Patient has shown regressive behaviors such as not paying attention to her appearance
14. Patient has shown unusual neediness
15. Patient has been drinking unusually
16. Patient has been taking drugs and medicines
17. Patient has become unusually active
18. Patient insists on changing her address or moving away
19. Patient has developed obsessive compulsive tendencies
20. Patient has been depressed and despondent
21. Patient shows unusual self-reproach, guilt, or shame
22. Patient has long-term chronic physical symptoms.

    Describe:
23. Patient has become detached
24. Patient has become paranoid
25. Patient has developed delusional thinking
26. Patient has developed hallucinations
27. Patient has developed thought disturbance
28. Patient has developed sexual problems.

    Describe:
29. Patient has problems with decision making
30. Patient has problems with self-confidence
31. Patient has problems with expression of her feelings
32. Patient expresses problems with sexuality:

    Aversion   Orientation change
    Dysparunia   Overinterest
    Vaginismus   Promiscuity
    Anorgasmia   Other
    Inhibition

Section II
Children as Victims:
From Six to Sixteen

The range of chronological ages in this section reflects the legal definition of childhood's spread; 16 is legally considered the end of innocence. This group also represents the variety of developmental levels with which workers in this area have to deal. The chapters in this section share a concern with the necessity for special handling of victims falling within these limits. It confronts the variety of variables that make assisting such clients so difficult.

In Chapter 4, Dr. Christine Adams-Tucker and Dr. Paul Adams support arguments against any current therapeutic practice that does not include the family as a unit in treatment of the child. Healthier alternatives are suggested in the interests of the child, and a number of innovative procedures are described which the authors have found to be effective.

Paul M. Fine, M.D., and Patty Carnevale, M.S.W., discuss in Chapter 5 social network aspects of treatment for incestuously abused children. They describe three distinct clinical settings in detail and the clinical experiences within each.

In Chapter 6, Dr. Carl M. Rogers and Ms. Terry Tremaine, M.S.W., discuss clinical intervention with male child victims, with attention to the presentation of case material appropriate to their research conclusions. Much of their material also concerns the role of the parents and the need to consider them as essential to the restorative relief of their child.

Lucy Berliner, M.S.W., and Elise Ernst, M.S.W., provide practical suggestions in Chapter 7 for selecting appropriate members for group therapy among a population of adolescent victims. The authors include appropriate techniques and the rationale behind applications of particular approaches which they have found successful.

4
Treatment of Sexually Abused Children

Christine Adams-Tucker, M.D.
Paul L. Adams, M.D.

ABSTRACT

Discussing father-daughter incest as a useful model for sexual abuse of children, this chapter considered these phases in the treatment of the incest victim: (1) case-finding, divided into sensitivity for the population at risk and the principles for detecting incest; (2) crisis help along with diagnosis and treatment planning; (3) extensions on individual therapy; and finally, (4) longer-term therapy.

Practical guidelines are set forth to deal with the incestuously abused child during the case-finding phase. A core set of data concerning the child who is vulnerable to incest includes her being a female who is coerced more often by conning than by physical assault, whose class and social level may be prosperous as well as poor, who may be of any age but whose credibility under age 11 or 12 years is virtually impeccable, and who may show a variegated symptom picture, or none initially, following her being sexually molested. Ways of reporting known and suspected cases of sexual abuse are considered, with recommendations for the professional working with children to be highly sensitive to the possibility of incest and liberal in reporting suspicions that incest has taken place.

Crisis help is depicted as of vital importance for the child during the crisis and for her future. The main things to be done in the crisis are to send the right person away from the home, to enfold the child in loving support, to do a proper workup with the father, to reinforce the mother's strength, and to do some explicit consciousness raising with the child victim. Diagnosis and treatment planning flow from all previous work with the victim and her family and herald aptly the treatment that must be given. Treatment itself is presented as individual therapy, conjoint therapy with mother and child, family group therapy, pharmacotherapy, and other modalities. A final description of some of the major themes of long-term psychotherapy with the incest victim demonstrates that the needed treatment is anything other than easy, quick, and routine.

... And what are the major obstacles to identifying the sexually abused child?

In practical terms, the answers are lack of recognition of the phenomenon, failure to obtain adequate medical corroboration of the event, and reluctance to report.

Suzanne M. Sgroi (1975)

The incestuously abused child provides a model for all sexually abused children. It sounds like a model that uses an extreme case but it is not: Most sexual abuse of children is incestuous — perpetrated by fathers and father surrogates against their daughters. Since our outlook is not favored by child molesters, it may appear illiberal to some readers, but in the interest of brevity we have opted to take up an attitude of extending first and foremost our helping empathy toward the child victims. In our daily clinical practice, we have found that mothers and children respond favorably to our approach — to case finding, crisis treatment, individual treatment planning, extensions on individual therapy, and a tried-and-true longer therapy with a psychoanalytic orientation.

Obfuscators and mystifiers often accuse any professional who wants to protect sexually abused children of being old-fashioned or too traditional or even of being opposed to children's sexual freedom. In reality, we advocate sexual freedom for children but believe that the issue of how professionals view childhood sexuality has no bearing on child rape, sodomy, and incest. We do not condone sex abuse of children by adults. Still, we know that regardless of whether children are seen as sexually innocent, ignorant, disinterested, willing partners, or craving for incest with their cross-gender parent, the particular ideology does not change the fact that incest and sexual exploitation of children have flourished through the ages of human history. Fashions in views on childhood sexuality may change with the times, but childhood sexual victimization remains, perpetually, in all eras. Child sex abuse is a potent reminder of our proclivities to be inhumane.

We view sexual abuse of children as one of many forms of exploitation arrayed on a continuum that spans from training or taming and brainwashing to — the most destructive — child murder. Unfortunately, we find that most often sexual abuse lies very near child murder on this continuum. Despite the gravity of such sexual exploitation, many professionals underrate and downplay sexual abuse of a child. The wary clinician can identify such "closet apologists" for sexual abuse because they take great pains to divide sexual abuse of a child into *assaultive* and *nonassaultive* categories. They are bent on raising exceptions, "yes, but. . . ." They rationalize an adult's duping and conning tactics to be less exploitative than the adult's brutal physical force used when a child is raped and battered. We try not to get mired in finding excuses, overt or covert, for the sexual exploitation of any child. In this discussion we present the treatment of child victims in four phases: (1) case finding, (2) crisis help, (3) extensions on individual therapy, (4) long-term therapy.

CASE-FINDING PHASE

Sensitivity to the Population at Risk

Throughout this discussion we shall use the paradigm of father-daughter incest when discussing the sexual victimization of children, not only because it is the most common form of bigenerational incest that we know about, but also because it stimulates most of the countertransference hangups and reticences among professionals.

The astute clinician will have done his or her homework whenever the clinician knows and anticipates the characteristics of sexually abused children and their molesters, encountered in emergency rooms, inpatient units (psychiatric or pediatric), outpatient clinics, classrooms, police stations, child welfare offices, and so on. We enumerate nine facts that professionals should store as knowledge and raised consciousnesses to carry with them.

1. Girls are victims more than boys.
2. Fathers and father surrogates are molesters more than mothers and mother surrogates.
3. A familiar and related person molests more often than a stranger.
4. Conning and coercion are used more than physical assault to make the child acquiesce to abuse.
5. Children of all ages — infants through teenagers — are incest victims.
6. One in four to one in three girls are victims of sex abuse by 18 years of age.
7. The younger child is more credible in his or her disclosure of incest than is the youngster over 12 years old.
8. Incest victims show a wide variety of symptom complaints or may show none at all.
9. Incest occurs throughout all economic and occupational strata of society and within all religious denominations.

Detection Principles

If the first principle in case finding is an alertness to the population vulnerable to sexual abuse, then the second is readiness to report the suspected case. There is dispute among professionals on this count; some are eager to be child advocates and to utilize existing statutes which mandate reporting of even suspected cases, while other professionals feel that they must break the law or that they have a prior duty to provide secrecy and confidentiality in all matters pertaining to client privilege. Our inclination is to report liberally and unrestrainedly since we are child advocates, not advocates for adults who sexually molest young children. We know that the statute exempts even false reports from liability. Indeed, we have found that a system of dual reporting best serves children. We report all suspected cases both to our local child abuse hotline and to the police or district attorney. That takes five minutes more but may spare a child much anguish. The child abuse hotline alerts the local child protection agency, often overworked and ineffective; the call to the police, for us, alerts an effective law enforcement agency with superbly trained personnel. A follow-up report in writing is the definitive step. The dual report sets in motion a system of checks and balances that serve the child's protection and may enhance criminal prosecution of the child molester. We guard against a light-handed approach because that often stacks the deck against an abused child, in favor of the molester. Liberal reporting is warranted because more cases are secreted away from our ken than ever enter our field of attention. Forces other than professionals are at work to prevent case finding.

Another principle of detection or case finding is: Provide thorough documentation of your findings. Photographs of vaginal lacerations are better documents than a written description. Too, one examination or history taking done with video or audio recording is superior to several done without taping. Laboratory examinations should be made to document the child's white blood count, smears and cultures from anal, oral, and pudendal orifices. The family physician needs to proceed boldly (all the while caring and supporting) in order to do an examination of the vaginal and anal areas on a sexually molested child and to document the findings of that inquiry.

One more principle of case finding is, interview any child of 2 or more years apart from the parents. It is time saving and legally prudent to have a police officer present to participate in the recorded interview with you; that spares exposing the child to multiple interrogations. Using dolls with anatomically correct genitals enhances the interview with a child and allows us to zero right into the core problem. A widespread attitude holds that children will not tell about their sexual molestation, but that is wrong. Children are relieved by talking out their traumas, almost as much as adults, but may need special encouragement to be candid, to use their own terms for what they are describing; many older children are positively delighted by the opportunity to talk to an empathic professional. Children can be competent and credible witnesses when they describe in detail the events of their molestation. We do well *not* to minimize and discount their reports of sexual abuse.

As the child is interviewed privately, away from parents, so each parent should be interviewed independently. Sometimes totally divergent stories will be told by mother and father when they are seen apart; when they tell one story together they have been given one rehearsal, to the child's disadvantage. Sometimes the mother will blow the whistle when her husband is not physically present but will be intimidated when he is with her. We must recall that men who sexually abuse their children are often wife beaters.

A sixth guide in detection of cases is to promote candor in all members of the family. Some persons proclaim that family secrets about incest should be left secretive and misty, but openness is preferable. If each child in the household knows about the incident (or chain of repeated events) each child can assist the mother and the abused child in preventing a recurrence of the sexual abuse. If a single person in the household is not told, suffering is more likely.

There are symptoms other than physical indicators of sex abuse to be expected, and our way of thinking about them is that some are proximate, others remote. The younger child often shows, very soon after being sexually abused, such clinical pictures as phobias and panic attacks, heightened irritability and alertness, problems with peers and schoolwork. The adolescent shows more often such phenomena as running away and becoming sexually promiscuous. Lines extend forward in time from these proximate reactions to being sexually abused so that as an adult, the woman who was sexually molested in childhood may show two major kinds of remote responses: sexual disorders, including prostitution; and severe mental disorders such as schizophrenia, multiple personality, and self-mutilation.

CRISIS HELP

Somebody Goes

Perhaps the most dramatic help given in the four or five weeks that a crisis lasts is residential change for the family members. For mere ease many professionals routinely hospitalize the little girl who complains about her incestuous father, or surrogate father. Yanking the daughter out of her ecologic niche "does not upset the whole family," family practitioners and pediatricians often say. What they correctly mean, in our opinion, is that some separation between molesting adult and molested child seems imperative; we agree, but choose to emphasize the option of removing molester, not molested.

Children can be made to feel guilty when they alert the authorities on incest, and as a consequence the father is sent away to live independently or to go to jail, and the mother gets upset or sad, or lashes out against her daughter. Sometimes professionals blame a child for "breaking up your family," as if the incest itself is not the thing that has destroyed the family; the child quakes at the awesome responsibility. Rarely can a viable family be reconstituted after incest, but family demolition is not the child's fault. Some child protection workers, not very protectively, say, "Your dad did not do that, did he? You just made it up, didn't you?" The child is out on a limb and feels so. Instead of further stressing the child by her removal from home, professionals would do better to strengthen her relations with mother and send father away.

District attorneys seem to have read Jean Piaget with greater understanding than many child care professionals, for they use the rule: *The younger the child, the more credible her testimony.* What a child under 11 years old says about her molestation can be taken as true. A child that age can be relied on to know experientally about sex abuse; if she supplies details it shows that she has experienced, not fantasied, her sexual molestation.

Enlightened judges are usually willing to send a father out of the home until the child's predicament is settled and clarified. Alas, many judges do refuse to keep a father away from his daughter, but child protection workers sometimes can influence such judges to consider the child's rights and welfare.

The Child

In the crisis period the young child needs all the support possible from her mother and siblings, from protective services workers, from primary care physicians, and even, perhaps, from child psychiatrists. Christine Adams-Tucker has found that the crisis responses for molested but healthy preschoolers are global stress reactions. Situations resembling crystallized neurotic responses occur mainly with older girls or unhealthy preschoolers, while with adolescents the patterns are again more chaotic, showing runaway behavior and sexual promiscuity. Close inspection reveals that all of these are desperate responses to the stress of incest, often lasting — when not properly remedied at the time of the crisis — throughout the lifetime of the victim. The mother especially needs to be shored up and brought to give care and encircling warmth to her daughter. For the mother to do this she often has to have an object lesson from someone, professional or friend, who can be loving and supportive to the mother herself. When incest occurs it is not a time for neutrality, for objectivity, for passivity. The mother needs to make quick decisions about her now-defunct marriage and family, to realize that she is now the head of the family group and must move with wisdom and decisiveness to nurture and provide security for her children. If professionals blame the mother for "not having her legs spread often enough" for her former spouse, no help is derived. If professionals waste too much effort in trying to reconstitute a dead marriage and family, they do disservice to both mother and victimized child.

Immediate work with the child consists in giving her assurance that a child does not bring on sexual abuse, that a father or any other grown man (or woman) has no right to abuse the trust of a child, and that she should not worry that her family will be destroyed when her father is arrested and jailed. In truth, her original family was destroyed precisely at the time the incest occurred. When adults acknowledge that children do not instigate incest, the adults can be ready, spiritually, to come to the assistance of a victimized child. In a Satyricon age or place, adults waffle and presuppose child blame and complicity, or worse still, assume that adults have a right to gull and brainwash children into sexual liaisons with adults. Our concern is with the rights and well-being of children, hence there is no place for hedging and emitting blather about Electra complexes of the small girls seduced by their fathers.

The Father

What of the father? Despite the evidence that child molesters are difficult to treat, resistant, evasive, corrupt, and perverted, a compassionate person must wish to do a proper diagnostic workup and to make humane treatment available to the child molester. The abuse and sodomizing of children is so firmly rooted in many adults that it has taken on a very human face. The molester is also my brother, someone has said, even if I hate his real sins.

Molesters need to have a psychiatric workup, a neurological workup including sleep EEG, and psychologic testing. Not to do these things is to leave some valuable stones unturned; to do them is to provide some valuable information about the psyche of the molester. Molesters fall into four groups, according to our experience with them: sadistic, brainwashing, pedophiliac, antisocial dyscontrol. Many child molesters show variegated responses that interweave these four types.

While our concern is principally with the victim, we wish to discuss some of the work to be done with the molesting father. We add this now because we see so many primary care physicians who go no further than to take the heat off the father without seeing to it that he is properly worked up and offered the best treatment accessible. In all instances, we insist that the father be evaluated by a psychologist, neurologist, and psychiatrist. Our rationale follows in sketchy format.

Psychologic testing aids the overall assessment. On the MMPI, his L-score is elevated — he lies, to put it bluntly. To state it more subtly, he is eager to present himself as a conventional and conformist person. Psychologic testing is quite indispensable because it has ways of detecting a person's attempts to outwit the test results. The Rorschach Psychodiagnostic Test is useful because it gives indirect information about the personality of the person being tested. The Rorschach also tells us the ways in which the person defends himself when afraid or anxious. For instance, when we know that the sequence of defenses is shock and denial, followed by "paranoid" projection, then by falling apart into random responses of poor quality, we have seen in microcosm on the Rorschach the sequence of actual behavior of the child molester as he goes from fright, rigidity, and denial to blaming others to saying he was out of his mind. Still other psychologic tests are very helpful to a compassionate, open-minded court. For a psychiatrist, the psychologist's assessment is an absolute requisite.

What is the point of a neurologic evaluation for the accused child molester? A neurologist checks out the brain functions of the patient as well as the functions of the rest of the nervous system. A neurologist makes subtle inquiries for head injury, for epilepsy, and for other kinds of episodes during which people lose control of their actions. Neurologic studies include X-rays, EEG, and other tests. A neurologic study can help a neurally impaired child molester to get appropriate treatment, that is, to stay out of prison and (it is hoped) to become a constructive member of society, taking medications and appropriately changing life patterns.

The psychiatric examination, also an important workup, can be truncated and be rather complete in one hour with some patients. With a resistive man, one who is out to dissimulate and make a false set of statements and inferences, often more time is necessary. The child molester does not know readily, however, how to fake or outsmart the professional examiner who sees the immaturity of the molester's genital development and activity. So a complete psychiatric interview gives a psychiatrist multiple opportunities to slip up on the child molester's unguarded, "blind" side.

The child molester often gives a history of an idealized mother to whom he was close, but the tight bondage with her did not give good preparation for his own development of free sexual expression. One historical fact that seems to be a common finding in child molesters is that many had their first sexual contact as adolescents *with a young boy or girl.* Babysitting provided them sexual outlets and opportunities that dating did not, they seem to believe. That early experience of sexual exploitation was like an induction that takes hold and can scarcely be altered subsequently. The child molester may have an extra complication of woman hating, so that while his chosen sadistic object is the little girl, he is homosexual at heart but stays in the closet.

The psychiatrist talks about personal biography with the adult alleged child molester. He discusses his close friends or the lack of them; also his marriage and its difficulties; work satisfactions and opportunities on the job to become sexually stimulated by either adults or children; his dreams, earliest recollections, interpretations of proverbs, disorders of thinking, presence of compulsive thinking or doings, drawings of house-tree-person; completions of beginning fragments of sentences; reactions to there-and-then confrontations, favorite jokes, and many more things. All the things that a psychiatrist does are integrated to form a total diagnostic opinion about the man. When brought together it is a description of an accused child molester which only a jurist with questionable motives would overlook, discredit, or decline to obtain. The full evaluation of a child molester is good preventive work, hopefully heading off his abuse of other children.

Consciousness Raising for Victim

Quite commonly, some sexually abused children believe it when they are told that they liked what their father was doing to them sexually (even if it was sadistic and hurtful), that father can do no wrong, and that what happened was done to promote their sexual liberation and enlightenment. Much as concentration camp internees identified with their Nazi aggressors, a young girl can be gulled and made to believe that cruelty is kindness and manipulativeness is tender concern. She introjects and identifies with her victimizer, her father.

Certainly, we must add, not all little girls are that gullible, and, consonant with their self-respect and autonomy, some fearlessly inform on their fathers. Still, even at that point, a girl with pronounced ego strengths can be made to feel implicated in her own exploitation as she sees her father (and others) bully and blackmail her mother into compliance with his wishes and emerge in a united front of parents against daughter; then in court to give a blanket denial to every charge the daughter makes; then to move to claiming that she wanted sex with him or seduced him; then finally, if ever, to admit — protesting that he did it because he was "beside himself" from marital discontent (the frigid wife theme), from alcohol or other drugs, or from temporary insanity. The daughter gets confused because she senses that in his heart he feels he is OK. Only *she* appears to have caused the trouble. If she, not the father, has been yanked out of her home, her dousing in guilt is complete.

What a girl needs at this point is a prompt exercise in demystifying consciousness raising. She must know from a concentrated three-way consciousness raising that she is a child, a female, and a victim. She must comprehend that as a child she is weaker than any adult; that some adults not only slaughter innocent children but also batter them in an infanticidal spirit, neglect and abandon them, brainwash them, seduce and sodomize them, exploit them in numberless ways. She must comprehend that "childism" — anti-child beliefs and practices — are components of our cultural heritage. She must understand that as a child she is entitled to certain liberties and protections from her parents. Her right to liberty certainly includes ownership of her own body. Her right to protection includes her right to safeguards against sexual abuse by grown-ups and older children. As a female she must raise her consciousness about the U.S. statistics showing that one in every four or three females has been sexually abused by age 18 years; she must see that many men exploit, restrict, and derogate females because it increases their share (as men) of power, prestige, and economic resources; that state legislatures dominated by men have refused to ratify the ERA and that churches dominated by men spread a sinful propaganda requiring females to be subservient to males; that the market for jobs is antifemale, and that collective action by women (and men) can bring not only good sisterly feelings but victory over sexism. As a victim, the young girl must perceive that she is a victim and not a perpetrator of sex abuse; that being brainwashed as a daughter is not the same as being in complicity; that victims often identify *unconsciously* with their aggressors and engage in role reversal, projective identification, narcissistic identification, and other distortions; that she will very likely show an alarming fascination, and penchant, for cruelty and for sadomasochism; that she will be prone to equate sexuality and brutality. She must glimpse that there is a way out for such victims if they identify with those who suffer, in helping other such victims and in preventing the sex abuse of all little girls, the exploitation of all children. That consciousness-raising effort is much more helpful, even at the time of the crisis, if it is buttressed by new family interactions and structural changes in the girl's everyday living — giving proof that her world is pro-child and anti-abuse.

DIAGNOSIS AND TREATMENT PLANNING

If the father, not the daughter, is sent away, the crisis tends to subside after about six weeks and a new family ethos takes over. If the crisis treatment has helped her the little girl has been able to resume her school learning, to fit back into her mother-headed family, to be able to play and to have fantasies and dreams as a mark of her own inner riches. If crisis help was salutary she may not have any serious residuals of victimization, neurosis, psychosis, or character malformation. We find in our clinical work that if crisis help has not been given, the girl after six weeks shows most often the signs of a posttraumatic stress disorder for which further treatment has to be planned. Many diagnostic classes may be appropriate, but according to the criteria of DSM-III (Diagnostic and Statistical Manual of the American Psychiatric Association) the posttraumatic stress disorder is highly appropriate. Often "posttraumatic stress disorder," subclassified as acute, delayed, or chronic, is more apt than the overworked "adjustment disorder," which should be assigned to milder, less stressful traumas than sex abuse by a parent.

Once a diagnosis has been established, a treatment plan is easier to formulate. Indeed, diagnosis and treatment planning clarify each other. One major treatment decision is about inpatient or outpatient modes. A few children are so upset after sex abuse that they need to be hospitalized, but we find that most are best served on an outpatient basis. Most of the treatment modalities now to be considered apply mainly to outpatient work with a sexually abused child.

EXTENSIONS ON INDIVIDUAL THERAPY

In between crisis therapy and the longer-term therapy given the individual child, there are several adjunctive or extension treatments worth considering. We shall be concerned whether they aid or abet the child victim as we discuss various treatments. We include the following and enumerate their benefits and drawbacks for child sex abuse victims: family group therapy; mother-child therapy; therapy for mother alone; peer group therapy; mother-daughter group therapy; pharmacotherapy; environmental manipulations; extended family supports and self-help groups.

Those who regard incest as arising from a dysfunctional family system envision the family of mother, father, and child(ren) as an interactive system of interrelated family members. This view focuses on the pathology of the family in contextual and dynamic modes. Proponents of a family systems approach utilize these theoretical underpinnings not only for understanding incest within a family context but also for evolving a treatment approach, family group therapy, geared toward reuniting the nuclear family unit of mother, father, and child(ren) and reorienting their interrelationships.

A logical fallacy is required for a therapist using a family systems approach to see an incestuous family as merely dysfunctional, not demolished and dead. We return to this later.

We do not laud family group therapy as very helpful for the child victim of incest. As a therapeutic modality, it is a behavioristic palliative in incest cases that perhaps helps molesters remain in the nuclear units with the exploited children or, at best, from the child's standpoint, curtails the molester's overt sexual behavior with the child(ren). Outwardly, such reunited families containing molesters may appear functional — they are all together again under one roof; he is not molesting his daughter; often he is financially supporting everyone. There is little intrapsychic change; only structural and behavioral realignments eventuate from such family group therapy.

Many family-focused professionals underrate incest in its undermining of "family" (of mother, father, and children) as a viable unit. How can a family survive when a father violates the taboo on both sex with a blood relative and sex with a child? We do not find this therapy to be helpful to the child because it focuses on the marital dyad as the dysfunctional locus and the site of needed repair, declining in that degree to focus on the child's special interests. Also we find this approach has behavioristic and structural goals that dictate *who* the family members are who need to form an integral group. Father has to be there. The outcome all too often is that the child gets heard only minimally, if at all, and she is *required* to live within an asymmetrical unit that includes her molester.

We have found the best accomplishment of family group therapy to be its success in alerting the child (as well as other family members) to monitor the behavior of the molester; it puts the household's children on guard against any unwanted sexual approaches that the molester might show. In the final analysis, clinicians who work with these victimized children must decide if family group therapy that includes the molester outweighs the paranoid hypervigilance of the children that necessarily follows. For example, how does one weigh their hypervigilance against their hoped-for success in heterosexual relationships as adults? Does hypervigilance aid coping? Having served as cops with father, can they accept and initiate pleasant sexual overtures later?

On the other hand, family group therapy that regards the family unit as those persons who help the child heal her wounds, after sexual exploitation, is an approach that provides the child with trustable and supportive adults and augments her voice within the family. That is the form of family group therapy that we have seen be truly therapeutic for child victims. These units for family therapy may contain adults who are grandmothers, aunts, uncles, foster parents, stepparents, or neighbors, but most often we find that they are composed of mothers and children.

The most appropriate unit for conjoint therapy is the mother-child unit, residing together after the disclosure of incest and the ejection of the father-molester from the child's home. In our experience, it makes no difference whether mother and child have the same or different therapist, provided they all meet regularly and often in conjoint therapy sessions. Beyond the crisis dilemmas mother and child victim must face, they need to work jointly on such issues as adjusting to the mother's being household head, the mother's handling of symptomatic behavior in the child victim (e.g., masturbation or fondling boys at school), and preparation for the criminal trial of the father, including securing warrants and talking with lawyers. Such joint work can help a mother and daughter to recognize that they can make changes and that the mother can augment her family's protection of its child members.

Moreover, individual therapeutic work with the mother is helpful to the mother and child through strengthening the mother's parental position of protector to her child. Individual time may be spent at first in hearing a mother's waffling about the dilemma of allying with the molester versus allying with the child. During this early period, it is important that the therapist not presume that the mother is always collusive in promoting the incest, or conclude that her waffling indicates that she is incapable of nurturing and protecting her daughter. Early on, a mother may voice worry about "making it" alone or she may be sorrowful at seeing her husband in jail. The helpful therapist waits to determine mother's ability to improve her alliance with her child over time.

We recommend two group therapy modalities to augment individual therapy for the benefit of child incest victims. The first type is peer group therapy for the victims themselves, in groups of children organized by age and gender. For younger children, such as preteens, we suggest a therapist of the same gender as the group members. For older youngsters, those who are teenagers, we suggest man and woman co-therapists. All child victims tend to identify the male therapist with their aggressor, the molester, and have a difficult time in surmounting this distorted identification. The older children can deal better with a male co-therapist.

The second type of group therapy involves mothers and daughters. This becomes an extension of mother-child conjoint therapy and utilizes some aspects of self-help groups. When combined in such group therapy mothers and daughters can explore the broader social stigmata of incest by fathers and father surrogates; can share practical issues of what or when to tell the child's school about the incest; can consider how to help siblings; and can discuss such problems as how much a mother should "hover" over her teenage victimized daughter. By the same token, many self-help groups have formed to aid victims and their mothers by providing support from volunteers who earlier had been incest victims and mothers of victims. We have found these self-help groups to be a very valuable extension to the child's individual therapy, provided they link with mental health professionals as resourceful group leaders or as supervisors. This linkage insures that victim and mother participants obtain needed psychiatric care in a timely fashion.

Yet another extension on individual therapy for the child is the support that can come from the child's extended family – those relatives, usually her mother's, whom the girl victim has known throughout her life. These persons may be her grandparents who augment her mother's financial resources until her mother finds employment or a better job. They may be aunts or uncles who provide a temporary residence for the victim and her family. Or, they may be relatives who provide time to hear out the child and her mother as they continue to cope with the ordeal brought on by incest.

Pharmacotherapy for the child incest victim often is considered an adjunctive treatment that aids the child. This is usually the case with family practitioners and pediatricians who encounter young victims during the time of crisis either in an emergency room or in their offices. Physicians choose medications such as hydroxyzine (Atarax or Vistaril) for the purpose of quieting or lessening a child's anxiety over the incest events. We do not consider that such anxiety is best treated by any pharmacologic agents that might act to "dope up" or "quiet down" a distraught child. Instead, we would urge family practitioners and pediatricians to seek alleviation of a child victim's anxiety through nonmedicinal candor, talking about the incest with the family, that is, by opening up verbal communications and not by shutting them down. A nighttime sedative might be the only pharmacotherapy needed for the hurt child.

The last type of extension on therapy we consider is that of environmental manipulation. There is a myriad of events for shoring up the new postincest family, arrangements that aid them in carrying out the daily events of their schedules and that help them in talking about and working through the incest episodes, making changes in their perceptions of themselves and others so that victimization will not be replicated in the child and in her future offspring. These environmental changes can be carried out by the family members themselves, by social workers, welfare workers, neighbors, self-help group members, clergy, teachers, lawyers, mental health professionals, and others. For example, a child's therapist might make a school visit with a mother and daughter to help the school better understand about the incest trauma and to anticipate some of the school-related problems that the girl might have. Or, a therapist could encourage a mother to allow her daughter to interact with kind and nonabusive adult men so that the girl experiences something other than the exploitative relationship she had with her own father. A social worker or self-help friend or doctor can lend immeasurable support by helping a mother sign up for AFDC income; obtain food stamps, housing assistance, homemaker services; arrange after-school child care; or seek better employment. A neighbor might assist a mother in some independence training by teaching the mother to drive a car, if she lacks that skill, or by providing transportation to driving lessons. A lawyer might arrange for mother and child to visit the courtroom where the criminal or civil (e.g., custody) trial will be held or a lawyer might role-play with mother and child the courtroom procedure of giving testimony. A religious counselor might lend emotional as well as spiritual support when he or she accompanies a mother and child to present evidence of sexual abuse to prosecutors so that a criminal warrant will be issued for the arrest of the molester, or so that a grand jury will be called to consider issuance of an indictment against him. It is of such practical details that human kindness is composed after a child has been sexually abused.

LONGER-TERM THERAPY

We find that some girls who have not been helped sufficiently in the acute crisis phase may show disordered behavior only belatedly. They go first to the primary care doctor and only afterwards get involved in the mental health system. These cases are always harder to deal with; too much has been internalized and too many neurotic constellations have begun to crystallize. Furthermore, some girls who have received crisis help simply are more prone to develop serious pathology, so they too will need longer-term help from psychotherapy. We have adopted a psychoanalytically oriented style but modified it to such a degree that it is probably better characterized as pluralistic or eclectic — it does not eschew home and school visits, environmental manipulation, court appearances, behavior therapy, supportive therapy or child advocacy, or pharmacotherapy. It is aimed to produce change, preferably with insight achieved, in ways that will give prompt and lasting relief to the child.

Besides symptom removal our longer-term therapy aims to protect the child against further victimization and prepare her for reduced suffering from any sexual assaults that may occur — alas — in her future. To accomplish the second means to go a bit further than the merest remediation of symptoms such as phobia, depression, fear, loneliness, rage, and disgust. Further, since we are dealing with so profound and so shocking a betrayal, it seems wise to gear our longer-term treatment toward some personality reorientation and to upgrade the child's ability to form loving interpersonal relations that are devoid of exploitation. Only the latter is a sure test of the treatment offered, we believe.

One of the major learnings from prolonged psychotherapy for a sexually victimized child is that her sexual feelings are not bad. Although work on sexual longings best follows work on anger, it becomes the keystone in long-term therapeutic work. When that learning about the sexual self is accomplished she will not have recrudescences of panic; she will be orgasmic and fulfilled, not becoming stuck in fearing men, hating males, or being promiscuous and indiscriminate in her relations with them.

The substance of long-term psychotherapy deals with several themes (sexuality, self-esteem, and hostility). Those are the recurrent themes that have to be considered, probed, analyzed, resolved, and, in a very important sense, transcended if the girl is to become a wholesome person whose ego strengths and id strengths are set free for living a good life. She will not be inhibited, coarcted, and cramped as a result of therapy but truly liberated to love and be loved, to be caring and compassionate about people, including herself. En route to that cheerful and rosy denouement she must do a lot of arduous work to permit such growth.

A theme that takes up a lot of productive therapeutic time is her rage, anger, hostility. It is a theme not fully covered by her work on man-hating, although it may seem to be integral to that feeling. She has to realize that it is warped to fuse or identify sexual with cruel impulses. Extricating the two is not easy for an abuse victim, one who has seen them to be inextricable, and in her own father.

She must see, in play and in talk, that she has incorporated cruel streaks that she did not dream of, that her inculcation in sadism was great — even if her father's sexual sadism was confined to only one act. Hers appears to have been a one-shot learning, but of course it was not. Very likely, she had a lifetime of tutelage in anger, revenge, and authoritarianism within her family; she learned well that violence is highly human because it comes to hand so easily when we are frustrated or punished. Consequently, there is a reservoir of anger that is unconnected to her sexual abuse by her father, but she may tend for a prolonged period to concentrate on her impotent rage over having been betrayed by her father. In general, this anger is best identified, clarified, interpreted, and in some instances accepted before any attempt is made to uncover her truly sexual feelings and impulses.

The whole issue of trust is another basic theme that makes up psychotherapy with a sexually abused child. If she cannot trust her parents, whom can she trust? The therapist has to show trustworthiness and dependability as a serious-minded professional, not as one more adult who uses hype to persuade a child that adults take good care of children and that policemen are their friends. The therapist, whether male or female, has to go through the father transference, helping the child to identify likenesses and differences between father and therapist and to sort out what the therapist-child relationship will be as a working alliance. Incestuously abused girls are truly afraid of repercussions from their taking action against their fathers; they may develop insomnia, fears of the dark, fear of prowlers and kidnappers and other thugs that will consume several sessions. But these fears will all be worked out, with the help of the therapist and with good support from the girl's mother. When the father as dreaded figure is laid to rest, the little girl often becomes starkly paranoid about her mother's role in her life, in her sex abuse, and in her future. That, too, requires therapeutic patience, skill, and incorruptible confidentiality about what the child tells the therapist during her private sessions. The therapist may become an auxiliary, benign mother for a time in the child's fantasy life. Eventually the girl accepts her own mother for what she is.

One more issue in long-term psychotherapy is the enfeebled self-concept of the girl following her informing on her dad. She feels that she is omnipotently evil; she feels that she is not a good person. She feels that she is at fault whenever her mother complains that father/breadwinner is gone, or when her sibs ask her questions in secret about what the father did to her. Shame is very much a part of her life, and that cannot be expiated and surmounted as easily as guilt. Still, she learns through therapy to see herself as a multifaceted, lifelike being who can resume her life as a growing person. New experiences in her world outside the consulting room give the best laboratory for changes in her self-concept; the dream gives the best mirror of her self-concept while she is in the consulting room.

Now, some comment about sexual lust and actions. She must come to terms with her fear of males even when it is masked in coyness and whorish hyperfemininity. She must grow to hate child abuse and the men who perpetrate it. She must engage in man-hating, letting it work through to a point that she ultimately gives up beating a dead horse; then she can conceive of male and female relations as cooperative and equalitarian and at times even platonic and not *erotic* in the narrow sense. The therapist facilitates her healthy development by accepting her man-hating (often not easy for a male therapist), as long as it must last. The therapist adopts the attitude that would say, "Hate males as long as you must and after that as long as you can!" The therapist aids her acceptance of sisterhood (affection and friendship among and between females) as truly beautiful, knowing that females are lovable as friends and allies in a way unmatched by the best male companions. When her extolling of sisterhood justifies an avoidance of males, that biggest of human minorities, the therapist helps her unload the compulsive part of her "feminism" in order to make freer and wiser choices. To stand so apart from males is to overvalue males, she discovers, and to minimize her own "masculinity," to degrade her own androgynous character. She decides neither to be nor to think in stereotypes.

Usually the girl patient, playing and talking, trying out new insights and behavioral changes, will be astonished by her hypersexualized behavior with her peers, especially in the middle stage of her therapy. She may even enact a drama to turn passive into active by "turning on to" grown men in order to rediscover how debased they are, or she may be driven to enact an identification with her aggressor by sexually abusing peers or younger children of either gender.

It is no wonder that hers is what psychiatric residents call "a sex case" since her original brutalization occurred in a sexual (or pseudosexual) context. She may spend endless therapeutic sessions in preoccupation with sexual matters, denying and squelching her sexuality or pushing her sexuality beyond its true range and focus. She moves, at the end, beyond this inordinate sexual concern, of sexualizing anything and everything except genitals — sexualizing in the way Freud's classic hysterics did since several of them, too, had been sexually abused by their fathers. By the middle phase of her treatment, the sexually molested girl shows eroticized dreams and play, eroticized transference onto the therapist, and great curiosity about the therapist's genitals and sex life, along with vigorous sexual experimentation of her own in masturbation, homosexuality, bestiality, heterosexuality, indeed every form of activity lifted out of Krafft-Ebing, or in line with the "polymorphous perversion" Freud attributed to neurotics during their childhood years. It seems like an iron law she must obey in finding her true self and subduing the false self built up around sexual trauma, childism, and misogyny. She learns to be herself and see through the sham of her shaping and conditioning by going through sexual overconcern during therapy.

It is clear that a young girl who has been sexually abused will be fortunate to have been given an opportunity to take part in a longer-term psychotherapy that is fitted to her special needs, that takes consideration of her entire life situation, and that enables her to overcome all the obstacles associated with having been a victim, a girl, and a child, and to go on with a full life as a result of treatment.

SUGGESTED READINGS

Adams, P. L., and Roddey, G. J. 1981. Language patterns of opponents to a child protection program. *Child Psychiatry and Human Development*, 11(3):135-157.

Adams-Tucker, C. 1981. A socio-clinical overview of 28 sex-abused children. *Child Abuse and Neglect, The International Journal*, 5(3):361-367.

Adams-Tucker, C. 1982, Proximate effects of sexual abuse in childhood: A report on 28 children. *Am. J. Psychiatry*, 139(10):1252-1256.

Herman, J. L., with Hirschman, L. 1981. *Father-Daughter Incest.* Cambridge, Mass.: Harvard University Press.

Rush, F. 1980. *The Best Kept Secret: Sexual Abuse of Children.* Introduction by Susan Brownmiller. Englewood Cliffs, N.J.: Prentice-Hall.

Sgroi, S. M. 1975. Sexual molestation of children: The last frontier in child abuse. *Children Today,* May-June: 18–21, 44.

Sgroi, S. 1982. *Handbook of Clinical Intervention in Child Sexual Abuse.* Lexington, Mass.: Lexington Books/D.C. Heath.

5
Network Aspects of Treatment for Incestuously Abused Children

Paul Fine, M.D.
Patty Carnevale, M.S.W.

ABSTRACT

Incestuously abused children present society with the unique clinical dilemma of protecting the children from intimate abuse, yet at the same time preserving their opportunities for normal family-social development and effective treatment. Three interrelated issues are central to this problem: First, incest intensifies relationships within the family, yet tends to destroy the family as a social system; second, traumas resulting from incest increase the child victim's needs for sensitive parenting, yet continuous parenting relationships may become less available when the child is removed from family ties; and third, the practice of placing child victims into foster care shields them from abuse, but also increases their risk for abnormal personal development.

A solution to conflicts surrounding incestuously abused children is suggested by the social nature of human beings. Children and families normally cope and develop under the broad influence of extended family and other social networks. Constructive networks can be identified, enlisted, or created in each instance of incestuous abuse to help provide support and protection for the child, models for the parents, and encouragement for the nuclear family.

This chapter discusses social network aspects of treatment for incestuously abused children. The authors of the chapter, a social worker-therapist and child psychiatrist, are experienced with network-oriented therapy at three distinct clinical settings. The settings, all of which serve abused children, include a community-based mental health clinic, a special program for therapeutic foster care, and a university-based child psychiatry service. Clinical experiences are discussed for each setting in terms of the nature, severity, and chronicity of incestuous activities, the child's developmental status, the presence or absence of family stability, and the availability of community supports for network-oriented treatment. General recommendations then follow.

Incestuous abuse presents society with the unique clinical dilemma of protecting children, yet at the same time preserving their options for normal family development and effective treatment. Three interconnected issues are central to this problem; First, incest intensifies relationships within the family, yet tends to destroy the family as a social system; second, traumas resulting from incest increase the victim's needs for sensitive parenting, yet continuous parenting becomes less easily available when the child is removed from family ties; and third, the placing of victims into foster care shields them from abuse, but also increases the risk for abnormal personal development (Johnston, 1979). Is it possible to reconcile these seemingly conflictual issues?

A solution to conflicts surrounding incestuously abused children is suggested by the social nature of human beings: Children and families normally cope and develop under the broad influence of extended family and other social networks (Rueveni, 1979). Therefore, constructive networks can be identified, enlisted, or created in each instance of incestuous abuse to help provide support and protection for children, role models for parents, and encouragement for nuclear families.

This chapter discusses social network-oriented treatment for incestuously abused children. The authors, a social worker-therapist and child psychiatrist, have facilitated network-oriented approaches at three distinct clinical settings, all of which serve abused children. The settings are a community-based mental health clinic, a special program for therapeutic foster care, and a university-based child psychiatry service. The chapter describes populations, programs, indications, and community supports for treatment at each clinical setting. General recommendations then follow.

TREATMENT AT A COMMUNITY MENTAL HEALTH CLINIC

Fifteen cases involving incestuous child abuse were selected for description from the case load at a mental health clinic in Sarpy County, Nebraska. Sarpy County, with a population of 86,000, includes semirural areas along with communities that are suburban to Greater Omaha, a metropolitan area of about 500,000. The county, which has been growing, has a disproportionately large military population. Many citizens of the county experience frequent changes of residence and may lack extended family supports.

Clinical Procedures at the Clinic

All cases described in this section were referred by the Child Protective Service for therapy, consecutively between 1979 and 1982, to one of the authors, Mrs. Carnevale. Prior to referral, each case was subjected to the following procedures: Following a complaint, the Child Protective Service worker locates the child, usually at school, and meets with her and a guidance counselor. The child is then asked to discuss the allegations of abuse, and, if appropriate, to make a written statement at the police station. This statement is used to ensure cooperation from the child's parents. The child's mother is then called to the police station, encouraged to support her daughter, and, in most cases, returns with her to the home.

The perpetrator of abuse, usually a father or stepfather, is picked up separately by the police. He generally spends a few days in jail, where his cooperation for treatment is sought. As a matter of policy, the Juvenile Court issues a restraining order limiting parental contacts with the family, and the abusive father is required to find a temporary residence outside the family home. Physical-medical and psychological evaluations, family therapy, and enrollment with "Parents United" are then court ordered. Under these conditions, criminal prosecution is not sought.

Parents United is a self-help group specifically designed to rehabilitate parents from incestuous families (Giarretto, 1978). After enrollment at Parents United, each member is expected to share an honest account of reasons for referral and to attend weekly meetings. Confidentiality within the group is encouraged. However, open communications are maintained between Parents United staff and Child Protective Service workers, and progress reports are shared with the court. Parents United sessions typically include a business meeting, followed by a formal presentation and small-group discussions.

As mentioned earlier, the court considers family therapy necessary and complementary to participation at Parents United. Therefore, an initial session is arranged with a therapist while the family is still in crisis, as soon as possible after the Child Protective Service receives a complaint. Regular sessions are then held by the therapist with family members until the family is considered rehabilitated. Since therapy is complex and personally taxing, the therapist requires formal support for his or her work from clinic administration, psychiatric and psychological consultants, and the community of other therapists engaged in similar work.

Two general goals are defined for therapy in each case. These are to help the child adjust to personal problems and to help the family develop appropriate ways of relating. Personal problems for the child victim typically include anxiety, guilt, depression, insecurity, fearfulness, unmet dependency needs, and pseudomaturity, as described by Herman and Hirschman (1981). Family problems usually include difficulties with impulse control, poor judgment, authority conflicts, manipulativeness, self-indulgence, confused intimacy, and a tendency to act out physically, as described by Anderson and Shafer (1979). Therapy addresses general as well as incest-related issues.

Sessions at the clinic are directed primarily toward the incestuous triad, in most instances consisting of a daughter victim, a father perpetrator, and a mother enabler. (For a discussion of incestuous triangulation, see Machotka,

Pittman, and Flomenhaft, 1967.) Initially, sessions are held with each individual from the incestuous triangle, as well as the marital couple as a diad, and the mother-daughter diad. In this way, the abused child is encouraged to work through personal feelings about herself and to discuss encounters with incest, first individually and then with the help of her mother. Meanwhile, the mother is encouraged to express herself, accept her position of authority in the family, and support her daughter. In sessions with her husband, she is encouraged to seek more equality in the marital relationship. For his part, the father is encouraged to acknowledge the seriousness of the situation, to control his actions, and, when possible, to experience appropriate emotions.

After a few weeks, siblings may be invited to participate in therapy sessions along with the mother and daughter. The main focus in therapy then shifts toward constructive family reorganization. During these sessions, the incest victim and her siblings are encouraged to confront and redefine relationships within the family. Finally, conjoint sessions are held with the father, and he gradually visits and reenters the home. Central to success in this approach to family reconstruction is the expectation that explicit new intrafamily rules will emerge under stress to be applied to self-healing and healthier extrafamily relationships. Family change as process has been described by Reiss (1982).

In cases where the father is incapable of change or the mother is unable to apply appropriate restrictions, it sometimes becomes necessary to place the victim temporarily with extended family or in a foster home. (For a discussion of intractable father-daughter incest, see Wells, 1981.) Basic clinical goals are then maintained while extended family or extended-familylike relationships provide an additional network for support to the child and her nuclear family. Because progress in these cases requires constructive contracts between the child's permanent and temporary families, the therapist carefully arranges visits among family members, at first in the substitute, then in the permanent home, and foster parents are included in therapy sessions.

Clinical experience at the Sarpy County Clinic have led us to believe that the combined approach to family rehabilitation under Juvenile Court supervision and including Parents United with family therapy and occasional temporary foster placements has been helpful to incestuously abused girls. Characteristics of cases served at the clinic are described below to clarify indications for this particular network.

Description of Cases at the Mental Health Clinic

All 15 incestuous abuse cases in Mrs. Carnevale's case load involved girls as victims. The girls ranged from 11 to 16 years of age, with an average age of 14. Thirteen out of 15 girls had been abused for two to three years, while two other cases were more acute. Eight stepfathers, five biological fathers, and one older brother were perpetrators of the incestuous abuse.

The average family in the program consisted of two parents with four children in the home. All families, with the exception of one oriental mother, were considered white. Blended families were not unusual. In 11 out of 15 cases, an oldest daughter was the identified incest victim. Other siblings were found to have experienced incest in only four cases.

The most frequent type of abuse in this group of treatment cases was fondling or genital manipulation. Seven cases included fathers who masturbated their daughters and daughters who were taught to masturbate their father or watch him masturbate. Other cases were more severe, including mutual oral sex, attempted penetration, one girl who was tied down while she was manipulated, and five cases of penetration with intercourse, usually by a stepfather under the influence of alcohol.

Fathers, by profession, were military officers (four), noncommissioned officers (three), small-business managers (three), truck drivers (three), a dishwasher, and a laborer. Seven mothers worked outside the home at the time of referral, five of them full-time. Eight mothers did not work outside the home.

Childhood histories of incestuous abuse were present but not prominent among parents from cases studied at the clinic. Six mothers recalled incidents of sexual abuse during childhood, but none was with a biological father.

When families were rated on scales for optimal, excessive, or inadequate closeness, structure, and contact with extended family, all were found less than optimal on one or more scales. However, there was no typical pattern. Seven families were rated enmeshed, but four were considered disengaged. Seven families were rated rigid, but four were considered disorganized. Seven families lacked extended family supports, but four were overdependent on extended family. Moreover, there were no correlations among these variables.

The typical dynamic for incestuous abuse from this group was passivity on the part of one or both parents. For example, a father in one case complained that the family dog frequently woke him while his wife was absent for the evening. At these times, he felt he had no choice but to molest his daughter. Before treatment, his wife chose to ignore this behavior.

Overt psychiatric disturbances were relatively absent among members of this group of incestuous families. There were no cases of schizophrenia, psychosis, gross organic brain syndrome, or retardation among parents or victims in the group. Victims and parents most frequently were assigned a diagnosis of adjustment or personality disorder. Cases of more severe abuse usually contained family members with more severe personality problems, but were not necessarily more difficult to treat. However, in the single case where the mother was found severely depressed, the family did not respond to therapy and soon left town. In general, as reported by Thomas and Johnson (1979), cases of incest involving intercourse were more difficult to treat.

Outcome for Cases at the Clinic

Four cases still in treatment at the time of study were evaluated. For outcome-to-date, ten were followed up and one was lost to follow-up. Criteria for success in treatment included a halt or reduction in incestuous activities, a reversal of self-defeating patterns by the victim, and constructive reintegration by the family.

The program appeared successful at reducing incestuous activities for this particular population. There were no instances of incest by parents during the program and no instances of incest in any foster home.

Foster placements became necessary to protect or treat the victim during treatment in eight out of fifteen cases. Placements were more frequent in cases with a history of overt abuse, including cases of intercourse, bondage, fellatio, and family orgies. However, such activities did not recur while the child was in treatment and were rare during the period of follow-up. In fact, the one instance of near-incest that became known to us on follow-up involved a treated victim who became pregnant by her mother's lover.

The program also appeared reasonably successful at rehabilitating victims. When victims were rated for general personal-social adjustment, we found five well adjusted, five fairly well adjusted, and five poorly adjusted. Not surprisingly, all five girls who were considered poorly adjusted also were among the eight who had required foster care. Since, in all cases, foster parents were considered helpful and cooperative, the five girls' poor posttreatment adjustment was attributed to more severe problems initially.

Effort to facilitate family reintegration also appeared reasonably successful in most cases. Six parental couples remained together and their family life improved, four couples remained together but considered their marriage dysfunctional, and in five cases the mother established a single-parent household. Placements under the program were not necessarily disruptive to family reintegration, but they tended to be lengthly. Only three placements lasted under a year. The remainder lasted a year or more. However, none of the girls in Mrs. Carnevale's case load remained permanently in foster care.

Indications or Treatment at the Mental Health Center

Our limited analysis of network-oriented treatment at the Sarpy County Clinic found the program suitable and indicated for incestuously abused youngsters who are adolescent or in middle childhood and from relatively functional homes where the family lacks severe psychiatric illnesses and overt sexual or physical abuse is not an ingrained transgenerational pattern. In other words, this particular combination of court supervision, Parents United, family therapy, and time-limited foster placements appears effective when a nucleus of family and personal strengths are available to respond to treatment.

The mental health clinic program is socially relevant because cases they treat are frequent, probably the most frequent type of incestuous abuse cases in clinical practice. Moreover, the program is applicable, with minor modifications, as a first resort for situations where children are younger, abuses more peculiar, families more deviant, patterns more ingrained, special problems present, or special resources required. However, even in a society where social services and mental health clinics are bountiful and effective, there probably always will be a minority of cases that require extreme protection and intensive treatment, yet children from extreme cases also require continuous parenting. Extreme cases, even more than others, call upon the community for a network-oriented approach.

TREATMENT AT A SPECIAL FOSTER CARE PROGRAM

Extreme case histories of incestuous abuse are not unusual among disrupted children in permanent foster care. This section describes treatment for incestuous abuse as one aspect of total care at a special foster care program. The program was established in Omaha in 1972 to provide care under five integrated guidelines for treatment. These guidelines, "The Creighton Plan," are: (1) Foster parents engage disrupted children in a predictable sequence of therapy to help them acquire adaptive social skills; (2) agencies and a foster care team support the foster family toward realistic commitments, resource control, family stability, and effective boundary maintenance; (3) broadly supportive social networks aid in therapy; (4) foster and adoptive parents include the child's biological family in the network when possible, or at least help the child work through significant past relationships and associated problems; and (5) the foster family draws upon the professional community for knowledgeable, relevant, and consistent services to meet any special medical, psychiatric, educational, and social needs. The treatment plan and the principles that underly it are described in other publications (Christensen and Fine, 1979; Fine and Pape, 1982; Fine, 1983). For a general discussion of special foster care see Bryant (1981).

Children were referred to the program for a variety of problems from hospitals, group homes, unsuccessful foster placements, and unworkable family situations. Characteristic problems included relationship disabilities, family disruptive patterns, frantic attention-demanding behaviors, and difficult-to-manage medical and educational disabilities. Incestuous abuse, itself, seldom was a primary reason for referral and sometimes became known only after the child had settled into treatment.

Clinical Population at the Foster Care Program

A study of all cases served by the program to date was undertaken in 1980. Sixty-eight long-term cases were identified for the study from a total of 91 referred to the program over an eight-year period. Complete results of the study are to be reported in a monograph by Fine, Blum, Kohn, Fain, and Eustice.

Histories of physical abuse and/or neglect were identified for over 70% of cases studied, and incestuous abuse was identified for 15%. The ten cases of incestuous abuse included eight girls and two boys who were victimized by biological, foster, and adoptive fathers and stepfathers, a grandfather. an uncle, and, in three cases, mothers.

The group of ten ranged in age from 6 to 15 years at the time they entered the program, with an average age of 11. Seven children were white and three were black. In terms of custody, only three were state wards. The mother was known in most cases, but in no case was a child living with the biological father.

Experiences with incestuous abuse tended to be extreme, chronic, and polymorphous. Cases included a 9-year-old girl who, following incestuous abuse during infancy, had resided in foster homes or institutions; a 6-year-old girl whose incestuous involvement with a stepfather was discovered after the borderline psychotic mother placed the child; a school-aged boy who had been abused by his promiscuous mother's alcoholic male friends; and a school-aged girl who was used for sex by adult inmates in an institution. Only two cases were adolescent at the time of abuse.

Other disruptions also were frequent for the group. For example, five of the ten overt incest cases had been removed from the biological home before age 7. On the average, they had experienced five temporary placements before entering our program. Medical, emotional, and social problems were widespread among biological parents of children in the group. However, only one biological parent, herself a foster child, had a clear history of childhood incest.

Sexual problems among the total group of 68 cases were not limited to overt incestuous abuse. An additional 31% of the group revealed histories of less abusive incest, probable incest, or a high risk for incest. These cases included mutually incestuous biological and foster siblings; girls who were placed because their siblings had been abused, or who were propositioned, or believed they had been propositioned; and boys who were so enmeshed with their mothers that incest was a distinct possibility.

Clinical Process at the Foster Care Program

Clinical procedures for this particular program were structured to facilitate corrective developmental experiences. Therefore, cases were evaluated, diagnosed, and carefully matched with therapeutic foster homes; the agency supported the basic premises of the program; the foster care team carried a small case load;

foster parents functioned as therapists in a process of corrective socialization; the integrity of foster homes was respected; regular group meetings were held with foster parents for training, case planning, and support; surrogate extended-familylike relationships between the child's foster and biological families were encouraged; and adequate professional backup was provided or located as required.

Diagnoses for the ten cases of overt incest included four undersocialized aggressive conduct disorders, four specific developmental disorders, three over-anxious disorders, two organic personality syndromes, and one case each of pervasive developmental disorder, attention deficit disorder, mental retardation, and adjustment disorder. Three of the ten cases also were experiencing one or more serious chronic illnesses including epilepsy, thyroid insufficiency, congenital brain anomalies, and cataracts. Special education was required for five of the ten cases.

Foster parents were selected to treat this group of children from a pool of 40 families. Characteristically, foster parents were mature and experienced, having, on the average, raised four biological offsprings and fostered over 20 children. Most parents from the group said they enjoyed fostering all types of children regardless of age or special problems. As a group, they were middle class and dedicated to their homes. Single parents were not excluded, but all parents maintained an extensive network of family and other supportive relationships. Most parents in the group were moral and structured in child rearing, but also patient and understanding. Many came to foster care through chance encounters before they were licensed.

Perturbations of problems were typical of therapy for most cases. The average victim of overt incestuous abuse remained in the program at least three years. Six required only one program placement, three required two placements, and one experienced four placements. However, in all cases, an attempt was made to preserve continuity of relationships for the child within the network of foster parents. Visits, phone calls, and helpful exchanges of services were not unusual among foster parents.

As a clinical impression, successful placements required about a year for children to settle into the home, followed by several more months or years during which they could internalize better ways of relating and come to terms with their backgrounds. In most cases, children were able to confront and work through experiences with abusive incest only after they came to love and trust a foster mother, and successfully experience new age-appropriate skills. Foster mothers then attempted to be understanding, matter-of-fact, instructive, and realistic in their approach to incest.

Corrective experiences with a foster father or father figure also were necessary. For example, in one case, a disrupted brain-damaged adolescent lifted her sweater to show her foster father newly developed breasts and rubbed against him. He discouraged this behavior and told his wife. The couple then discovered that their foster daughter had been boasting to peers about a nonexistent sexual relationship with her foster father. Much discussion with many people in a variety of embarrassing situations followed. Perhaps the incident was inevitable. As a result of it, the patient was able to work through lifelong attitudes and feelings concerning inappropriate sexual experiences, beginning with her biological father. In the long run, the process was helpful and corrective.

A child psychiatrist and caseworkers contributed treatment and other technical suggestions during foster parent group meetings. Intense reactions to incest were frequent among foster parents, but could be worked through in the group. Individual sessions for the child with the psychiatrist or mental health therapist sometimes also were required for specific problems. Such problems included enuresis, encopresis, depression, anxiety, and school refusal. Visits to the psychiatrist's office also were used for occasional sessions with the entire foster family or to help the patient reestablish constructive relationships with the biological family.

Biological family members, when they were known and available, were included in network aspects of the treatment program. In these instances, other treatment programs could be offered as needed. Relevant programs might include Alcoholics Anonymous, Parents Anonymous, social services, psychotherapy, psychopharmacology, and psychiatric hospitalizations. However, despite sincere efforts, only 30% of the incestuously abused group was able to return to the biological family. Nevertheless, in most instances, the victim seemed able to achieve a better understanding of past experiences and to accept parental disabilities. In any case, patients always feel better knowing that their parents and siblings had received needed care.

Outcome for Cases in the Foster Care Program

One part of the 1980 study of special foster care was to follow up 30 sequentially selected cases. Follow-up cases included 5 who had been incestuously abused, 13 who had been abused nonincestuously, and 12 who had not been abused.

All 30 follow-up cases were located and interviewed concerning current adjustments and attitudes toward the program; each individual also was rated for developmental disruption; and, in addition, an abbreviated form of the Minnesota Multiphasic Personality Inventory was administered to 24 who were capable of taking the test.

The five follow-up cases of incestuous abuse appeared reasonably representative of all ten cases of incestuous abuse from the inclusive study of 68 cases. Four were white females and one a black male. Their average age was 14. Three of these five former victims were still residing in a Creighton Plan foster home, one was in a small group home, and one was in a state-operated group home.

None had experienced incestuous abuse during the program or after. When asked about the effects of special foster care on their lives, all five responded that the foster care program had helped them, that they maintained a good relationship with the foster family, and felt attached to the foster parents as parent figures. All five said they remembered their biological families and that the program either had a good effect or no effect on their relationship with biological parents. Three indicated that they also felt attached to their biological parents as parents, but only one maintained frequent contacts. Four said they had close friends of both sexes. However, only two indicated that they were doing well at school or on the job. We concluded from the interviews that, considering the groups' age and background, their adaptation was relatively positive.

Rating scales and testing tended t confirm this impression. On follow-up, none of the five were rated to have regressed behaviorally when compared to behaviors from the time they had entered the program; this despite the fact that three carried potentially disabling psychiatric diagnoses.

Findings from the MMPI, illustrated in Figure 5-1 were particularly instructive.[1] As part of the follow-up study, we compared mean MMPI profiles for the incestuous abuse follow-up group with MMPI profiles for nonincestuous and nonabuse follow-up groups.

A clinical interpretation of results shows that all three groups were within the subclinical range for pathology, and that patterns for the three groups were more similar than different. All groups showed subclinical profile elevations that identified the average respondent as defiant, disobedient, devious, impulsive, mischievous, self-centered, selfish, needy for affection, and likely to act out underlying feelings of inferiority, anxiety, or depression. In other words, the basic pattern of pathology for incestuously disrupted individuals was specifically similar to other disrupted individuals.

Mean MMPI profiles also indicated minor differences among the three groups. Subjects with a history of nonincestuous abuse most closely exemplified the action-oriented subclinical pattern shared by all three groups; subjects from the incestuously abused group showed an additional tendency to be pessimistic, demanding, and concerned about their health; and subjects with no history of abuse revealed the most severe pattern for severe psychiatric vulnerability. Closer investigation of the nonabuse group indicated that their more vulnerable picture correlated with time spent in placement prior to entering the Creighton Plan: The more the adolescents had experienced disruptive childhood placements, the more at risk they were for psychopathology.

Outcome results from this limited study may be helpful for clinical practice. They suggest that incestuous disruption, as a subset of general disruption, is

---

[1] For discussion of the MMPI, the abbreviated MMPI, and their significance, validity, and interpretation, see Marks, Seeman, and Haller (1974) and Ward (1980).

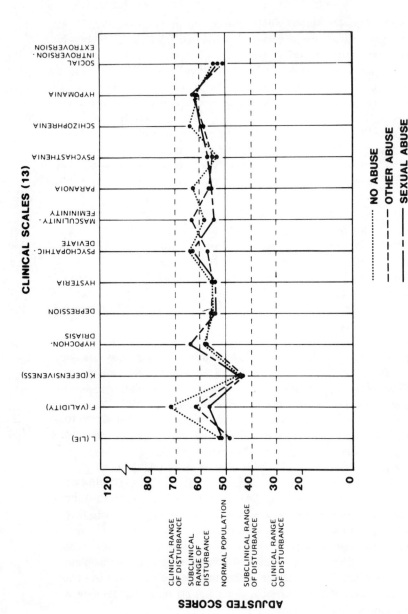

Figure 5-1. Minnesota Multiphasic Personality Inventory results comparing average scores for 24 children in long-term foster care, 5 of whom had experienced sexual abuse, 10 of whom had experienced abuse but not sexual abuse, and 9 of whom had not reported abuse.

secondary for purposes of therapy to general disruption: Incestuously disrupted children, in common with all disrupted children, primarily require secure and consistent reparenting. However, as a subgroup with special needs, they also may require help for pessimistic feelings about their bodies and sexuality.

TREATMENT CONSIDERATIONS AT A CHILD PSYCHIATRY SERVICE

Psychiatric facilities are an important resource for incestuously abused children. Cases from the Creighton University Child and Family Psychiatry Service, a facility that offers network-oriented services, illustrate an integrated approach to psychiatric care.

Clinical Population at the Child Psychiatry Service

The Child and Family Psychiatry Service is a university-based multidisciplinary outpatient clinic that utilizes standard diagnostic, therapeutic, and consultation procedures. The service has integral connections with child and adolescent psychiatric units at a general hospital and close connections with community-based programs. In this way, the service acts as an interface between technically intensive, community-removed resources and less intensively staffed community-based resources.

Over 500 cases were seen at the service in 1980. Ninety-four cases at risk for developmental disruption were selected from this population: These were cases in foster and adoptive care or involved in custody disputes. Twenty-two cases from this group involved incestuous abuse.

Forty-one percent of the 22 cases involving incestuous abuse were referred to the service directly by foster, adoptive, or biological parents; 32% were referred by private or county social service agencies; 23% by a state foster care unit; and 4% by the courts. Reasons for referral included problems with learning, behavior, or emotions in 59% of cases; problems concerning the process of substitute care in 32%; and evaluations concerning the suitability of a home in 9%. Most of the patients were living at foster homes, but substantial minorities were in adoptive or biological homes. One girl was in a group home.

Children from these cases ranged in age from 4 to 21 years with an average age of 14. Fifty-nine percent were female. Seventy-three percent were white, 23% were black, and one was oriental. Diagnoses ranged from adjustment disorders to organic personality disorders, and in most instances, pathology was similar to other groups of incestuously abused disrupted children.

Clinical Experiences at the Child Psychiatry Service

Cases at the service are evaluated for biological, psychological, family, and network factors. Then they are formulated for recommendation of priorities and relevant procedures. Options for this particular group of cases included: focused outpatient therapies; case management suggestions directed to agencies, schools, or parents; hospitalization; and opinions regarding custody. Each of these options is illustrated below to demonstrate how the service functions in the community.

Outpatient therapy was provided for nine cases from seven families. For example, in one case, an elderly foster mother brought her 12-year-old foster son to the service requesting help for his passivity, enuresis, and minor thefts, and her concern that he might once again molest younger relatives. The boy had been abandoned by his mother at age 8 following molestation by a stepfather. He was adopted, but his behavior in the adoptive home caused them in turn to abandon him. Bright and talented, in his heart he was loyal to his biological family. Psychotherapy was recommended and begun. In therapy, he focused on escapist science fiction fantasies. Attempts were made to help him reengage with the world of reality and to control his life, but these were only partially successful. However, in this context, the foster mother and caseworker could be encouraged to help him achieve an emotional reconciliation with the adoptive parents and his biological mother.

In another case, family therapy sessions were held with a mother and five of her children when they were reunited after eight years in the foster care system. The abusive alcoholic father was now dead. Among other things, the family needed to mourn him.

Suggestions to parents, agencies, or schools were focal for eight cases from six families. For example, in one case, previously unrecognized learning disabilities were uncovered by psychological testing. The problem was discussed with the parents, and recommendations sent to the school and family physician.

In another case, a 4-year-old foster child was referred by a county foster care worker to evaluate her possible return to the biological parents. The child had been removed because of physical neglect, but there were vague suspicions of sexual abuse. On evaluation, we found that the girl was intensely attached to her biological parents and there was no evidence for sexual abuse. However, we also found that her biological mother was depressed, demoralized, and over-whelmed by pressures. She herself reported a horrendous history of sexual abuse by her father and in foster homes. Despite these experiences, she remained a capable woman. Advice to the worker in this case included therapy for the mother, counseling for the couple, and a return home for the child. The mother benefited from therapy and began to cope. Eventually, she insisted that her husband find a job, which he did. The child was then returned home with an apparently good result.

Custody evaluations were performed for the court in two cases. For example, in one case a multiply displaced, abused, learning-disabled 9-year-old boy was referred for determination of his suitability for a preadoptive placement. After the evaluation, permanency and therapy were recommended.

Hospitalization was required in two cases. One case involved a chronically assaultive retarded 19-year-old state ward who was abused and abandoned early in life. She had never achieved a successful attachment in a substitute home and was thought to be hopelessly institutional. However, after six weeks in the hospital, spent helping her control behaviors and assessing vocational skills, an extraordinary home was found. She lives there now, reasonably well adjusted.

In another case, hospitalization was required for a 14-year-old diabetic foster child who was self-destructively negligent of her health. She simply was unable to cope with the combination of abuse, neglect, incest, displacement, and physical illness. For her, temporary hospitalization was a needed retreat.

CONCLUSIONS

Incestuously abused children are not a homogeneous group. Rather, they face the community with a variety of problems and strengths. Each case merits careful evaluation for severity, chronicity, and associated factors.

Cases beginning during adolescence frequently can be treated in the community under court supervision utilizing parent support groups and family therapy.

Family reconstruction is a goal in every case. When an incestuous couple requires separation, it is more constructive to remove the perpetrator than to remove the victim. However, if placement for the victim becomes necessary, it should be temporary and integrated with treatment.

Cases beginning early in life are more associated with severe personal and family problems. Psychiatric illnesses, alcoholism, and marginality are more prevalent in these cases, and children are more vulnerable.

When young children are removed from the home, permanency for the child and rehabilitation for the family always are important goals, and developmental continuities should be preserved whenever possible. Options for permanency include a return home, adoption, and special foster care.

Children who are incestuously abused and multiply displaced may develop severe personality problems. Corrective socialization in a network of caring biological and surrogate family relationships is suggested as primary for these cases. Therapeutic foster homes, a logical base for these services, require special structure and extra support.

Community-oriented psychiatric services can play an integrative function in many cases. Physical, emotional, and family disabilities should be identified and treated in an effective manner.

Humane treatment, balance, and appropriate experiences are necessary for all human beings. Incest challenges the structure of the family. Incestuous abuse distorts normal child development. Social measures to support family life and normal child development may be the most effective method for prevention and treatment in the long run.

REFERENCES

Anderson, Lorna M., and Shafer, Gretchen. 1979. The character-disordered family: A community treatment model for family sexual abuse. *Am. J. Orthopsychiatry,* **138**(7): 967–970.

Bryant, B. 1981. Special foster care: A history and rationale. *J. Clinical Child Psychology,* **10**(1):8–20.

Christensen, G., and Fine. P. 1979. Corrective socialization in foster care of children. *Child Psychiatry and Human Development,* **10**:15.

Fine, P. 1983. Clinical aspects of foster care. In M. Cox, and R. Cox, eds., *Foster Care: Current Issues and Practice.* Norwood: Ablex, in press.

Fine, P., Blum, M., Kohn, E., Fain, P., and Eustice, S. 1984. *A Ten Year Follow-up of Therapeutic Foster Care.* New York: Child Welfare League of America, in process.

Fine, P., and Pape, M. 1982. Pregnant teenagers in need of diagnostic parameters. In I. Stuart, and C. Wells, eds., *Pregnancy in Adolescence.* New York: Van Nostrand Reinhold.

Giarretto, Henry. 1978. Humanistic treatment of father-daughter incest. *J. Humanistic Psychology,* **18**(4):60–76.

Herman, Judith, and Hirschman, Lisa. 1981. Families at risk for father-daughter incest. *Am. J. Psychiatry,* **138**(7):967–970.

Johnston, Mary S. Krentz. 1979. The sexually mistreated child: Diagnostic evaluation. *Child Abuse and Neglect,* **3**:943–951.

Machotka, Pavel, Pittman, Frank, and Flomenhaft, Kalman. 1967. Incest as a family affair. *Family Process,* **6**:98–116.

Marks, P. A., Seeman, W., and Haller, D. L. 1974. *The Actual Use of the MMPI with Adolescents and Adults.* Baltimore: Williams R. Wilkins.

Reiss, David. 1982. The working family: A researcher's view of health in the household. *Am. J. Psychiatry,* **139**(11):1412–1420.

Rueveni, Uri. 1979. *Networking Families in Crisis.* New York: Human Science Press.

Thomas, George, and Johnson, Clara L. 1979. Developing a program for sexually abused adolescents: The research-service partnership. *Child Abuse and Neglect,* **3**:683–691.

Ward, L. 1980. Conversion equations for modified scoring of the MMPI-168. *J. Person. Assess.,* **44**:644–646.

Wells, Lloyd A. 1981. Family pathology and father-daughter incest: Restricted psychopathy. *J. Clinical Psychiatry,* **42**(5):197–202.

6

Clinical Intervention with Boy Victims of Sexual Abuse

Carl M. Rogers, Ph.D.
Tremaine Terry, M.S.W.

ABSTRACT

Little attention has been paid to the patterns and characteristics of sexual victimization of boys and the crucial role of parents in helping them cope with the resulting trauma. The special and unique treatment concerns in managing these cases are related with appropriate case material to illustrate anticipated reactions of both. A number of guidelines are suggested for intervention to cope with the typical emotional and physical reactions to the assault on the part of both victim and parent.

He sits tensely in our playroom avoiding eye contact and speaking only when spoken to. Slowly, the complete story emerges, one little piece at a time. This afternoon Leroy, a 14-year-old neighbor, forced him into a stairwell and rectally sodomized him. He is hurt, embarrassed, afraid, but above all angry. He says if he were older or stronger he'd kill Leroy. He's 6 years old.

Regrettably, this scenario or one very much like it is all too common to those who work daily with sexually victimized children and youth. Although in the past two decades increased professional attention has been given to the problems of sexual abuse and incest, little attention has been directed to the problem of sexual victimization of boys. This is true despite the fact that perhaps as many as one-fourth of all child victims of sexual assault or molestation are boys — an estimated national figure of 100,000 boy victims every year.

There are two principal reasons why we have collectively tended to fail to address the problems of boy victims. First, professional concern for sexual victimization of children has its roots in two different social service movements: child protective services and services for victims of rape. Sexual assault of boys has not been a primary concern of public protective services for the most part due to the fact, as will be seen later, that few of the boys are victimized by parents or guardians. The rape crisis center movement, in contrast, has historically been closely tied to the feminist movement and legitimately concerned with the rape of women regardless of age; only recently have rape crisis centers begun to see sexual abuse of boys as an additional area of concern.

The second and perhaps more crucial reason for professional neglect of the problem has to do with out collective reluctance to identify the sexually molested boy as a victim, per se. Our societal reaction is quite different for a case involving a 12-year-old girl seduced by a 35-year-old man than for a case of a 12-year--old boy seduced by a 35-year-old woman. Most cases involving boy victims, however, involve male perpetrators who are often juveniles themselves. This often leads to a hasty presumption on the part of health care, social services, and law enforcement personnel that an incident constitutes "inappropriate sex play" rather than a true victimization or abuse situation, even in cases where the age differences are extreme (e.g., six or ten years) or where force or threats of force have been used. While we routinely identify the 8-year-old girl engaged in intercourse by a 16-year-old boy as a victim, we often fail to apply the same standard when the victim is a boy.

Perhaps more importantly, there exists a cultural bias toward blaming the victim of sexual crimes in general and of blaming boy victims in particular. The underlying dynamics of this phenomenon are too lengthy to discuss in detail. As it relates to boy victims, it generally takes one of three forms. First, because physical trauma is infrequent with boy victims – as with girl victims – there is often a tendency to deny that the boy was truly victimized. In particular, there is a tendency to blame the boy who fails to forcibly resist the assault. Passive acquiescence in the face of demonstrable threat is reformulated in terms of the victim's own lack of masculinity: "A real boy would never let someone do that without fighting back"; "He must have wanted to do it because he didn't resist"; and so forth. Second, we often fail to identify boys who are bribed or who prostitute themselves as victims. A physician, for example, related the story of an 11-year-old boy he had seen (who was concerned that he might have gonorrhea). This boy, from an impoverished background, was engaging routinely in sex with a 40-year-old man. In exchange, the adult lavished gifts, clothing, and money on the child. The physician in this case did not perceive the child as a victim, but rather as a "hustler." Finally, there is a pervasive denial of the victimization of homosexual boys; self-identified homosexual boys when recounting a rape experience or a seduction experience by substantially older adults are disbelieved or more commonly are lectured regarding how their sexual preference makes such victimizations inevitable.

In part for the reasons enumerated above, little attention has been given to the patterns and characteristics of sexual victimization of boys or to the special or unique treatment concerns in managing these cases. In the following sections we hope to partially clarify the situation, first by discussing some of the common patterns and characteristics of victimization of boys, then by discussing particular victim and family reactions in these cases, and finally by suggesting some specific guidelines for intervention.

PATTERNS AND CHARACTERISTICS OF SEXUAL VICTIMIZATION OF BOYS

Estimates regarding the frequency of sexual victimization of boys differ substantially as a function of study setting and definitional criteria employed. Many studies (e.g., De Francis, 1969; Jaffe et al., 1975) place the figure at 10% or less of identified cases. The National Incidence Study conducted by the National Center on Child Abuse and Neglect (NCCAN) (OHDS, 1981) places the figure at 17% of all cases. Our own data, based on cases seen at Children's Hospital National Medical Center in Washington, D.C. between March 15, 1978 and December 31, 1980, reflect a figure of 25% of identified victims being boys (101 of 401 cases). The true incidence is probably substantially higher in that boys are substantially less likely to report their victimization (Swift, 1977).

In our experience, although there are many areas of similarity, there are fundamental differences in patterns of sexual victimization between boys and girls. Eighty-three percent of the boys seen were under the age of 12, compared with 70% of the girls. Twenty-six percent of the boys were under 6 years of age. Boys and girls are equally likely to suffer some physical trauma such as bruises (8%) or lacerations (10%). Few clear differences emerge between boys and girls in terms of how offenders engage the child in sexual activity, with physical force being the most common means (48% and 50%, respectively), although girls are less likely to be threatened with physical harm (37%) as a means of obtaining compliance than are boys (51%). Boys and girls are almost equally likely to be abused over time (43% and 47%, respectively), but boys are more likely to be abused by multiple offenders (20%) than are girls (13%). Girls, however, are more likely to reside with the offender at the time of the abuse (42%) than are boys (21%).

The most striking differences between cases involving boy and girl victims, however, are in terms of offender characteristics. Thirty-one percent of all girl victims are abused by a parent or parental surrogate, compared to only 8% of the boys. Boys are primarily victimized by nonfamily members who are known to either the victim or his family (63%) or by strangers (15%), while girls are most likely abused by a family member (52%). Similarly, while only 28% of the girls are abused by a juvenile, this figure is 56% for the boys. Fifty-six percent of the boy victims are subjected to anal intercourse.

VICTIM REACTIONS

Child reactions to being sexually victimized are complex and difficult to predict. some children appear little affected by the experience, while others may demonstrate marked personality and behavior changes. Despite the diversity of reactions or ability to cope, situational variables appear to be related to how the child copes.

Generally speaking, the older the child, the more difficult the adjustment. Similarly, the use or the threat of force, a close relationship with the offender (e.g., parent, grandparent), repeated sexual abuse over time, and nonsupportive reactions on the part of parents, professionals, or others, can all lead to more difficulties in adjustment in the postabuse phase.

Common reactions of child sexual assault or abuse victims, irrespective of the child's sex, include both emotional and behavioral impacts. Feelings of guilt are often present and may be exacerbated if they found the experience pleasurable, if they were enticed or bribed into cooperation, if they were engaged in a forbidden activity (e.g., visiting the park against parental orders), or if others assume a blaming or accusatory stance with the child. Guilt over disclosure of the incident (or incidents) is also common in those situations where there is a close positive relationship between the child and the perpetrator or in situations where parental reactions are hysterical in nature, with the child assuming responsibility for the impact of disclosure on others. Other common emotional reactions include shame, depression, a variety of fears (fear of men, fear of sleeping alone, fear of the dark, fear of specific places or situations), anger, and general anxiety.

Behavioral reactions of child victims to either the sexual incident or the disclosure are also varied and marked. Preoccupation with sexuality, reflected in increased masturbation, increased sex play, or, in older children, promiscuous behavior are not uncommon. Disturbed sleep or eating patterns including nightmares and depressed appetites are frequently noted. Young children may evidence behavioral regression such as a return to bed-wetting, thumb-sucking, and similar previously discarded behaviors. Older children often resort to drugs or alcohol as an escape mechanism. There may be marked changes noted in the child's interpersonal behavior ranging from withdrawal from peers and family to, in younger children, increased dependency and demands for nurture from parents. School-age children may manifest a radical decrement in school performance or an increase in school avoidance. Although less common, older children may also run away from home, particularly in situations where the offender is another family member or where parents are perceived as nonsupportive or blaming.

More detailed discussions of victim reactions are available from other sources (e.g., Thomas and Rogers, 1981; Burgess et al., 1978; Schultz, 1980). While boy victims may manifest any of these common emotional or behavioral reactions to the experience, in addition they frequently exhibit behavioral changes that are more or less unique to male victims. These changes appear to be directly related to the homoerotic implications of the sexual contact and our differential cultural expectations of behavior for boys. Specifically, three common reactions of boy victims are: confusion/anxiety over sexual identity, inappropriate attempts to reassert masculinity, and recapitualation of the victimizing experience. In the following sections, illustrative examples and a discussion of each are provided.

B. J., an 11-year-old boy, was orally and rectally sodomized by an adolescent relative who is self-identified as having homosexual tendencies (prior to the assault, B. J. was unaware of these tendencies). According to B. J.'s parents, he had always been very masculine in behavior — they described him as being "all boy." In the postabuse period, B. J. began adopting feminine mannerisms and increasingly withdrew from previous "masculine" games, became involved in playing more traditional "feminine" fames, such as doll babies and house, where he assumed the role of the mother. The parents were appropriately concerned but somewhat at a loss as to how to deal with these substantial changes.

Confusion over sexual identity is a particular reaction for some boy victims. The experience of a homosexual act contradicts the child's understanding of normal sexual relationships. As a result, the victim frequently seeks an explanation for why he was selected, internalizing the incident and blaming himself for its occurrence. These boys often believe that the assault occurred because of their physical appearance (slight build; lack of muscles), or because of their speech (soft or unobtrusive), or because of their personality (warm or friendly), or even because of their clothing (i.e., wearing shorts made the offender think he was a sissy). These so-called feminine attributes are perceived as substantially contributing to the assault. Particularly for those characteristics that the child is unable to change, he may come to identify with the notion that he is effeminate or is perceived as either effeminate or homosexual by others.

This concern of the boy victim that he may himself be effeminate or homosexual can be reinforced by a variety of factors. First, to the extent that he previously identified with strongly masculine standards or expectations for conduct, failure to physically resist even in the face of clear threat of harm may be internalized as indicating that he is not really a "man." Second, anxiety over sexual identity may reinforce itself if the child victim finds the experience pleasurable. The emergence of such feelings, particularly in the older child, threatens the child's self-concept as a sexual being. He is aware that our society defines only heterosexual contacts as acceptable, and subscribes to the general mythos that only those of a homosexual orientation can find pleasure in sexual contacts with members of their own sex. On the other hand, he cannot deny his feelings or sensations at the time. Once again, the child may misinterpret the situation as implying a latent homosexual orientation rather than correctly understanding normal physiological sexual responses.

T. R., a 10-year-old boy, was rectally sodomized by an adult male acquaintance of the family. While this case was still active in the courts, with its attendant pressures, T. R. was again sexually assaulted, this time by an adult male relative. In both situations, either force or the threat of physical harm was used to attain T. R.'s compliance. Prior to the first assault, according to his parents, T. R. was a generally easygoing, friendly, and inoffensive child who got along well with others. After the first assault, T. R. became more assertive and unruly in his relations with adult males. Following the second victimizing experience, T. R. appeared to undergo a profound change in his social relationships, adopting an aggressive and hostile posture toward both male and female peers. School fights, with T. R. as the instigator, became common, and his relationships with both of his parents and his siblings deteriorated as he became increasingly argumentative, recalcitrant, and aggressive.

The emergence of inappropriately expressed attempts to reassert masculinity through aggressive behavior is perhaps the most common behavioral reaction of boy victims. Although patterns and forms of aggression differ, there appears to be a very strong tendency for these boys to attempt to resolve their confusion or anxiety about their sexual identity through overidentification with the masculine stereotype. Many boy victims who were passive or unassertive individuals prior to the assault become aggressive afterwards; they tend to feel that their previous behavior contributed to their victimization. They both perceive that they have somehow lost their "manhood" through the assault and also tend to project this perception onto others. Aggressive behavior, therefore, becomes a means both to convince themselves that they are masculine and to reestablish their masculinity in the eyes of others. This aggressive behavior also serves a limited protective function. The child believes that if he presents a mean or "tough" image no one will attempt to take advantage of him again. One victim made such a point of wanting it known that he wasn't a pushover that he routinely picked fights with substantially older and stronger boys.

Although picking fights and attempting to bully other children are the most common forms of aggression encountered, a variety of other aggression-motivated behaviors have been observed in our clients. These include the destruction of property; confrontive and obtrusive behavior with parents, teachers, and other adults; and similar behaviors. Chronic disobedience, particularly of a deliberate nature, may become common. Many of these children appear to be seeking punishment, not for its own sake, but rather to project a masculine image to others.

O. M., a 12-year-old boy, was forcibly assaulted and rectally sodomized by two older boys while he was temporarily residing in a shelter care facility.

Upon being returned home to his natural family, O. M. sexually assaulted two 5-year-old neighbor boys. Although O. M. expressed his own feelings of fear and shame during his own assault, he could not articulate why he assaulted the two neighbor boys nor did he appear capable of empathizing with his two victims.

Although less common than the preceding male victim reactions, there is a tendency among boy victims to recapitulate their own victimization, only this time with themselves in the role of the offender and someone else as the victim. Although this reaction can be conceptualized as a displaced aggression phenomenon with the victim, being incapable of direct retribution against the original offender, displacing his aggressive impulses onto others, the particular mode of aggression chosen makes such an interpretation suspect. Similarly, although these events are often assaultive in nature, neither force nor the threat of force is always used — the victim turned-offender seems most interested in recreating a scenario similar to his own victimization, with modes of inducing compliance, specific sexual acts, and even age difference being patterned after the original incident.

In its most common form, the apparent need of the boy victim to reenact his own victimization appears to be but a variation upon inappropriate attempts to reassert his own masculinity. The boy victim feels that he was "robbed" of his masculinity and in a very real sense seeks to regain it through overidentification with the offender. In its most extreme manifestations, the child internalizes a world view that there are only two choices — to be an abuser or a victim — and elects to give rather than receive abuse.

The inability of many of these victim/offender boys to empathize with their victims may reflect a denial process in which the child essentially denies his own experience and his own feelings. Denial of the offense itself, even in the face of overwhelming evidence, is not uncommon.

Recapitulation may occur most commonly in situations where the boy victim perceives, rightly or wrongly, that others doubt or question his masculinity following his victimization. Alternatively, the event can also be construed as an attempt by the victim to either impress upon others the impact of his own victimization or merely to try to understand his own experience — the activity must be desirable if someone was willing to subject him to it. The event may also reflect an acceptance of a negative self-concept — "I'm no damn good because if I were good this wouldn't have happened to me" — with the child acting out the most negative behavior of which he is aware. Recapitulation, in our experience, is most common when the legal system fails to take appropriate steps against the original offender. While the reason for this apparent relationship is unclear, it may be related to the child's perceptions that he, rather than the offender, is to be blamed and that society tacitly condones such behavior.

PARENTAL/FAMILIAL REACTIONS

Child and parental reactions to a sexual abuse incident constitute a complex transactional process where each mutually influences and to some degree determines the other. Undesirable child reactions may be either heightened or ameliorated by how other family members, particularly parental figures, react. Parental reactions in turn, however, often appear to be influenced by the child's reactions.

In general, the reactions of parents and other family members are similar regardless of sex of the victim. Needless to say, parental reactions are also influenced by situational factors related to the assault such as the age of the child, type of sexual contact, whether force was used, the relationship of the offender (family member, friend, etc.), and so forth. Common parental reactions include anger, which may be directed toward the offender, the child, or both, or may be displaced onto intervening professionals. When the parental reaction is anger directed at the offender, it can generate to the point where the family seeks direct physical retribution. Guilt, particularly in situations where the parent perceives that his or her behavior contributed to the victimization (e.g., failing to believe the child when he or she reported an earlier, less serious, contact) is also common. It should be stressed that many parents react with appropriate concern and support for the child irrespective of other reactions. Parents may blame themselves for not monitoring the child's activities better, for failing to heed explicit or implicit indicators of sexual abuse, for not teaching the child more adequate approaches to securing safety, or for other factors that the parents perceive as being under their control.

Anger directed toward the child can result in physical abuse. A small yet important percentage of cases involve the parent assaulting the child following disclosure, often because the child was disobedient and this contributed to the sexual abuse (e.g., leaving the house against parental directive). Obviously, this reaction only heightens the child's tendency toward guilt and self-blame. Parents often express anxiety about what family members, neighbors, and others will think about the situation, as well as anxiety about the impact of the experience on the child's subsequent development. In extreme situations these anxieties may be come manifest as unrealistic fears or expectations for the child. In contrast parents may either deny the sexual assault or minimize the significance of the event if it is acknowledged.

Generic parental reactions and approaches to managing them with cases of child sexual assault are amply discussed elsewhere. Three harmful patterns of parental reactions appear to be particularly common, although not unique, in cases involving male victims. These are denial or minimization, blaming of the victim, and unrealistic fears regarding the impact of the event.

T. M., a 7-year-old male, was orally and rectally sodomized by an adult male neighbor. Despite physical medical findings consistent with the child's complaint, Mrs. M. initially reacted by refusing to believe that the incident took place. Eventually, Mrs. M. acknowledged that the abuse must have occurred, but then maintained that everyone, including her son, was over-reacting to the incident, and that everyone should just "forget about it and pretend it didn't happen."

In the case of T. M., the mother's initial refusal to believe that the incident took place appeared primarily to reflect an ongoing conflictual relationship with her son typified by a general perception of him as being untruthful and incorrigible. In working with the mother, it became clear that this conflictual relationship manifested itself in her devaluing her son and his experience in most arenas. Specifically, in terms of the sexual assault, she appeared more concerned with the impact upon herself and other family members than upon him. Her desire to minimize the seriousness reflected this devaluation; she perceived cooperation with social service and criminal justice agencies as an unfair burden on her and a waste of her time, irrespective of her son's needs.

Parental denial can take many forms, ranging from denial that the alleged incident took place, through refusal to believe the particulars of the abusive experience, to denial of the observable impact of the experience on the child. It should be stressed that almost all parents in these situations engage in some denial, however minimal. A significant yet small percentage will engage in denial to the degree discussed here.

The underlying motivations or dynamics of denial or minimization are varied and complex, ranging from a general maladaptive or nonsupportive relationship between parent and child to a need to defend against one's own feelings regarding homosexual behavior. Denial may reflect the parent's own inability to cope with the stress of the situation, or it may reflect the parent's inability to constructively address his or her own anxieties and fears about the impact of the assault on the child. A close personal relationship with the offender also may contribute — as in incest cases, it is often difficult to accept that a well-known, liked, and trusted individual is capable of such behavior. Other factors that appear to contribute to the denial process include a fatalistic world view and a lack of belief in positive or constructive intervention.

In our experience, denial or minimization of impact is much more common for parents of boy victims than it is for the parents of girl victims. In particular, parental needs to defend against their own feelings regarding homosexual behavior seem to play an important part in this process. Parents harboring strong feelings of disgust or revulsion regarding homosexuality or homosexual behavior find it extremely difficult to accept that their son has been sexually victimized by another male.

J. S., an 8-year-old boy, was accosted by a 12-year-old neighbor boy while on his way home from school. The older boy pulled J. S. into an alley and threatened to beat him up if he did not perform fellatio on him. J. S. was frightened of this older boy, and complied. J. S. told his parents what had happened when he got home. Although both were upset, their reactions differed markedly. While the mother was appropriately angry about the incident and concerned for J. S.'s well-being, J. S.'s father reacted with anger and hostility directed at J. S., accusing him of being a homosexual and stating that "any real man would die before he did that." In his father's eyes, J. S. was a sissy and weakling for submitting to the threats. Weeks after the assault, Mr. S. still refused even to talk to his son.

Although an extreme example, the case of J. S. vividly illustrates the frequently encountered problem of parents blaming the boy for being sexually victimized. While girl victims are also frequently blamed, the problem appears more common and widespread for boy victims. Derogatory labeling is usually although not always associated with blaming the victim. We find this to be a problem in approximately 5% to 10% of our cases involving boy victims.

Blaming the victim, particularly the boy victim, can serve a variety of parental needs. Occasionally it represents direct displacement of anger from the offender to the child. More commonly, it constitutes a self-protective mechanism for avoiding self-blame either for the incident or for holding the child to unreasonably high standards of behavior. Blaming parents tend to have rigid and high expectations for their child's behavior — they expect the child to perceive and react to situations as they themselves would. They make frequent erroneous attributions regarding the purposiveness of the child's behavior. In the case of J. S., the father, perhaps accurately, perceived the situation as one in which the offender may have hurt but not seriously injured J. S. His unwillingness to fight back but rather submit was interpreted in terms of adult perceptions of risk and adult perceptions of the degrading and dehumanizing nature of the sexual contact itself.

There is often a kernel of truth in parental blaming in that the child may have shown poor judgment. This is particularly true in situations where bribery, nonphysical threats, or other means are used to elicit the child's compliance in the sexual contact. Again, however, the parents are frequently applying adult logic and understanding as the yardstick against which the child's behavior is judged. Typically, the parent is assuming that the child clearly understands the full implications of his or her behavior and is electing to participate despite this understanding. Similarly, the parent of the self-identified homosexual child frequently chooses to blame the assault on the child's homosexuality rather than on the offender.

Blaming of the child victim for the sexually abusive experience can seriously aggravate problems the child has during the postabuse adjustment phase regardless of the child's sex. A particular danger with boy victims, however, is that labeling that calls their sexual identity into question can lead to increased confusion over sexual identity, inappropriate attempts to reassert their masculinity, and occasionally recapitulation of the abuse itself. Similarly, it is not uncommon when dealing with boy victims to discover that male peers are similarly labeling the child, often leading to comparable behavioral reactions.

L. M., a 7-year-old boy, was rectally sodomized by an adult male friend of the family. As with many victims, L. M. temporarily became more withdrawn from peers and from adult males, and expressed a variety of ongoing fears related to the assault. L. M.'s mother began to report marked changes in his behavior, including the withdrawal and fears, but extending to perceived changes in mannerisms and voice tonal qualities — both of which were seen as becoming more feminine. Mrs. M. was convinced that her son was becoming a homosexual as a result of his experience. Clinical assessment failed to verify these more extreme perceived changes.

Parents of sexually victimized boys, particularly those of latency age, tend to experience a great deal of anxiety and often specific fears relating to the impact of the assault upon the child's normal sexual development. Most commonly, there is fear expressed that the child will become a homosexual as a result of the experience. Other fears are often present, however. These fears are frequently extreme and may elicit a discounting response from the helping professional because of their patent absurdity. One mother, for example, in all seriousness was afraid that her son's abnormal sexual experience would lead to his becoming a "mass murderer" when he grew up. This fear appeared to be based upon her understanding of a few sensationalized accounts of the lives of individuals who had committed heinous crimes.

Misinterpretation of behavior and transference processes play an important role in the development and reinforcement of unrealistic parental fears. It is to be expected that the child victim will go through a period of psychological and behavioral disorganization after an assault and its disclosure. During this time, the child may engage in behaviors that were not part of his previous repertoire, such as acting fearful or withdrawn in relationship to others or becoming more dependent on his parents. Parents, projecting their own anxieties about the experience and its impact, can misinterpret these changes and ascribe either more meaning or a totally different meaning to these changes than would a third party. When parental anxiety is extreme, a heightened focus on observing the child can also lead to distorted perceptions where normal and routine behaviors of the child are suddenly perceived as sinister manifestations of fundamental personality change. In the case of L. M., Mrs. M. accurately perceived her son as being more withdrawn and more fearful than he had been before the incident, but she interpreted these changes as supporting her own fears that her son would now become a homosexual. The more anxious she became, the more carefully she scrutinized her son's behavior, reinterpreting and perceiving her son's normal characteristics in light of her own fears. Neither L. M.'s voice nor mannerisms were more "feminine" than most 7-year-old boys'. Others who had known L. M. before the assault failed to note these purported changes. Mrs. M's fears were such that her perceptions were becoming increasingly distorted, yet she was appropriately seeking help to ensure that her fears would not be realized.

Transference phenomena also contribute to the emergence and reinforcement of unrealistic parental fears. Sources of transference are most commonly personal experience or past knowledge of friends, neighbors, or relatives who were sexually assaulted at an early age and who apparently developed later problems in sexual adjustment. They indiscriminately presume that these results are fixed and inevitable and that their child will therefore experience the same conflicts. The transference of parental fears seems to be most important if the parent was assaulted at an early age, with the parent having evident difficulty in separating his or her own unresolved feelings regarding the experience from the feelings of the child. In one case, for example, the boy's mother had herself been sexually molested when she was 10 years old. She blamed this incident for her subsequent inability to develop a meaningful fulfilling sexual relationship with men. She expressed fears, stated in terms of her certainty that her son would be incapable of forming meaningful relationships with women.

Unrealistic parental fears can substantially interfere with the child's ability to transcend the experience. Most frequently, they reinforce the boys' often inappropriate approaches to reasserting their own masculinity. Parents who have extreme fears regarding the potential for homosexuality often implicitly or explicitly reinforce aggressive antisocial behavior on the part of their sons, thereby reducing their own anxieties. Less commonly, but particularly when the fears are accompanied by extreme perceptual distortion, the child may internalize the parental projections and come to see his own behavior as abnormal or homosexual, and a self-fulfilling prophecy may result.

GUIDELINES FOR INTERVENTION

For the most part, clinical assessment and intervention with boy victims should proceed in accordance with generic intervention approaches for child sexual assault victims. These approaches are well presented in other chapters as well as in other sources (e.g., Thomas and Rogers, 1981; Burgess et al., 1978; Schultz, 1981), and in any event are too lengthy to discuss in detail here. Particular characteristics and problems encountered with boy victim cases suggest some additional steps and modification of approaches.

As in any child sexual abuse or sexual assault situation, it is important to initially and subsequently assess both the child and the parents in terms of their coping capacities, progress, and general postabuse adjustment. With boy victims in particular, it is important to carefully assess their own cognitive understanding and interpretation of the event to identify ongoing or emergent confusion and anxiety relating to sexual identity. While it is common for clinicians to rely heavily upon parental report to gauge the child's postabuse adjustment, the dual problems of parental minimization or denial and the emergence of unrealistic parental fears suggest that parental reports are less reliable with cases involving boy victims. Direct clinical assessment of the child and, if possible, external validation of reported problems from other sources (e.g., other relatives, teachers) should be standard procedure in these cases.

For boys experiencing sexual confusion or anxiety as a result of the experience, direct reassurance and provision of a thorough cognitive framework to enhance the child's understanding are often helpful. Erroneous understanding of the motivations and actions of the offender and their own feelings play a central role in victim self-labeling, inappropriate attempts to reassert masculinity, and recapitulation of the offense. If the child is provided with a better understanding of offense dynamics, self-blame is minimized — the boy comes to accept that neither his behavior nor his personal characteristics are to blame.

When parents are assessed, particular attention should be given to the identification of tendencies either to blame the child for his victimization or toward harboring unrealistic fears regarding the impact on the child. Often these tendencies or feelings are well defended and are only reluctantly disclosed. Continuing parental depression, lack of parental support for the child, increased complaints about the child, or substantially altered patterns of parent-child interaction are often surface manifestations of unresolved parental anger or fears directed toward the boy victim. Careful probing will usually elicit the underlying concern. Obviously, it is of central importance to the child's favorable adjustment that parental feelings and fears be quickly resolved. Here, too, providing the parent with a thorough understanding of the problem and its dynamics is helpful. In addition, it is frequently useful to work carefully with the parent in terms of enhancing his or her understanding of the event from the child's perspective, rather than the parent's own. Exploration and discussion of feelings regarding homosexuality may also further alleviate these problems by more clearly allowing parents to identify their own projections onto their son.

Boys who as a result of their victimization are engaging in inappropriate attempts to reassert their masculinity, such as fighting or being disobedient, can often benefit by careful channeling of their need for self-assertion into more socially acceptable outlets. Sports, particularly contact sports, as well as courses in boxing or other self-defense techniques can prove beneficial to the child in terms of helping to reestablish his masculine self-concept. Care must be taken, however, in terms of how such channeling into these activities occurs. Unless handled tactfully, the boy may perceive such attempts as further implicit criticism of his sexual identification, or blame for his inability to defend himself from the original assault.

As noted earlier, not all boys who are sexually molested or their parents experience the problems briefly discussed here. They are frequent enough, however, to warrant particular clinical concern and sensitivity. Although our focus has been upon clinical mental health issues, it is important to remember that careful case coordination and case management are also of major importance. How professionals in the health care, mental health, social services, law enforcement, and judicial systems react and relate to these children and their families can significantly affect their eventual adjustment. Regrettably, all too often the responses of these professionals when confronted with the boy victim are also denial, minimization, or blaming of the victim.

Although any final conclusion would be premature, increasing evidence suggests that many adolescent and adult sexual offenders were themselves sexually molested as children (Swift, 1977; Thomas and Rogers, in press). Certainly, the vast majority of sexually abused boys do not develop such problems. Careful assessment, monitoring, and intervention with boy victims may, however, be the best long-term approach to preventing sexual crimes.

REFERENCES

Burgess, A., Groth, A., Holstrom, L., and Sgroi, S. 1978. *Sexual Assault of Children and Adolescents.* Lexington, Mass.: Heath.

De Francis, V. 1979. *Protecting Child Victims of Sex Crimes Committed by Adults.* Denver: American Humane Association.

Jaffe, A., Dynneson, L., and tenBensel; R. 1975. Sexual abuse of children: An epidemiological study. *Am. J. Dis. of Chil.,* 129:689–692.

National Center on Child Abuse and Neglect. 1981. *Study Findings: National Study of the Severity of Child Abuse and Neglect.* Washington, D.C.: U.S. Govt. Printing Office. DHHS Pub. No. (OHDS) 81-30325.

Schultz, L. (ed.). 1980. *The Sexual Victimology of Youth.* Springfield, Ill.: Thomas.

Swift, C. 1977. Sexual victimization of children: An urban mental health center survey. *Victimology,* 2:322–326.

Thomas, J., and Rogers, C. M. 1981. Clinical assessment of the sexually-abused child. *Nursing Clinics of North America. Washington, D.C.*

Thomas, J., and Rogers, C. M. A treatment approach for intra-family juvenile sexual offenders. In I. Stuart and J. Greer eds., *Sexual Aggression: Current Perspectives on Treatment.* New York: Van Nostrand Reinhold, in press.

7
Group Work with Preadolescent Sexual Assault Victims

Lucy Berliner, M.S.W.
Elise Ernst, M.S.W.

ABSTRACT

Group treatment may be the best therapeutic approach to address the victimization issues for children who have been sexually assaulted. Sexual activity with an adult is considered abnormal and unhealthy for children and is prohibited by both custom and law. To be sexually abused removes children in experience and knowledge from their peer group. It makes sense to address the most elusive yet persistent effect of abuse, the sense of "differentness" from others, in a group setting. The authors propose that to have such an abnormal experience without a peer forum to understand and resolve this "differentness" may prevent a child's full recovery. The victims become survivors when the experience no longer negatively defines a child's sense of self.

The shocking prevalence of child sexual abuse has been recently reported at 38% of females before the age of 18 (Russell, 1982b). In spite of this, most victims feel isolated from others and as if they are the only ones who have had such an experience. Only with the current increase in reporting has a true picture of the numbers and patterns of abuse become clear. It is now known that generally, sexual abuse consists of adult or significantly older males, who are known or related, using nonviolent means of involving children in progressive sexual activity. The children are either explicitly threatened or believe that there will be negative consequences for telling about the abuse. In many cases, the children do not even directly reveal what has happened, but it is discovered, witnessed, or elicited because someone recognizes that either the children's behavior or the offenders' behavior is indicative of sexual abuse (Conte and Berliner, 1981).

The impact of sexual abuse on children can only be understood in the context of the children's perception of what has happened, and their perception is limited by their developmental stage, the information they have about this kind of behavior, and the response once the abuse is known. What has actually happened to the children is not sufficient to define the experience because social judgments about sexual assault and victims are ambiguous and inconsistent.

Adult victims of sexual assault have to contend with the view that women are likely to make false accusations of sexual conduct, and even when it is acknowledged that there has been forcible sex, it may be considered acceptable or at least understandable under some situations. It is still the case that if women act in ways that are not considered proper or have a preexisting relationship with the assailant, their victimization is seen differently. It is well known that sexual assault in marriage is not even against the law in most states (Russell, 1982a).

The impact of sexual assault is related not just to the horror of experiencing a coerced sexual act, but to the expectation or fear of not being believed or being held responsible for one's own victimization as well. The literature is full of references to the feelings of blame and guilt that are seen in rape victims (Burgess and Holmstrom, 1979).

This same problem exists for children, but is compounded by the factors of immaturity and dependence, making children reliant on adults for understanding and explaining their experiences to them. Many of the same beliefs about adult victims are applied to children as well. There is a widely held (although completely unfounded) attitude that children are also likely to make false allegations of sexual assault. Again, when the offender admits to the behavior, it is often suggested that the children were participants, or in some way contributed to the activity. Adult offenders frequently intimidate the children into cooperating or keeping quiet by telling them how others will react if they tell. As is true with adult victims, children commonly report fearing that no one would believe them, or that they would get into trouble or be the cause of trouble to others should they report their victimization.

A sense of alienation from oneself and others is produced when an abnormal and externally imposed event must be understood and lived with in the absence of a clear framework. The critical elements that define sexual abuse of children are that it is sexual and that it is coercive because it is done in a context where true consent is not possible. This makes it wrong, and makes the adult or older person entirely responsible. It is unknown what difference the impact of abuse would be if there were general agreement about these ideas and children could count on a believing and supportive response. But this is not the case, and probably much of the distress that victims experience is directly attributable to such attitudes.

Adults, both the caretakers of children and society in general, do not necessarily agree on even the most basic issues. Some professionals claim that child molestation is not a sexual crime or is not sexually motivated behavior, although by any definition it is sexual activity that is arousing to the adult (and sometimes the child). There is also substantial empirical evidence of physiological arousal to children in those who have committed sexual offenses against children (Abel et al., 1979). This is not to say that other motivations and factors are not also present, such as personality defects, childhood experiences, situational stresses, or most likely a combination of these.

There are also some who claim that sexual activity with a child is not inherently bad and social attitudes against it should be changed. This point of view holds that children are sexual beings and that introduction to sexual experiences conducted in a nonviolent manner as a sort of educational experience may be beneficial. Generally, it is only applied to incest situations, where it is advocated that the parents engage in sexual activity with their children. It is also reported that there are advocates of early introduction to sex with adults among a certain group in the gay male population (*Time Magazine,* 1980). Of course, this stance ignores the reality that there is a fundamental inequality of position and knowledge between adults and children in society that eliminates the possibility of a child ever being able to give real consent, no matter what the context (Finkelhor, 1979b).

Even if there is agreement by adults that what is done is sexual assault, the children may still not have adequate information to understand the meaning of the sexual behavior. In many families, there is little or no discussion about these matters. It is no coincidence that most families use euphemistic labels for sex organs, have no terms at all, or refer vaguely to "down there." If children receive any information beyond naming body parts and learning the mechanics of reproduction, it is usually minimal and accompanied by all manner of negative connotations. There are warnings about sexual drives and desires and advice on how not to be sexual (at least until marriage). Masturbation or exploratory activities between peers is condemned. Children are given the message that any kind of sexual activity is bad and is to be avoided.

Since all sexual activity by an adult with a child is illegal, the offenders generally use some means of legitimizing their actions. This often consists of convincing the children that it is acceptable or normal (e.g., sex education, physical inspection, to help them in adult life). Children's developmental limitations and position in society promote the idea that adults are always right. Most children are regularly made to do things, or prevented from doing things, because adults have determined it was in their best interest. Even when the sexual activity is uncomfortable or clearly understood by the children to be wrong, if the offender is someone who meets important physical or psychological needs (e.g., a parent), it is impossible for children not to go along. It has often been reported in the literature that children will tolerate extreme abuse and even defend the abuser when it is a parent (Butler, 1978).

In other words, children are neither developmentally nor socially prepared to understand or resist sexual behavior imposed by adults, especially known or trusted adults. Thus, if they know the activity is sexual, they assume that it must be wrong; but if an adult is doing it, then they, the children, must be at fault because adults are never wrong; and even if adult offenders were wrong, they would not admit it. As a result, most children reason that it is they who are wrong or bad to have been involved in the situation at all. This feeling is compounded in older children, because once they are out of the abusing situation they think that by not fighting back or by not telling they are guilty of causing their own victimization. It is this aspect of the sexual assault experience that a group approach is specifically designed to address.

The feeling of complicity that children have while the abuse is going on is frequently not resolved by telling. Studies show that most child victims never report at all, and of those who do, many believe it was worse afterwards (Finkelhor, 1979a). These children feel they might not be believed when they do tell. They know that the accused offender will very likely deny the allegations, minimize what happened, or blame the victim. Further, societal intervention often exacerbates the children's feelings of self-blame. They may be subjected to repeated interrogations, removed from their home and family, or blamed by others for causing all the ensuing problems and complications.

Clinical experience shows that even when there are not specific signs of emotional or behavioral disorder, the abuse experience is one that is indelible. Parental or therapeutic suggestions to forget about it are not successful. Abusive experiences, even in earliest childhood, are remembered by many victims. Now that there is more openness about abuse, adults who were victims of sexual abuse in childhood are seeking treatment for the first time. Many functioning and apparently well adjusted survivors report a continuing sense of shame and guilt about what was done to them. They feel unable to escape the feelings of "badness" (Brady, 1979).

Beyond the impaired or damaged sense of self, the entire range of disturbance in child functioning has been identified as being associated with a history of sexual abuse. Clinical programs have seen children with acute traumatic reactions, sleeping and eating disturbance, loss of concentration, regressive behavior, nightmares, fear responses, and phobic reactions. Other children demonstrate sexualized behavior by acting out with toys, animals, and playmates. There may be disturbance in peer and family relations, ranging from withdrawal to aggressiveness. Such school problems as poor achievement, truancy, or drug and alcohol abuse are seen. More serious conduct, such as running away, prostitution, shoplifting, and subsequent involvement in antisocial and delinquent behavior, has been connected with abuse. Depression, suicidal thoughts and behavior, and self-mutilation are not uncommon clinical manifestations. Victims may have somatic problems (such as abdominal pain, headaches) and conversion reactions. Some psychoses in adolescents can be linked to sexual abuse. Sexual dysfunction and other sexual difficulties, such as aversion to sex or compulsive sexualization of all relationships, are reported by victims. Victims are at higher risk to be revictimized, become offenders, get involved with offenders, or produce offenders. Most survivors say they have a continuing difficulty in forming and maintaining intimate relationships (Herman, 1981).

In some children the problems are evident before the abuse is uncovered. Professionals working with children are increasingly finding that the explanation for children's abnormal behavior is undisclosed sexual abuse. Teachers, day-care providers, health care professionals, counselors, police, probation officers, juvenile courts, pastors, and psychiatrists are now identifying many more victims by recognizing the symptoms of disturbance and asking about abuse. Other children have no overt evidence of having been assaulted and do not appear noticeably affected. Some children develop symptoms immediately after disclosure, and others not until after a period of apparent adjustment. The symptoms' severity can range from minimal to the ultimate in severity, suicide.

The reasons why a given child responds in a particular way is unknown. Professionals speculate that a combination of variables combine to produce certain patterns of reaction. It is likely that an interaction between characteristics of the abuse situation (duration, offender relationship, etc.), the child's developmental stage and personality, the family's situation, and the response to disclosure form the child's coping style. At this stage there is no reliable information on exactly what influences how a particular child reacts, or on what is a normal versus an abnormal response to sexual abuse.

CLINICAL INTERVENTION

The mental health professional's primary concern in treating a victim of sexual assault is to reduce or prevent any negative effects of the abnormal and coercive experience. There may be a range of approaches to addressing the many possible types of reactions that are seen in child victims. Depending on the specific situation, a particular type of intervention may be indicated. A behavioral intervention might be most appropriate where there is a clearly defined problem, such as refusing to go to bed or being aggressive with others. For younger children with a more generalized anxiety or insecurity, play therapy could be used. If family relationships and roles are impaired, then family treatment is important. Some children respond to having a supportive, dependable adult who can give feedback, information, and reassurance in a one-to-one counseling relationship. Other more intensive interventions would be necessary in some cases, such as psychiatric hospitalization, day treatment, residential treatment, or medication.

Group therapy is probably best used in addition to other treatment approaches designed to address specific problem areas. For some children the group may be the primary treatment, while therapeutic efforts are directed at the other family members (the nonoffending parent, or the offender). In some cases, it has a diagnostic purpose. When a child's behavior is significantly different in comparison to other victimized children, it may be an indicator that more intensive therapy is needed. It could also identify the areas of clinical concern, for example, the child who is unable to join in group activities or who is out of control in peer settings.

RATIONALE FOR GROUP TREATMENT

A crucial aspect of child development is the establishing of an identity as an individual. This process occurs through an interaction with others and the world. At about school age, relationships with peers start to become important, and their significance increases until at adolescence, peer relationships become a major source of meeting basic emotional needs. Being able to make friends, belong to a group, share activities, and be accepted by others is an important — indeed, necessary — part of developing a positive sense of oneself. When children are cruel or humiliating or rejecting toward another child, it can contribute to lifelong problems with self-esteem, which itself leads to ostracization of the particular child. Not being part of a peer group is a major loss in the developmental process.

A sexual abuse experience automatically makes these children feel different from other children. In fact, like adult victims, they often report feeling branded, or as if others could tell that they were being or had been abused. A big fear of most victims is that others will find out and make fun of them, or stop liking them. The knowledge of being a victim, or the need to keep it a secret, is a barrier to establishing close relationships with others. Sadly, many children have found out that when they do share in confidence about their abuse, it is all over the school by the next day. It is usually not repeated maliciously, but curiosity, fascination, and fear all contribute to making it difficult information to keep private. So child victims become alienated from peers because of what they know, or what they fear as the inevitable consequence if others knew. Even if they are accepted by the peer group, acceptance may not be as validating to these children because they suspect it would not be available if their experiences were revealed.

A group for abused children provides a group of peers who know about the sexual abuse, who share the experiences, and whose acceptance is therefore guaranteed. It gives the intervener a natural learning setting in which to correct the distorted thinking children usually develop by giving information, clarifying misunderstandings, and allowing expression of feelings and fears. It is hoped that the damage to the children's psyche can be lessened if they come to believe that they are not at fault in any way for having been victimized, even if the actions of others do not communicate this. For example, a goal would be that even if the offender denies the abuse, the child victim would really know that what was done was wrong and that he or she is believed by the therapists and others. Just knowing that there are others who have experienced something similar and yet look and act like "regular kids" makes the abuse experience less alienating for victims.

Group approaches have been used by many programs offering services for sexually abused children. Ongoing support and education groups for adolescent female victims has been the most widely reported group approach with children. These groups are usually for victims of ongoing incest situations, frequently as part of a family reunification program's approach. Groups are also used for offenders and nonoffending parents as a primary treatment modality (Giaretto, 1976).

THE THERAPIST

There are no particular clinical skills necessary besides generic group skills, experience with children, and an ease with and knowledge about the topic of sexual assault. Obviously the group leader must be able to talk freely and frankly about sexual abuse. Since children may have a lot of questions or incorrect information about what has happened or what will happen next, the group leader must have a basic working knowledge of the causes and explanations of this kind of behavior, common victim reactions and feelings, and what the laws and usual legal procedures are. For example, many children will ask, "Why do they do it?" Or, "What happens in court?" An important function of the group experience is to offer a better understanding of the experience and a sense of mastery over it. Answering questions and giving accurate information is an essential component of this process.

The sex of the therapist, or whether there are cotherapists, undoubtedly has an impact, but not enough is yet known to suggest any particular format over others. Having a cotherapist clearly eases the burden by allowing a division of labor between observing, facilitating, and participating. It makes sense that it would be valuable for children who have been abused to have a safe situation in which to interact with someone of the sex of the offender, since generalization is a common sequela of sexual assault. In other cases, it might be too frightening.

Because the groups are time-limited and not intended to substitute for other treatment, there is the opportunity to involve non-mental health professionals as cotherapists. Anyone interested in and skilled with children could be a leader, as long as there is an experienced professional with primary leadership responsibility. In one group, a prosecuting attorney was the cotherapist and in another a Children's Protective Services worker. Some communities use teachers to help lead the groups. The group can offer a valuable learning experience for the cotherapist, as well as provide an opportunity to participate in the more positive aspects of intervention on behalf of the child victims. It could be especially helpful for the investigative or legal personnel, Children's Protective Services personnel, police, and prosecutors, whose usual role is often limited or coercive by nature.

Since sexual assault is a legal issue as well as a therapeutic one, it is possible that the group leader could become involved in legal proceedings. It might be as simple as providing a limited evaluation based on the children's behavior and expressed concerns in the group. Occasionally, there will be subpoenas, depositions, or actual courtroom testimony. Typical questions therapists are asked are: What is the goal and purpose of the group? What is said by the children? Could a child be influenced to exaggerate, make up, or change an allegation because of contact with other victimized children? In one case, the defense lawyer charged that the group experience had caused the child to elaborate, when in fact the child had only become more free to tell the complete story. It is always difficult to express and justify therapeutic issues in a legal setting, but the responsible therapist should be prepared to do so if necessary. Children's right to have treatment should not be contingent upon the offender's admissions or the status of a legal case. In many jurisdictions a case can drag on for months or even years. It is important for the leader to express the value of telling the truth to the children and to be scrupulous about not in any way trying to influence the facts the children are reporting.

Going to counseling is in itself a somewhat abnormal experience and could imply to the children that something is terribly wrong with them. This is particularly true if the setting is one associated with sickness, such as the program where the authors work, which is hospital-based. This effect can be countered by presenting the group as a class or educational experience. It should also be presented as fun and should *be* fun. The authors' experience is that the children look forward to the group sessions and really enjoy coming to them. The group sense of belonging can be enhanced by having children bring things to share, such as baby pictures, family photos, or special possessions. Having food to share is the best facilitator of all. With something to drink – it should have to be poured out by the children – and something to pass around and eat, a bond is established.

As is always the case with therapy for children, scheduling and transportation are frequent obstacles to participation. Single parents who are working may not be able to take time off from work, or they may have other children who would require a sitter. If car pooling can be arranged, or if there is a volunteer system for bringing children in, participation is more consistent. The time-limited aspect is often easier to sell to parents than an open-ended counseling contract. Parents are more cooperative when presented with a specific program while knowing that, if necessary, subsequent treatment can be pursued.

GROUP STRUCTURE

With adolescents, an ongoing group model is effective. A loose-knit, unstructured, easy-entry group that teens can belong to for varying lengths of time seems to work best for this age. For some participants, it becomes a primary support system that replaces or enhances the children's basic family support. The sexual abuse experience, although the common factor, is not the basis of the group interactions all of the time. The problems and concerns of all adolescents, with their changing bodies, roles, and relationships, are addressed in the group. From a developmental perspective, it is appropriate that teenagers have significant relationships with people outside their families on an ongoing basis. There are many normal adolescent questions and problems that are only addressed in peer settings. It is beneficial to teens to have a peer context that is structured and influenced (however minimally) by responsible adults, where the information is accurate and support available (Berliner and MacQuivey, 1982).

A time-limited group makes more sense with preteenagers for developmental reasons. First, relationships outside of the family, although important, do not usually have the same level of meaning or influence in this age group. Peers are significant as playmates and companions, not as the source of meeting primary emotional needs. Second, the open-ended quality might be more difficult for younger children to grasp, whereas knowing how many sessions are planned might structure and provide for closure on the abuse experience. The more concrete and specific thinking of preteen children is more consistent with a time-limited approach to group therapy. Placing children in a group of a similar level of social and personality development is necessary. There is quite a bit of difference in developmental sophistication between the youngest children, who are just beginning school, and the pubescent sixth or seventh grader. Otherwise, too great a difference between the children might reinforce rather than reduce feelings of being different. A two- to three-year span is best, although there might be good reasons to put a particular child in an older or younger group. For example, very immature children might be so out of place in an age-similar group that it is preferable to have them in with a younger one. Similarly, pubescent children who already feel older than those their own age and do not share much with peers could be disruptive in such a group, or might not gain much from the group experience.

The children's ability to tolerate information or understand the subject matter varies. How to talk to group participants about the legal system is determined by their level of development. Explaining concepts such as "innocent until proven guilty" to a child who is asking, "Why are the lawyers trying to make me look like a liar?" is much more difficult with younger children who cannot grasp the idea behind basic principles of law. It is hard enough with any age to explain the workings of the legal system.

Not only is the age issue important in terms of what is covered in the group, but also in terms of how the group is conducted. The younger children will need more playing and physical activity as part of group process. With older children, discussion can be the more primary communication means. For all ages, a variety of ways of interacting is good, including art work, drawing, therapeutic games, role-playing, exercises, nonverbal and physical contacts, didactic presentations, films, and demonstrations.

The groups should be structured in leader style and functioning. Since individuation and authority issues are not yet primary, the school-age children respond without much resistance to a structured approach. Children of this age tend to become disorganized and unruly very quickly in group situations, especially if they are nervous or unsure. It is a good idea to have a number of different possible activities planned for each session so that there is never a situation where the group cohesiveness completely disintegrates, or where the group coalesces around something negative or destructive. Throwing things, running out of the room, and making fun of someone are less likely to happen when children are busy doing something else.

The gender of the group members seems to be less important with the younger children, and co-ed groups work just as well. As they get closer to puberty, embarrassment, sexual stimulation, awkwardness, and self-consciousness become so overriding in boy-girl settings that this inhibits the group's functioning. In some cases, the children strongly prefer same-sex groups, and it is worthwhile to accommodate this.

Child victims also seem to have different fears and concerns at different ages. The group focus should be on the issues that are most relevant to the group members. The younger children are much less aware of or interested in the sexual meaning of the contact. They are often mystified about why grown-ups would even want to do those things, and will refer to sexual behavior as "yucky" or "silly." Pubescent children, on the other hand, are very much aware of sex and may be having sexual feelings themselves. As a consequence, the 6-year-old may fear getting into trouble for what happened, but the 10-year-old fears that something about her body's changes may have caused her to be molested.

Although many of the same issues will be raised with all ages, they might have different meaning for different groups, and the depth or level of sophistication of the information will be dependent on the children's ability to comprehend. For example, it is important for all children in group to get information about normal sexuality to replace the deviant "education" they have received by being victimized, but a 5-year-old's need to make this distinction should be handled differently from the 12-year-old's. With the younger children sexual relationships will not develop for many years to come, and sexuality is thus a less urgent concern. Detailed information is unnecessary for this age group, whereas the early adolescent has already probably thought about sexual matters, and more discussion about boyfriends/girlfriends and values clarification about relationships is relevant.

SETTING UP A GROUP

In setting up a group, the first task is to identify and cultivate sources of referral. It is desirable to have a relatively steady flow of potential group members. It is not good to ask children to go on waiting lists for groups that will not be starting for months. In the authors' situation, the specialized program serves a large number of sexual assault victims, and this provides an immediate supply of available candidates referred by other staff. Groups can begin at regular intervals as soon as there is an adequate number of children. About three or four is the smallest size, and six or seven the largest for effective group process to occur. In the case of a less specialized setting, it is necessary to have contacts with organizations or programs who can refer children, or to be such a large program that there are enough abused children already identified. This might be the case in a residential treatment center or a mental health center within which a specialized group could be offered. The Children's Protective Services is almost always very pleased to find a reliable and specialized counseling service for child abuse situations. In many communities, there is an organized network of agencies dealing with sexual abuse, including police, CPS, prosecutors, and advocates. They are likely to be a source of referrals, as well as to know how child abuse and child victims are treated in the community, and who is working in the field.

The therapist(s) should have worked out the format, structure, content, and purpose and be able to present it in plain language before actually scheduling a series. It is very likely that the parents will want to know in a general way what will be happening. they may be worried about the topics to be discussed or the kind of information that will be given. They will be especially sensitive to issues around values about sexual behavior or how the offender should be viewed. A useful approach is to have a parents' meeting (not including the offender) before beginning the children's series. The parents' concerns could be anticipated and addressed, and their questions answered. Parents will want to know what to look for in their children and how to be helpful. This is a good opportunity to reinforce the importance of their attitudes and responses in shaping the children's recovery. It is important to state that no matter what the children's conduct was, they were not responsible for the abuse and that they need to know that their parents are completely supportive. Children fear the loss of parental support more than anything, and this kind of supportive message cannot be given too often.

It can be anticipated that during each group series there will be at least one occasion where a child returns from group and says or does something the parent does not understand or approve of. Because of the subject, it is likely that children will be talking about things that are not usually discussed openly. They may begin to use new words or learn about aspects of sexual behavior from other children. This is inevitable and not necessarily undesirable, but parents should be forewarned. A child might come home and ask a parent, "Do you have a clitoris?"; or say "Suzy's daddy had oral sex with her." Sometimes children get overstimulated by conversation or an exercise, or misunderstand something. For example, J. went home and told her mother she didn't want to return to group because they were going to take off their clothes and look in a mirror the next week. She had misunderstood a suggestion to do this in privacy at home. During another group, D. revealed a reattempt at offending by her visiting brother, which the parents did not know about. The leader informed the child's primary therapist several days later because there was no immediate danger, but the parents felt they should have been informed directly at the time. Establishing a system for communication in case the parents notice unusual responses, or become concerned, will avert some of the complications.

As with any group, the issue of confidentiality has to be settled. There must be some guarantee of privacy, or children will not share; yet children are not in a position to accurately assess what information their parents must have in order to help. Generally, the parents should be told that what is said in group is private unless someone's safety is at risk. For example, if the offender is making unauthorized visits, or the child has been thinking about suicide, there should be immediate communication with the parents or the authorities. Children will also be told this. They should also be encouraged to protect each other's privacy by not talking about people outside of group.

SELECTING PARTICIPANTS

Some therapists require an intake interview before children join the group. It may be possible to substitute a report or assessment by consultation with whoever is providing the primary care. It is not always necessary to know the complete history and circumstances of the assault in order for group participation to be useful. As long as someone else is working with the child on an ongoing basis or where an assessment has already been made and other intervention completed, the group leader does not have to take primary responsibility. In a mental health center children might be referred by the primary therapist to a group conducted by another staff member, or a rape crisis center might offer periodic groups as an adjunct to other more traditional treatment. It is important to be sure that someone — the parents, a caseworker, therapist, or advocate — is taking responsibility for making sure that the children are safe, or that the legal case is proceeding.

The group leader does need to assess the appropriateness of group treatment for the particular child at that specific point in time. A very severely disturbed child will not benefit from the experience and is likely to distract the group. It could cause further alienation and rejection rather than being helpful. It is necessary for participants to be able to communicate with children their own age. A child who is very resistant, or in a phase of denial, may need to wait until another time for group treatment.

Clinical experience has not shown that the relationship of the offender is a significant factor in group composition. Since most of the time the offender is someone with whom the children had a preexisting relationship, there are common issues of betrayal of trust and ambivalence for the children. Whether the child will have a continuing relationship with the offender does seem to matter, and this can be a subject for group discussion. Sometimes the children in that kind of situation will benefit by a mini-group session to share the feelings that inevitably come up about seeing the person who molested them again. The children who will never have contact with the offender again are probably not as interested in what happens in the future relationship. The actual specifics about the sexual assault experience do not seem as important to the children as the fact of having been molested. They rarely talk about what actually happened or how often it occurred.

In selecting children for group it is important to consider the balance of the group, if possible. It is a good idea to avoid having only one child in a particular situation, or of a particular sex. For example, in one group W. was the only boy with four girls. He went home and told his mother about another boy participant who did not exist. If everyone has been molested by a family member except one (or the reverse) the different one may feel his or her feelings are not addressed, or are not as acceptable as the others'. In one group, a follow-up mini-session was held for the three (of six) whose fathers were offenders. They had specific concerns about their future relationship with their fathers, which was not relevant to the others (offenders were a school janitor, an uncle by marriage, a friendly horse farm owner). This kind of planning is not always possible, however, and it is probably better to take the chance and go ahead rather than have no group at all.

SETTING

A good-sized group room is desirable. Children will prefer sitting on the floor and pillows to sitting on chairs. There should be enough room to accommodate moderate physical activity, but the room should be small enough to foster group cohesion. Children in groups may get loud or boisterous periodically, and it is preferable to be in an area where activity will not disrupt others. If the group leader is constantly trying to keep everything under tight control or is worried about others outside, it interferes with a positive and fun atmosphere. It should be possible to have food and drink without great concern for messes, because they are inevitable.

The equipment that is necessary is standard: art supplies, crayons, markers, pencils, paper, etc., all in ample supply. A blackboard or big poster paper that can be taped on the wall is helpful. Therapeutic games, pencil and paper exercises, movie projector and/or video equipment, and books are useful.

CONTENT

Every group should cover some basic themes in age-appropriate ways. Some are assault-related and should be part of any group: acknowledgement of the assault experience ("I am here because I got molested"), understanding of the responsibility of the abuse ("It's not my fault"), recognition and labeling of feelings about being sexually abused ("It was hard to keep the secret"; "I was afraid"; "I still love him"), sense of affinity with other victims ("I am not the only one"), and what they have learned that might protect them in the future ("I'd say no if it happened again"). Covering these subjects is designed to restructure the children's understanding of their experience and their reactions.

The other important aspect of group is that damage to the ego or sense of self is assumed to be a potential consequence of sexual assault. It is believed that children will benefit by a structured opportunity to have ego-enhancing and positive interaction with other victims. General discussion, exercises, and activities should have the basic purpose of enhancing self-esteem. Some important areas are healthy body image, psychological sense of self, skill building, sharing, and giving.

GROUP FORMAT

Each session follows a format. At the start of each group, the children are reminded why they are there in age-appropriate language. Each child then reports on a positive event that has taken place in the previous week (e.g., good test score, no arguments with brother, birthday party). The food is introduced at the beginning, and the children share in passing it out or pouring. After the first session the members can select the next week's treat. After a brief period of eating and sharing (10 to 15 minutes), a group activity, either art or drawing, is introduced. Then there may be a discussion, demonstration, or mini-lecture. A final group exercise or activity closes the session. This format does not need to be rigidly adhered to because there should always be the flexibility to continue with a particular activity if the children are absorbed and are enjoying it. A lively discussion with a lot of participation or a particularly elaborate role play might take up most of one session.

SUGGESTED FORMAT FOR A SIX-SESSION THERAPY GROUP

SESSION ONE

Introduction of leaders and children.
Statement of common experience ("Everyone is here because someone molested/ assaulted/touched them in a wrong way/place").
Ground rules:
   No one has to talk about what happened if he or she doesn't want to.
   No physical or verbal violence in group.
   What is said is private unless it affects their safety/respect for each other's privacy.

Food:
Pass out/discuss/plan for next week.

Art:
Children draw a picture name tag — things, activities, places, that have special meaning to them.

Discussion:
Labeling/defining sexual abuse:
"Can anyone say what molestation is?"
"What's the person it happens to called?"
"Who is responsible?"
"How many people were molested by someone they know?"
"How many by a parent?"
"How old were you when it started?"
"How many people had it happen one time and how many had it happen a lot of times?"
"Who did everyone tell?"
"Did they believe you?"
"Is it better before you tell or after?"
"What does it feel like when you're keeping the secret?"
"What does it feel like when someone thinks you're lying?"

Group exercise:
Little kids:
Whisper down the line, squeezes around in circle, London Bridge.
Older kids:
Physical exercises (stretching, touching toes, etc.).

Closing:
"Does everyone know everyone's name?"
"What did you learn about each other?"

SESSION TWO

The offender/what happens.
Introduction/sharing something positive, food.

Art:
Draw a picture/representation of opinion about the offender. Put up on wall for rest of group (rogues' gallery).

Discussion:
What did you think about him before he molested you?
Did your feelings change?
Why do you think he did it?
How did he make you?
What did you think would happen if you told?
What should happen to the sex offenders?

Role Play:
Act out courtroom handling of case. Children are given tags (judge, victim, defendant, defense attorney, lawyer, bailiff, juror, prosecutor). They make up the scenes and case. Have them change roles/do several.

Relaxation exercise:
All members lie on floor with heads in center and imagine happy place, practice relaxation techniques.

Closure:
Ask children to bring picture of self as baby for next session.

SESSION THREE

Body image.
Introduction, sharing, food.

Art:
Draw self-portrait. Use mirror/have children talk about what part of body they like. Share baby pictures.

Discussion:
Label body parts/functions.
What are all the names you can think of for where a boy (girl) goes pee?
What is the real name?
Which parts of your body are private?

Note: With pubescent children there will be much greater interest and a whole session might be directed to changing bodies:
Who has her period?
What did you think when it started?
Who knows what masturbation is?
What are the changes a boy (girl) goes through?
Who can you ask questions about these things?
Who went to a doctor? What was the exam like?

Have books available:
Teen Body Book.
Changing Bodies.
What's Happening To Me?

Activity:
Active game/play for younger children.
Relaxation exercise.

Closing:
Ask children to bring family photos or mementos from friends/family.

SESSION FOUR

Family/friends.
Introduction, sharing, food.

Art:
  Kinetic family drawings.

Discussion:
  What is a family?
  Who is in your family?
  What is the most important thing about mom (dad)?
  Are you mad at/feel let down by anyone in your family?
  What would you like to be different?

Friends:
  Tell something about your best friend.
  What would your best friend say about you?
  What is a good friend?

Role play:
  How to be a friend if someone tells you they are abused.

Closing:
  Children to bring a joke to share next week.

SESSION FIVE

Ego enhancement
Introduction, sharing, food.
Joke telling.

Group game:
  The Ungame.

Problem solving:
  List all the problems from being abused (put on paper on wall).
  Choose one problem for group to help solve (e.g., being afraid at night: group
  discussion on techniques to fall asleep, night-lights, hall light, warm drink
  before bed, checking doors, parents reading story).

Physical contact/activity:
  Group hug relaxation exercises.

SESSION SIX

Prevention.
Introduction, sharing, food.

Activities:
Prevention.
What would you do if: (molest scenario, rape scenario).

Discussion, role play, movie:
Little kids — who to tell.
Bigger kids — how to fight back/get away.

Preoffense warning signs:
How to know if someone may molest you (e.g., treating you different, wanting to be alone, accidentally-on-purpose touching you).
Mini-self-defense ideas (how to get out of wrist, neck hold, how to walk confidently, shouting for help).
List places/people who can help if it ever happens.
Party.
Closure, goodbyes, sharing names and numbers (older kids).

SOME SUCCESSFULLY USED EXERCISES

Art Work
Picture tag.
Self-portrait.
Kinetic family drawing.
Offender representation.
Group mural.

Self-Esteem Exercises
Self-affirming statements/sentence completions:
    "I am wonderful because. . . ."
    If repeated each week the therapist keeps a record and at end of group children can take list home.
    "What I do well is . . ." (better with older children).
Guided fantasy (Wait until third or fourth session when children are comfortable and secure. Have children draw the place they imagine.)
Ask children to name a wish. (One 5-year-old said: "I wish my dad would stop playing with my weiner.")
Ask who was the loudest, the quietest, the funniest?
At the last session ask how each child contributed.

Read a story:
    Theres' a Monster in My Closet.
    Sylvester and the Magic Pebble.

Therapeutic games:
    Ungame.
    Talking-feeling-doing game.

Bring camera and take pictures of individuals/group. (Caution: In one group a 9-year-old girl said, "You aren't going to take dirty pictures?" Many cases of sexual abuse involve pornography.)

Mirror — have available in room.

Have children bring in baby pictures/family photograph album.

SKILL BUILDING ROLE PLAYING

Learn to problem solve:
Identify problem, list alternatives, select choice, etc., learn to negotiate.
Relaxation.
How to make a friend.
How to say no/assertiveness.

Movies:
Who Do You Tell.
Child Molestation: When To Say No.
No More Secrets.

No group will or should go exactly according to plan. Some groups are verbal and creative, and coalesce immediately, while others require more effort. It is important to have in store a number of ideas, games, and exercises that can be used when needed. Special needs or concerns for children in a group may have become apparent throughout the course of the series. This information must be communicated to the parent or primary treatment person. Sometimes a group may need an additional session or to meet at some time in the future.

A follow-up meeting with parents is useful when feasible. Evaluation of the group from the parents' perspective is good feedback for group leaders. Parents can be given information so that they can recognize whether their children develop problems at some point in the future. One group of parents liked the support from each other so much that they organized a picnic for the families.

REFERENCES[1]

1. Abel, G., et al. 1979. "Identifying Dangerous Child Molesters," a paper presented at the Eleventh Banff International Conference on Behavior Modification.
2. Berliner, L., and MacQuivey, K. 1982. A therapy group for female adolescent victims of sexual abuse. In Robert A. Rosenbaum, ed., *Varieties of Short-Term Therapy Groups.* New York: McGraw-Hill, in press.
3. Brady, K. 1979. *Father's Days: A True Story of Incest.* New York: Seaview Books.
4. Burgess, A., and Holmstrom, L. 1979. *Rape: Crisis and Recovery.* Bowie, Maryland: Robert J. Brady.

[1] Readers needing further information on games and exercises should contact Ms. Berliner directly, at 325 Ninth Ave., Seattle, Washington 98104.

5. Butler, S. 1978. *Conspiracy of Silence: The Trauma of Incest.* San Francisco: New Glide.

6. Conte, J., and Berliner, L. 1981. Sexual abuse of children: Implications for practice. *Social Casework: The Journal of Contemporary Social Work,* December.

7. Finkelhor, D. 1979a. *Sexually Victimized Children.* New York: Free Press.

8. Finkelhor, D. 1979b. What's wrong with sex between adults and children?: Ethics and the problem of sexual abuse. *Am. J. Orthopsychiatry,* 49(4):692–696.

9. Giarretto, H. 1976. Humanistic treatment of father-daughter incest. In Helfer and Kempe, eds., *Child Abuse and Neglect: The Family and the Community.* Michigan: Ballenger Publications, 1976.

10. Herman, J. 1981. *Father-Daughter Incest.* Cambridge, Mass: Harvard University Press.

11. Russell, D. 1982a. *Rape in Marriage.* New York: Macmillan.

12. Russell, D. 1982b. The incidence and prevalence of intrafamilial and extrafamilial sexual abuse of female children. *Child Abuse and Neglect: The International Journal,* October.

13. The pro-incest lobby. *Time Magazine,* November, 1980.

Section III
Adult Victims of
Sexual Assault

The seven chapters of Section III are concerned with treatment of adults from a variety of environmental settings as well as both sexes. The approach is both broad and deep in scope, and provides the reader with the opportunity to become aware of not only those persons traditionally associated with such experiences but some who are commonly ignored in this respect.

Dr. Donald J. Cotton and Dr. A. Nicholas Groth present in Chapter 8 the problems faced by therapists within the restrictive environment of a correctional institution. They describe the nature of imprisonment as activating sexual victimization and discuss some of their prescriptions for coping with such situations. They detail a program for prevention, intervention, and prosecution of perpetrators of such aggression, as well as the treatment procedures.

In Chapter 9, Arthur Kaufman, M.D., contrasts reactions of males who have been raped within the community with reactions known to occur in females suffering the same assault. The chapter includes suggestions for interview techniques to alleviate the reluctance of males to verbalize their indignation and provides a victim data sheet for possible use by the reader.

Dr. Dorothy J. Hicks and Ms. Denise M. Moon contribute Chapter 10, a chapter valuable for its detailed description for physicians, psychologists, police, and social workers of the necessary procedures to be followed by the physician and social worker if the older woman victim is to be truly restored to some reasonable state of mental health. The older female victim requires special handling if she is to recuperate from an attack at an age when there are few available significant supporting friends and relatives available for such purposes. It is a valuable guide.

In Chapter 11, Dr. William R. Miller and R. Ann Marie Williams provide an extensive view of the psychodynamic consequences of sexual assault upon the partner of the victim, with instructive examples from case histories whom the authors have assisted. They describe in detail not only the victim's reactions as reported to them but the often ignored, and yet vitally important, reaction of the spouse or boyfriend to the assault. Suggested techniques that they have found effective in coping with these "significant others" in the lives of such women are particularly instructive.

Dr. Judith V. Becker and Dr. Linda J. Skinner illustrate in Chapter 12 informative techniques as they are practiced in cases of sexual assault. They are based upon behavior modification applications to the particular problem. Anticipation of and coping with reactions to assault form the core of this valuable chapter.

Edward L. Rowan, M.D., and Dr. Judith B. Rowan describe in Chapter 13 some practical applications of behavior modification techniques to clients referred for assault experiences within the confines of a university town. It is a rewarding exposition of how to evaluate and meet the crisis presented by such clients, who must remain within their circle of friends and acquaintances where knowledge of the assault is difficult to conceal.

Dr. Mimi H. Silbert provides us with a most informative chapter, Chapter 14, on a client population who are more often derided or ignored yet demand from all of us some greater measure of attention and concern. The factors to be considered in counseling prostitute victims of sexual assault are detailed via a unique program for such women. The chapter is illustrated with samples of questionnaires that the author has constructed to measure progress in treatment procedures as well as sample interviews describing the intervention models found most successful with these clients. The use of clients who have overcome their emotional and physical trauma as supportive counselors is a valuable part of this program.

8
Sexual Assault in Correctional Institutions: Prevention and Intervention

Donald J. Cotton, Ph.D.
A. Nicholas Groth, Ph.D.

ABSTRACT

Correctional facilities are high-risk settings for male rape. The extent and seriousness of this problem often goes unrecognized due to the nature of prison conditions, inmate codes, and staff attitudes. Inmate rape is not primarily a sexually motivated act but instead constitutes the sexual expression of aggression. Such aggression may be retaliatory, compensatory, or erotic, and the act of rape is more one of hostility, status, or domination than one of passion or desire. Male rape may be psychologically devasting to the victim in that it devalues him in regard to two primary sources of male identity: sexuality and aggression. Furthermore, the victim is confined to the same institution as his offender and therefore continues to remain at risk of further assault. Civil litigation regarding institutional liability is increasing, and it is incumbent upon correctional institutions to train their personnel in regard to identifying, treating, and preventing the sexual abuse of inmates. To this end the major issues to be addressed for a model protocol are presented in this chapter.

Correctional facilities such as jails, detention centers, reformatories, houses of correction, prisons, and the like constitute high-risk settings for the sexual victimization of males. Inmates in both juvenile and adult institutions are subjected to sexual harrassment, intimidation, and assault. Although a number of researchers[1] have addressed this issue, it continues to remain a subject more of academic interest than of practical concern. Yet inmate sexual assault is a serious problem that constitutes a major undercurrent in incidents of institutional

[1] This chapter is an expanded version of a paper entitled "Inmate Rape: Prevention and Intervention" which appeared in *The Journal of Prison and Jail Health,* (Vol. 2, No. 1, Spring/ Summer 1982), and is reprinted through the kind permission of Human Services Press.

violence, a problem that can only escalate as correctional institutions become more crowded. If staff are not adequately trained to recognize and address this issue they are caught off-guard and unprepared to handle such incidents when they occur. This, in turn, poses greater risk to the Department of Corrections, the prison administration, and the institutional personnel of civil liability for not preventing its occurrence and/or not providing adequate services to the victim.

This chapter addresses the problem of inmate sexual victimization in regard to identification, intervention, and prevention. It concentrates on this problem in male correctional settings due to the greater frequency of reported sexual assaults among male inmates. Its findings, however, may also to a large extent be relevant to correctional facilities for females.

INCIDENCE

The actual extent of male sexual assault in jails and prisons remains unknown. The best estimation to date was done by Davis (1968), who projected an annual rate of 1000 sexual assaults in the Philadelphia prison system. However, any available statistics must be regarded as very conservative at best since discovery and documentation of this behavior are compromised by the nature of prison conditions, inmate codes and subculture, and staff attitudes. These factors serve to limit access to accurate information on the incidence of inmate sexual assault. As a result, the prison administration as well as the general public may fail to appreciate the extent and seriousness of this problem in regard to its occurrence or its impact. Without accurate information on sexual assault within their institution, correctional staff are at a serious disadvantage to remedy this problem.

Prison Sex

Sexual behavior in prison encompasses autoerotic, homosexual, and (in co-ed institutions or where conjugal visits are permitted) heterosexual activities, and wide differences exist among institutions in regard to their tolerance of such behavior. Interpersonal sexual activity may be engaged in through consent or coercion. Whereas consenting sexual activity is an issue that requires an appropriate in-house institutional policy, nonconsenting sexual interaction is an entirely different matter. From a clinical or psychological frame of reference, consensual sex is normal whereas coercive sex is pathological. Nonconsenting sexual interactions in prison may be classified into three basic types.

1. *Sexual harrassment,* where the inmate is treated as a sexual object and comments are made about his physical attractiveness: "Guys would whistle at me or say I got a nice ass. Sometimes they would grope me or put their hand on my leg or just stare at me in the shower and this would really shake me up."

2. *Sexual extortion,* where the inmate is pressured into repaying his indebtedness to another inmate by relinquishing sex: "I owed this guy gambling losses and he has supplied me with some pot, cigarettes, and other things — now he told me I could settle the account by giving him some head."

3. *Sexual Assault,* where the inmate is overpowered or threatened with physical injury unless he submits sexually: "I was writing a letter in my cell when three guys came in; while the other two held me face down on the bunk each guy took a turn fucking me in the ass."

Victim Response

The most serious problem associated with coerced sex in prison is the "no-win" situation it creates for the victim, which is the primary issue that prevents inmate victims from reporting the offense and limits the ability of the institution to effectively remedy this problem. When faced with sexual victimization, the inmate has four available options, each of which has certain negative consequences:

1. He may try to escape the situation by going into protective segregation which will in turn further confine him, restrict his activities, and reduce whatever privileges he may have in prison. He cannot move about the institution without escort and thus he will lose canteen and recreation privileges. He will not be able to attend school, job training, or mental health programs. His attending church or receiving visits will be curtailed, and the like. In some extreme cases the victim may try to escape sexual assault by physically breaking out of the institution, attempting suicide, acting out violently, or becoming psychotic so that he is removed from the facility.

2. He may try to defend himself by fighting back. This may increase the risk of more serious physical injury being done him by his attacker(s) and/or he risks disciplinary action (loss of good time, punitive segregation, etc.) for violation of institutional rules. Some victims try to fight back. Sometimes they attack the offender when he is asleep or they get help from others to retaliate against him. Other victims try to change their image by becoming more aggressive in general, perhaps even sexually assaulting someone more vulnerable than they. This response only precipitates more institutional violence, violence that could be reduced or eliminated by dealing more directly with the problem of sexual assault.

3. He may submit to the assault, but then he acquires a reputation that makes him vulnerable for as long as he is in the institution. He will be stigmatized as a "punk" and will henceforth be subjected to one form or other of sexual exploitation. He may be forced to "hook up" (provide sexual services) to one inmate (his "jock" or "dad") in exchange for protection from sexual victimization by other prisoners. He may have to continually exchange sex with everyone and anyone for survival. If he reports the victimization to the authorities, he

acquires the label of a "snitch" or informer and places his life in jeopardy. This "jacket" will follow him while he remains in the correctional system and will expose him to further abuse and harm.

4. He may endure the sexual assault in silence and secrecy. He may refuse to report the assault, or to identify the assailant(s), or to seek treatment. As a result, the trauma of sexual victimization may have long-lasting after effects for him. As David Rothenberg (1978), founder and director of the Fortune Society, has stated:

> The agony remains . . . as does the bitterness, the need for vengance, the self-loathing and self-shame. We probably will never be able to measure the rippling effects of each single assault. But we are self-deceptive if we do not think that there is a correlation between inexplicable and sudden street violence and the incendiary emotions evoked from prison sexual violence [p. 466].

One of the basic and tragic observations about human behavior is that aggression elicits aggression, especially in males. Victims become victimizers. Traumas that are not treated persist; what is not talked out is acted out, and the cycle of sexual violence is perpetuated; the prey must become the predator or risk remaining a prey. Society, then, has a vested interest in this issue in that some of the men in prison are so characterologically traumatized and angry that they retaliate when they return to the community by committing acts of physical and sexual violence. Studies of sex offenders reveal frequent histories of their own sexual assault, abuse, and exploitation, often while incarcerated in juvenile institutions.[4]

DYNAMICS OF INMATE RAPE

Rape is not primarily motivated by the frustration of sexual needs. It is more the sexual expression of aggression than the aggressive expression of sexuality. The gratification of sexual needs and the release of sexual tensions in jails and prisons are possible through autoerotic sexual activities and consenting same-sex (and in some prisons, opposite-sex) encounters. The rape of male inmates occurs in correctional settings not because it is a substitute for sex with women, but for the same reasons it occurs in the community: to hurt, to humiliate, to dominate, to control, and to degrade. Sex becomes the expression of aggression and the aggression may be retaliatory, compensatory, and/or erotic. Inmate rape is complexly determined and serves a number of purposes in the psychology of the offender. It becomes a way of expressing who is in control and who is controlled; sex thus signifies the power relationship. It becomes a way to vent anger, to get even, to hurt and degrade someone. And this release of anger and expression of power can provide an intense sense of excitement when it is sexually discharged. The nature of imprisonment becomes a catalyst in the activation of sexual victimization, for it confronts the inmate with his personal inadequacies and the pervasiveness of external (institutional) controls. Consequently a hierarchy becomes established based on the inmate's available resources: physical strength, gang affiliation, access to contraband, his crime of record, institutional reputation, and the like. Davis (1968, p. 16) notes that this power need is characteristic of a "subculture that has found most nonsexual avenues of asserting their masculinity closed to them" which results in a feeling of emasculation. He describes the consequences of this power need:

These frustrations can be summarized as an inability to achieve masculine identification and pride through avenues other than sex. When these frustrations are intensified by imprisonment, and superimposed upon hostility between the races and a simplistic view of all sex as an act of aggression and subjugation, then the result is assaults on members of the same sex.

MALE RAPE TRAUMA

The trauma of sexual victimization for a male in prison for the most part is identical to the biopsychosocial impact of sexual assault on a female in the community. There may be physical, emotional, cognitive, psychological, social, and sexual sequelae. Physical consequences may include injury and disease infection. Emotional disruption may be manifested by increased anxiety, fear, depression, shame, anger, mood swings, phobic reactions, etc. Disturbance in cognitive functioning may take the form of flashbacks to, or preoccupation with, memories of the assault, impaired ability to concentrate, difficulty in attending to tasks at hand, and the like. Psychologically the inmate may experience discomfort in regard to his feelings of safety and adequacy, devaluation in regard to his identity and self-esteem, and disruption in social relations with increased distrust, withdrawal and isolation, or intensified aggressiveness. Then, too, there may be specific social-sexual issues that become concerns for the victim pertaining to his "manhood" or sexual identity, impaired sexual functioning, negative sexual attitudes, and the like.

The trauma of sexual assault for a male victim may be even more psychologically devastating in some respects in regard to impact and recovery than it is for a female victim. Socialized to be powerful and in charge, and to equate manhood with power and control, a male who is sexually assaulted not only suffers a defeat in combat where he is rendered physically helpless, he also forfeits his sexual role, is "used as a woman," and loses his "manhood." Not only does he see his sexual violation as a personal defeat in a contest of physical strength, he perceives his sexual identity has also been tampered with. He is devalued in the two primary sources of his male identity: sexuality and aggression. In addition, having been socialized to "fight their own battles," many men regard the seeking of assistance in the form of rape crisis counseling yet another indication of personal defeat and disgrace. To ask for help is tantamount to an admission of helplessness or weakness. Such attitudes consequently impede the recovery process for male rape victims. While he remains in prison the inmate victim remains under the surveillance of his attackers, who continue to have sexual access to him. If he does not know the identity of his offender(s), this intensifies his feelings of vulnerability. Unlike the rape victim in the community who can change address, job, life-style, and relationships, the inmate victim is not able to make such changes to regain a sense of self-control. The recovery process may be delayed until he is released from the institution and is able to regain a feeling of personal control once again. Even then, the recovery process may remain incomplete.

INSTITUTIONAL RESPONSE

Liability

The correctional institution is not immune from responsibility to address the problem of sexual assault within its walls. Court decisions are increasingly awarding civil damage suits to victims as well as making determinations of criminal responsibility.[5] Some decisions have found the correctional staff, as well as the institution, personally liable for their actions. The institution has three primary areas of responsibility in dealing with sexual assault: (1) prevention, (2) intervention, and (3) prosecution.

Prevention

While this chapter addresses the issue of institutional services more directly, it cannot be understated that the problem needs to be controlled by a strong policy towards prevention. There are such strategies that have been reported to be successful in decreasing reported incidents.

One strategy is to identify the profile characteristics of victims and offenders and to segregate these groups as much as the physical plant and resources will allow. The experienced housing assignment officer routinely makes these intuitive decisions. However, he is frequently not supported by a clear institutional policy that will persist even when less experienced officers make housing decisions or when space limitations demand compromises. Usually the screening and classification process will sort out the most vulnerable inmate: the obviously physically or mentally disabled, the identifiable homosexual, and the transsexual male.

Many vulnerable inmates, however, pass through this crude screening. The potential victim is typically vulnerable by age, size, body build, culture, and life-style. The Davis study describes the average victim as being younger and smaller, and having more attractive physical features than the offender. Irwin (1970) describes victims being vulnerable because they are not "street-wise"; they do not know the street language, roles, and games and do not know how to protect themselves. The vulnerable inmate is usually a middle-class first offender who, while heterosexual in sexual orientation, is insecure about his masculine identity.

The offender, in contrast, is experienced in institutional life, has done time before, has a history of institutional violence (sometimes clearly including prior sexual attacks), and has a need to establish or defend a reputation. The ethic of "ripping off anything you can from whoever you can" and "doing anything you can get away with" results in vulnerable inmates being forced into a prescribed subordinate sexual role in the prison subculture, to be used and abused by those momentarily above them in the hierarchy. This is the process of "punking" or "turning out" vulnerable males into a lesser class of prisoner and thereby enhancing one's own status.

The argument against a defined classification system that claims physical plant limitations, time factors, and lack of criteria may well be valid. However, the reduction in subsequent violence and liability may be seen to make these changes cost-effective.

One experimental solution tried by the San Francisco County jails was to identify jail areas for those who are first-time and/or nonaggressive inmates, in order to separate them from the more aggressive repeaters. Under this system, in addition to the usual protective custody classification, an area would be identified for younger, less aggressive inmates to be housed with other vulnerable inmates, such as the elderly and disabled. The procedure for this selection process would be in the form of a written housing assignment protocol to which each placement must conform. In the event of a sexual assault resulting from an inappropriate assignment, officers who failed to follow procedures could be effectively disciplined for the then obvious violation of the protocol.

Another means of prevention is to provide more adequate surveillance of institutional blind spots. Outside of the cell blocks, sexual assaults occur in any area not routinely watched: transportation vans, holding tanks, shower rooms, stairways, and storage areas. There needs to be a careful allocation of hardware (such as video cameras) and personnel resources to minimize the risk in these areas.

Intervention

Once a sexual assault victim is identified, the institution is responsible for adequate treatment services to that victim. These services not only psychologically assist the victim but also serve to document the offense, provide forensic evidence, and help intervene against further violence. For the victim, such services facilitate the recovery process. As with women rape victims, insensitively conducted intervention services are reported to be as traumatizing, if not more so, than the actual assault. Given that there is physical and emotional injury, the institution needs to respond in an appropriate, professional, and consistent manner.

Crisis Intervention Protocol

The staff's personal discomfort in regard to dealing with male sexual assault can interfere with providing even simple services to the victim. Unprepared, the staff member's intervention may compound rather than ameliorate the impact of the victimization. One solution, which has been effective in the San Francisco County jail system, was to institute a specific interagency protocol[7] for dealing with sexual assault victims. Staff then do not have to go through personal confusion to decide if and what they should do. Their responsibilities are then very clearly and directly spelled out, to which they can be made accountable.

Once a sexual assault protocol has been established and staff trained to dispel the myths and misconceptions about male rape, the problem can be addressed more rationally. The staff will understand that men do get sexually abused, are not asking for it, and are victims of a vicious struggle for institutional dominance. When attacked, the victims are in extreme stress and conflict. They require specific services. The services are directed towards both the victim's biopsycho-social needs and the institution's investigative needs.

The San Francisco jail protocol has been developed with the cooperation of several county agencies, particularly the Sheriff's office and the Public Health Department. A detailed procedure was developed which identified what services the staff in each agency would provide and under what circumstances. In addition to the protocol, material was included that provided references, investigative techniques, and counseling guidelines.

The protocol identifies and addresses the following victim needs:

a. Medical:
   - Examination and treatment of injuries
   - Documentation of injuries
   - Collection of medical evidence
b. Psychological:
   - Crisis counseling for emotional trauma
   - Referral for long-term counseling, if needed
c. Legal:
   - Investigation and prosecution of suspect(s), if appropriate
   - Legal counseling about options

- Information about case prosecution
- Alternative legal recourse

d. Social:
- Engaging social system for support
- Postrelease planning

e. Protection:
- Prevention of further attacks and retaliation
- Segregation from assailants

Intervention Phases

The protocol specifies the procedures required to meet victim needs during the following five phases of intervention.

1. *Initial intervention:* Upon discovery of an offense or verification of suspected sexual assault the most important steps are to provide protection for the victim, to arrange medical assessment, and to document the incident. Investigation then proceeds to identify the assailant(s) and to collect evidence according to standard procedures which ensure labeling of evidence and maintaining its chain of custody. If an assailant is identified he must be segregated from other vulnerable inmates, interrogated, and once the case is prepared, booked on the appropriate charges, and prosecuted.

2. *Preliminary jail medical evaluation:* Triage is provided in regard to the degree and seriousness of physical injury and recency of assault. Referral is then made to the appropriate medical facilities. Institutional medical staff should be trained to do rape examinations and forensic evidence collection, and notified so they can carry this out immediately after the assault. While physical evidence has been collected in female victims up to 72 hours after assault, there is no baseline for males. There is increased risk of losing evidence the longer the wait — if the victim alters the assault site; by washing, gargling, or defecating. Follow-up testing for VD infection should be arranged and crisis intervention and support services for the traumatic impact of the sexual assault should be available.

3. *Medical referral:* If the institution does not have medical services adequate to address the victim's needs, referral to an appropriate facility should be made for emergency medical care. Such agencies will usually have their own protocol for sexual assault victims but often will need specific guidelines for working with victims under custody. The services usually required include immediate crisis intervention, medical treatment, and evidence collection. Occasionally, referral to another medical service may be indicated for evaluation of psychological reactions or medical complications.

4. *Institutional follow-up:* A designated case manager, from internal affairs, nursing, or social service staffs, is responsible for arranging and ensuring that the inmate victim is placed in a reasonably secure area of the institution away from the suspect(s). In addition it is the responsibility of the case manager to follow up medical treatment, to monitor psychological reactions, to provide liaison with the legal system, and to help the victim develop some support system.

5. *Postrelease referral:* The victim may, following release, continue to require assistance to recover from the sexual assault trauma. Many victims' recovery process will be stalled while they are in the institution where they were assaulted. If they are transferred soon after the assault, follow-up care should be arranged at the new institution. If they are released to the community, referral to an appropriate agency may be indicated.

The success of a protocol such as the one described here is dependent on its implementation. Each agency involved should have an opportunity to participate in its design and to work out conflicts of priorities, such as between medical and security needs. The staff should have an opportunity to have in-service training on the procedures and have input on its revisions when there are problems. Finally, the protocol should be enforced and staff held responsible if procedures are not followed. Some staff should be responsible for routinely monitoring procedures in selected cases to identify problem areas and suggest modifications.

Prosecution

Upon admission to a correctional facility the inmate should be advised and counseled in regard to the risk of sexual victimization, how he can help reduce this risk, and how he can receive help if he is sexually hassled, exploited, or attacked. In addition, clear warnings should be given regarding the consequences of sexually victimizing a fellow inmate, and the inmate should be told how to get professional help to keep from sexually harrassing or assaulting other inmates. Sanctions need to be enforced through institutional disciplinary actions and/or prosecution.

The procedures spelled out in the protocol provide a description for conducting the investigation of a sexual assault. When such cases are prosecuted, court procedures should be explained to the inmate victim and he should be kept informed of the status of the case and its ultimate outcome. The prosecution of such cases makes a clear statement to inmates that coercive sex is not acceptable and will not be tolerated even within correctional institutions.

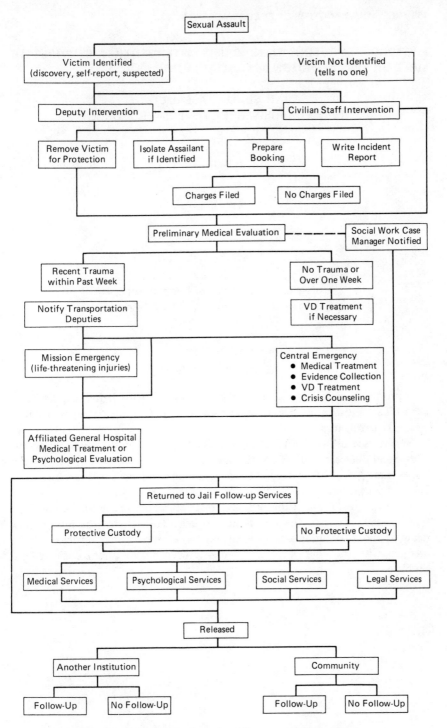

Figure 8-1. Sexual assault service delivery protocol flowchart.

137

PROTOCOL FOR PROVIDING CRISIS INTERVENTION SERVICES TO MALE VICTIMS OF PRISON SEXUAL ASSAULT

JAIL SEXUAL ASSAULT:
REVISED CRISIS INTERVENTION PROTOCOL

July 1981

A program of the Office of Forensic Services
San Francisco Department of Public Health

ACKNOWLEDGMENT

This protocol was written in collaboration with the participating jail agencies, particularly the San Francisco Sheriff's Office and the San Francisco Public Health Department.

This revised protocol is based on a crisis intervention model developed by the author and funded by NIMH's National Center for the Control and Prevention of Rape grant No. 1-R01-MH2962-01 and administered by San Francisco State University's Frederic Burk Foundation, October 1978.

Since the institution of this protocol, three convictions have been obtained in sexual assault cases in the San Francisco jails. The victims, the investigating deputies and prosecuting attorneys, as well as the agency staff involved, can be credited with the courage to apply new procedures to a long neglected jail problem.

CONTENTS

I. INTRODUCTION

The development of this protocol serves two functions. First, it provides a standardized procedure for identifying and meeting the service needs of victims of sexual assault in the San Francisco County jails. Second, the protocol also serves to standardize procedures for conducting the investigation and processing a case for prosecution.

Initial use of the protocol has proved to be effective in meeting these goals. Within three months of its implementation in 1978, two jail rapists were charged and convicted. Identified victims now receive services through this procedure. Current reports suggest that the problem of jail sexual assault has been curtailed by the implementation of this protocol, and as a result of a revised classification system that identifies vulnerable inmates.

We are only beginning to understand the major role that jail sexual assault plays in the maintenance of inmate violence and in the perpetuation of an anti-social, violent-prone population. The victims, who are often only in jail for light charges, experience severe trauma. All too frequently, the victim can only cope with the trauma by using violence in turn, either towards himself or towards others.

A reasonable effort must be made to reduce this violence. The courts are defining increased liabilities against those institutions and staff personnel who do not meet their responsibilities in limiting the occurrence of sexual assault in correctional institutions.

The numbers of jail rapes, while great, are difficult to determine. The exact number of incidents cannot be determined because victims do not report for fear of retaliation or are ashamed to tell other people. Only a fraction of the victims utilize jail services after the assault. For each case that is reported or otherwise discovered, one can assume that many more go unreported. There were 45 reported sexual assault incidents in the San Francisco County jails in the period from 1969 to 1978. These incidents involved various types of inmates. Regardless of the victims' background, age, charges, race, and sexual preference, patterns do emerge, and the commonality is that all the victims were vulnerable in some particular manner.

This protocol identifies procedures that coordinate and standardize services in the San Francisco County jails for sexual assault victims. These procedures can help jail administrators and personnel to identify and meet responsibilities in providing services to sexual assault victims and may reduce possible civil liability.

This protocol specifically addresses the service needs of male inmate victims because there are few reported cases of sexual assault on female inmates. These crisis intervention procedures, however, can be used as basic guidelines for any woman inmate victim as well.

The importance of victim services is indicated by the serious, acute, and long-term reactions resulting from the trauma of assault that victims may experience.

In addition to physical injury, the victim may experience severe emotional reactions to the assault. These reactions, some of which are described in the concluding section of this protocol, are compounded by the jail setting. The sexually assaulted inmate may act out to compensate for his concern about his masculinity, his self-worth, his vulnerability, and his jail reputation.

Having professional and sensitive services available also helps with prosecution. Without the victim's participation, there is a limit to the physical evidence available, and he is often reluctant to testify against the assailant.

Increased prosecution of assailants is one of several ways to reduce inmate sexual assaults. Other methods include revising classification procedures, monitoring isolated jail areas, and educating potential victims. Effective services for rape victims can be developed by establishing standardized procedures for the staff to provide services with understanding and sensitivity to the trauma experienced by the victim.

There are five basic service areas for which victims will need assistance. These five service areas, described below, are the bases for the crisis intervention protocol and the procedures for the delivery of these services.

MEDICAL: examination, documentation, and treatment of injuries; evidence collection

PSYCHOLOGICAL: crisis counseling for emotional trauma reactions and identity concerns

LEGAL: consultation about prosecution of assailants and other possible legal and civil recourse

SOCIAL: follow-up planning and dealing with family concerns and personal support system

PROTECTION: prevention from further attacks and retaliation

These service needs are described more fully in the protocol. Following the protocol are pages with additional information about victim reactions and suggestions for counseling victims.

The following terms are used frequently in the protocol and are defined here to clarify their application to these procedures.

SEXUAL ASSAULT: Any threatened or completed sexual act forced on another against his will. Forced sexual assault may also include situations in which the victim was coerced into a sex act.

CASE MANAGER: The medical social worker specifically assigned by the Forensic Services Director to coordinate follow-up services of inmate sexual assault cases.

PROTOCOL: A detailed list of procedures, administratively approved to be followed for providing specific crisis services.

CRISIS INTERVENTION: Immediate delivery of services related to a specific acute need. The services provided include assessment, treatment, referral, follow-up, and evaluation.

II. CRISIS INTERVENTION PROTOCOL FOR JAIL SEXUAL ASSAULT

PHASE 1. DISCOVERY

A. *Victim Identification*
Note: The following are usual ways of learning that a sexual assault incident has occurred:

1. Deputy discovers a sexual assault in progress.
2. Victim reports a sexual assault to a deputy.
3. Victim reports a sexual assault to civilian jail staff.
4. Sexual assault is reported by another inmate or rumored.

While some sexual assault victims will be clearly identified, most will probably need some sensitive investigation to verify a suspected sexual assault. Jail staff may hear of an inmate being threatened with sexual assault or one rumored to have been assaulted. Some victims of sexual assault may be suspected because of unexplained injuries, changes in physical behavior due to injuries, or abrupt personality changes such as withdrawal or suicidal behavior. The following guidelines may be used to provide assistance to a suspected victim.

1. Jail staff should check out a suspected victim without jeopardizing the inmate's safety, identity, and confidence.
2. Remove the suspected victim from the immediate area for interviewing.
3. Ask the suspected victim open-ended, neutral questions such as "How are you doing?" "Are you being hassled?" or "Would you like to be moved to another tier or cell block?"
4. If there are no indications of any problems, suggest that if help is ever needed, the inmate can contract a deputy, the medical staff, the jail psych team or prisoner services staff.
5. If the inmate has had problems, consider the following:
   a. Advise the inmate that jail staff can help him.
   b. If he is scared of being labeled a "snitch" (informer), advise him that he does not have to identify the assailants to get help.
   c. If he was sexually assaulted, mention the importance of getting help to deal with the assault and to be checked out medically for VD and any injuries, and that trained staff are available.

d. Determine together with the victim what services he needs.

e. Make arrangements for the appropriate services as agreed to. Refer to the following guidelines for intervention.

B. *Procedures for Deputy Intervention and Investigation*
Note: The following procedures apply for recent victims of sexual assault. If the inmate was threatened with sexual assault or was sexually assaulted some time before, not all of the following steps may be appropriate.

If an inmate claims to have been sexually assaulted, you do not necessarily have to make a judgment about whether or not it did happen. Unless there are intervening security reasons, proceed with these procedures so that corroborating medical evidence can be documented.

The most important steps are to arrange protection for the inmate, to refer him to the medical staff, and to write up an incident report.

It is important that all contact with a sexual assault victim be sensitive, supportive, and nonjudgmental. Refer to the suggestions that are attached.

1. Securing the victim(s)
   a. Remove and refer the victim for services.
      1. Identify the victim(s).
      2. Remove the victim from the area immediately and place in a protective area until he can be brought to the medical area.
      3. Bring the victim to the jail infirmary for a medical evaluation as soon as possible. The medical staff will refer the victim to the appropriate emergency facility. They will also inform the case manager to coordinate other needed services and to do follow-up.
      4. If the assault was recent (within the past 48 hours) inform the victim not to shower, wash, drink, eat, or defecate until he has been examined if medical evidence is to be collected.
      5. Get a brief statement of what happened. (The victim may be too much in shock to give much detail at this time. It is important to be understanding and not too forceful. There will be opportunity later for more details.)
      6. The victim may not want to report the name of the assailant(s), but he is nevertheless entitled to protection as well as medical and support services.
      7. When the victim returns, arrange reassignment to a secure area, either in protective custody or to another secure jail area. Be sure that the assailant(s) and previous cellmates are not located in the same area.
   b. Collect Evidence.
      1. *Cell area:* Look for any presence of semen that can be used as evidence. For example, collect blankets and sheets if there is

semen present. Place each item in a separate paper bag. Seal and
label as indicated below. If semen is present on the floor, etc.,
collect samples using a cotton swab. Place the swab in a test tube
which has 1/2 cc of saline solution. These items can be obtained
from the jail medical staff.
2. *Victim's clothing:* When convenient, have the victim change into
clean clothes. Place each item of clothing into a separate paper
bag. Seal and label as indicated below.
3. *Medical evidence:* All medical evidence will be collected at a
public health facility and will be sent to the crime lab.
4. *Labeling and chain of custody:* All evidence should be sealed and
labeled with the following:
   • Collected from whom and/or where
   • Date
   • Time
   • Location
   • Type of case
   • Description of the item
   • Collected by whom (name and badge number)
   This procedure begins a chain of unbroken custody of the evidence.
   The evidence is to be brought to the crime lab as soon as possible
   or lock-up in the police property room.
5. *Photographs:* If the victim has bruises and other indications of
physical assault, arrangements can be made to have photos taken
on or by the police photo lab after the medical examination. If
the assault was particularly violent, it may be necessary to photograph the attack area if it is possible to isolate the area.
2. Securing the assailant(s)
   a. Isolate the assailant(s).
      1. Identify the assailant(s) if possible.
      2. Place the suspect in administrative segregation. Be sure that the
      suspect is not placed with any other vulnerable inmates.
   b. Collect evidence if the assault was recent.
      1. *Suspect's clothes:* Have the defendant change into another set of
      clothes. Place each item of the clothing into a separate paper
      bag. Seal and label as indicated below.
      2. *Weapons:* Collect for evidence any objects used in the assault that
      served as a weapon, such as sharpened toothbrush, brush handle,
      etc.
      3. *Labeling and chain of custody:* All evidence should be sealed and
      labeled with the following:
         • Collected from whom and/or where
         • Date

- Time
- Location
- Type of case
- Description of the item
- Collected by whom (name and badge number)

This procedure begins a chain of unbroken custody of the evidence. The evidence is to be brought to the crime lab as soon as possible or lock-up in the police property room.

3. Preparation for booking

Note: Booking does not have to be done immediately and can be done any time during the suspect's incarceration. Prepare the case before booking.

a. Arrange for all evidence to be brought to the crime lab.

b. Arrange to keep witnesses separated from the assailant. Interview and obtain statements from witnesses as soon as convenient.

c. Obtain a fuller statement from victim and indicate if the victim is willing to testify.

d. Determine whether to question the suspect. If the suspect is to be questioned, do so as soon as possible. Before conducting the questioning, read the defendant his Miranda rights.

e. File an incident report.

f. Obtain criminal records of both the defendant and the victim.

g. Identify the appropriate penal code violation to be used in the complaint. See the attached list of codes for the most suitable violation.

h. Consult with the rebooking officer if there are any questions or problems.

i. If the evidence indicates, you or the rebooking officer should then book the defendant.

j. The D.A.'s office will determine if the case is to be prosecuted. If the case is to be prosecuted, it will proceed as any other case.

C. Procedures for Civilian Jail Staff Intervention

Note: Some inmates may not want to tell deputies that they have been sexually assaulted because they fear retaliation. However, they will want to do something to prevent further assaults. They may tell you because they trust your or because they do not know what else to do. The following procedures will give some guidelines for providing that help.

The most important steps are to arrange protection for the inmate and to refer him to the medical staff.

If an inmate claims to have been sexually assaulted, you are not being asked to make a judgement about whether or not it did happen. Unless there are intervening situations, proceed with these procedures so that collaborating medical evidence can be documented.

It is important that all contact with a sexual assault victim be sensitive, supportive, and nonjudgmental. Refer to the suggestions that are attached.

1. Advise the victim of services available and determine with the victim what services are needed.
2. It is important that the victim's safety and health be provided for as soon as possible. The following steps should be taken if needed. If necessary, the case manager for the sexual assault victim can make these arrangements.
   a. If protective custody is needed, contact the jail assignment officer on duty.
   b. If medical evaluation is needed, contact the jail medical staff on duty. In addition to being examined for possible injuries, the victim should be tested for VD.
   c. If the victim has any interest in having the assailants charged, medical evidence will need to be collected. Contact the jail medical staff on duty.
   d. If counseling is needed, or any other follow-up services such as legal or social services, contact the case manager for sexual assault victims directly through the medical staff.

PHASE 2. PRELIMINARY IN-JAIL MEDICAL ASSESSMENT

Note: All victims of sexual assault should be referred to the jail medical staff for evaluation and referral for services. Some victims may have been critically injured, others may need routine examination for injury and testing for VD. Most victims will require supportive services for the trauma experienced as a result of the assault.

Services for sexual assault cases that have occurred within the previous week and all VD follow-up testing and treatment should be given at Central Emergency unless a medical emergency. (Note: "Central Emergency" refers to location of sexual trauma service; "Mission Emergency" refers to county hospital emergency room service.)

It is important that all contact with a sexual assault victim be sensitive, supportive, and nonjudgmental. Refer to the suggestions that are attached. Advise the inmate of services available and together agree on the services that are to be provided.

A. *Triage (Determine Seriousness of Injuries and Refer)*
1. If critically injured, refer to Mission Emergency. (Life-threatening injuries may require going to the nearest hospital.
   a. Notify custody to arrange transportation.
   b. Notify medical staff at the emergency room.
   c. Notify case manager when convenient.
2. If victim is not critically injured but is traumatized, and/or the assault was within the previous week, refer to Central Emergency, the county facility for sexual trauma services.
   a. Write up a medical consult to be taken by the transportation deputy.
   b. Notify custody to arrange transportation.
   c. Notify staff at Central Emergency by phone.
   d. If evidence is to be collected and the assault was within the past 48 hours, have the inmate present himself as nearly as possible in his present physical condition. Request that the inmate not shower, wash, drink, eat, or defecate. Deputies will collect the victim's clothes.
   e. Notify case manager for follow-up.
3. If the victim is not critically injured and is not traumatized, and/or the assault occurred in the previous week, arrange the following:
   a. Refer to Central Emergency for VD testing and treatment.
   b. Arrange for protective custody if needed.
   c. Refer to counseling if appropriate.
   d. Notify case manager for follow-up.

B. *Follow-up Medical Services*
1. Provide whatever medical follow-up care is indicated.
2. Arrange follow-up VD testing at Central Emergency 10 days after the initial VD tests.

PHASE 3. MEDICAL TRANSFERS FOR EXAMINATION AND TREATMENT

A. *Transportation Arrangements*
Note: The medical staff will notify the appropriate jail staff to arrange transportation to the indicated medical facility. Sexual assault victims have next priority after acute medical cases.

1. Transport inmate to the medical facility indicated by the medical staff. The choice of facility will be dependent on the condition of the inmate.

Life-threatening and acute cases will be sent to county general hospital. Some medical emergencies may have to be taken to the nearest hospital. Non-life-threatening cases of sexual assault are to be seen at Central Emergency.

2. All contact with the victim should be supportive and nonjudgmental.
3. The victim may be referred to county hospital security ward after treatment. Notify the jail medical staff of any moves or any problems.
4. Information about the sexual assault is sensitive and, as with all medical information, is confidential and should be given only to those who are involved in investigation or in providing direct services to the victim.

B. *Mission Emergency – County Hospital*
   Note: These are the routine hospital procedures.

   1. Registration.
   2. Triage, diagnosis, and immediate treatment.
   3. Treatment continued:
      a. In-patient admission.
         i. Hospitalize on security ward or on hospital ward with security guard.
         ii. Notify jail medical staff to inform case manager.
         iii. Notify medical social worker on ward.
         iv. Contact Central Emergency to send sexual trauma services staff to the hospital for evidence collections and/or crisis counseling.
      b. Out-patient care (victim is not admitted).
         i. Arrange treatment follow-up such as medication, appointments, etc.
         ii. Referral:
            a. If sexual trauma services are needed and have not been provided, refer to Central Emergency.
               • Arrange transportation with custody officer escorting the victim.
               • Notify jail medical staff, who will inform the case manager.
            b. If no other medical services are needed, refer the victim back to the jail and notify jail medical staff that the inmate is being returned so that protective custody can be arranged.

C. *Central Emergency or Facility for Sexual Trauma Services*
   Note: These are routine clinical procedures for all adult victims of sexual assault.

   1. Registration (not necessary if the victim has a medical consult form).
   2. Victim asked to sign medical service permission form and medical information release form.

3. Medical examination and treatment.
4. Opportunity for inmate to make a police report.
5. Opportunity to collect evidence and sperm samples.
6. Crisis counseling for emotional trauma.
7. VD testing and preventive treatment if indicated.
8. Discharge planning and referral.
   a. Psychological evaluation – county hospital
      i. Arrange admission for psychological evaluation and/or decompensation.
         • Day shift: Phone ward psychiatric nurse, ward social worker, or ward psychiatrist.
         • Evening shifts: Refer to psychiatric emergency admitting service or notify ward psychiatry staff on call (call ward to get beeper number).
      ii. Arrange transportation with the custody officer escorting the victim.
      iii. Notify jail medical staff, who will inform the case manager.
   b. Medical Service – county hospital
      i. Arrange admission.
         • Afternoons (1 to 4 P.M.): Use medical screening clinic. Send victim directly with a written consult.
         • All other times: Call medical resident at the emergency room.
      ii. Arrange transportation with the custody officer escorting the victim
      iii. Notify jail medical staff, who will inform the case manager.
9. Medical Reports
   a. Fill out the medical consult to be returned with the victim with only a general description of the treatment.
   b. Fill out medical report and distribute copies as follows:
      i. Central Emergency files
      ii. Jail medical files
      iii. Sheriff's office (give to deputy or send to booking officer).
   c. Fill out third party confidential report if indicated and distribute copies as follows:
      i. Jail medical file
      ii. Sheriff's office (booking officer)

D. *Security Ward – County Hospital*
   Note: These procedures are the same for both medical and psychological evaluation services.

1. Admission and registration.
   a. Medical examination.
   b. Psychological evaluation.
   c. Initial treatment.
2. Impatient services (as required).
   a. Medical treatment by hospital staff if indicated.
   b. Crisis counseling and short-term counseling, coordinated by psychiatric staff. Deal with issues of:
      i. Self-identity.
      ii. Survival skills and coping with jails.
      iii. Life issues and goals.
      iv. Ventilation of feelings.
   c. Medical social services coordinated by ward medical social worker.
      i. Social needs: support system, family contact, property, etc.
      ii. Legal needs: Assess case and other legal issues, make referrals, and explore alternate placements.
3. Discharge planning coordinated by ward medical social worker.
   a. Arrange protective custody with assignment officer at jail site.
   b. Arrange with case manager needed follow-up of services:
      i. Medical services.
      ii. Psychological services.
      iii. Social services.
      iv. Legal services.
      v. Custodial services.

PHASE 4. IN-JAIL FOLLOW-UP

Note: The case manager should coordinate the delivery of follow-up services required during the remainder of the jail sentence. The major concerns are the continued protection of the victim and provision of counseling for the post-trauma stages after the assault.

A. Arrange protective custody with the assignment officer as needed.
B. Monitor progress of victim, particularly in terms of reentry adjustment.
C. Coordinate the continuation of needed services.
   1. Medical: medication, nursing care, routine examinations, and VD follow-up.
   2. Counseling
      a. Conduct postcrisis counseling or arrange with the jail psychiatric team.

b. Counselor contact for crisis counseling:
   i. Counselor should be prepared to be available for frequent contact after the assault and continuing on an "as needed" basis.
   ii. Contact may be needed as follows:
      • Every other day for the first few weeks.
      • Weekly contact up to the third month.
      • Continue as needed.
c. Counselor should be aware of reaction stages and provide support as needed for each stage. (See counseling materials attached.)

3. Social services.
   Note: The victim may feel particularly powerless because of the assault and because of the nature of the jail institution. For this reason, social work may be more critical in meeting the following services. Referral and follow-up can be arranged with various jail agencies such as prisoner services or service league. The victim should be encouraged gradually to provide for his own service needs.
   a. Help deal with outside support system such as family and friends.
   b. Help deal with institutional problems such as phone calls, property, protective custody issues.
   c. Arrange postrelease planning if needed.

4. Legal services.
   Note: The assault may generate a number of legal processes that involve the victim. The victim may need specific advice in determining the procedures and resources for each legal process involved. The case manager can help to identify the legal need and refer to the appropriate resource.
   a. Determine victim's legal status.
      i. The legal status of the victim may be needed to arrange follow-up services.
      ii. Determine the charges, his public defender or attorney, the pending court dates, sentencing date or sentence, release date, and possible holds for pending cases.
   b. Identify the legal concerns and refer to the appropriate resource.
      i. Prosecution of the assailant (refer to the district attorney's office).
      ii. Legal implication on victim's charges and sentence (refer to the victim's public defender or attorney, or to the prisoner services attorney).
      iii. Civil remedies and suits (legal assistance agencies usually do not get involved in civil suits. The victim may find them helpful to identify precedures and to locate available private attorneys).

PHASE 5. POSTRELEASE REFERRAL

Note: Some victims will require continuation of follow-up services after they are released from the county jail facility. They may be released back to the community or transferred to another institution. The case manager should attempt to identify appropriate resources where the victim may continue to get support and services.

A. Transfer to another institution, that is, state or federal prison, another county jail, mental hospital, etc. Before the transfer, the case manager should arrange for the following:
1. Ensure that all alternative placements have been exhausted.
2. All records should be checked to avoid labeling of the inmate as a victim of sexual assault for his protection.
   Note: Many institutions have inmates process records, which can result in exposing the inmate as a victim or having made a report of the assault.
3. Arrange follow-up medical and psychological services as needed, discreetly if possible to protect the victim's reputation. (This can be done through phone calls.)
4. Victim may need counseling on survival techniques and formation of life goals in preparation for the transfer.

B. Release to the community.
   Note: In addition to follow-up services, a victim who is released with no resources for survival may be particularly vulnerable after the trauma of the assault. Postrelease services can help the victim assume control over his life and make the life changes necessary to stay out of jail. The following follow-up services may be facilitated by the case manager as needed:
1. Postrelease plans for housing, meals, employment, or welfare and social support.
2. Referral for continued intervention services.

III. PROTOCOL IMPLEMENTATION

A. Obtain approval of Protocol draft by jail agencies.
B. Institute jail personnel in-service training workshops.
C. Post notice for jail inmates (see Appendix) advising:
1. Risk of sexual assault in jail.
2. Sexual assault services for sexual victims.
3. Prosecution of sexual assaults.
D. Ongoing evaluation and revision of protocol.

IV. APPENDIX

SUGGESTIONS FOR ASSISTING VICTIMS OF SEXUAL ASSAULT

Sexual assault and attempted sexual assault are viewed as a crisis resulting in the disruption of the individual's physical, emotional, social, and sexual equilibrium.

The trauma of sexual assault may continue to emotionally effect the victim for many years. These effects may impair the normal functioning of the individual, who may continue to have chronic reactions such as depression, damaged self-esteem, and phobias, as well as the inability to maintain routine activity such as work, sleep, and sex. There may be a general reaction of constant fear, guilt, anxiety, and frustration.

These consequences can be minimized by supportive counseling available soon after the assault. Support can be given by helping victims express their feelings, by expressing understanding about what victims have gone through, and by helping victims to use a personal support system to regain control over their lives.

The following information may help to deal more effectively with sexual assault victims.

A. Penal codes for sexual assaults.
B. Guidelines for investigating sexual assaults.
C. Summary of victim responses.
D. Counseling suggestions.
E. Model jail warning notice.

E. Model Jail Warning Notice

ABOUT YOUR SAFETY

While in jail, you might be hassled by other people.

Some of these hassles are against the law. Some hassles deny your human and civil rights. You have the right to do your own time in jail without being hassled.

The following steps may help you avoid thefts, attacks, and forced sexual hassles:

- Avoid jail areas that are out of the way and not safe.
- Try not to get into debt with other inmates or accept gifts and favors.
- Be direct and firm if other people ask you to do something you don't want to do.

- Be alert at all times.
- If you are gay or transsexual, you may ask a deputy to be placed in the gay tier.

If you are attacked or fear that you will be attacked, tell someone who can get you help. You don't need to name the attackers to get help.

- A deputy may move you to a safer area.
- If you are hurt or need someone to talk to, tell the nurse at pill call.
- You can also get help from other people in the jail such as your lawyer, public defender, or the jail services worker. If these people can't help, you can file a grievance notice.
- If you want, you may press legal charges. Tell a deputy that you want to do so.

If you are forced into having sex, you should have the doctor examine you and you should be tested for VD. You should talk with a counselor about what happened to you. Tell the nurse at pill call what help you need.

If you are released before you can get help in the jail, you should contact someone at one of the counseling centers. They have low or no charges for their services.

BEFORE YOU ATTACK ANOTHER INMATE, REMEMBER . . .

- The Sheriff's Office will file legal charges against inmates who are found attacking or sexually hassling other inmates. You may lose good time or get more time. You may be locked down.
- You may need clinical help to keep from attacking and sexually hassling other inmates. You should talk with someone on the jail psychiatric team. Tell the nurse that you want to see them.

REFERENCE NOTES

1. Weiss, C. and Friar, D. 1974. *Terror in the prisons.* New York: Bobbs-Merril.
   Scacco, A. 1975. *Rape in prison.* Springfield, Ill.: C. Thomas Books.
   Lockwood, D. 1980. *Prison sexual violence.* New York: Elsevier.
2. Davis, A. J. 1968. Sexual assaults in the Philadelphia Prison System and sheriff's vans. *Trans-Action,* December, 8-16.

3. Rothenberg, D. 1978. *Hearings on research into violent behavior: overview and sexual assaults.* Hearing of Subcommittee on Domestic and International Scientific Planning, Analysis, and Cooperation of the Committee on Science and Technology, U.S. House of Representatives. (Testimony presented). Washington, D.C.: Government Printing Office, **64**, 464-488.
4. Groth, A. N., with Birnbaum, H. J. 1979. *Men who rape: the psychology of the offender.* New York: Plenum.
5. Zeringer, B. D. 1977. Tort-liability of the state for injuries suffered by prisoners due to assault by other inmates. *Tulane Law Review,* **51**, 1300-1306.
   Sexual assault and forced homosexual relationships in prison: cruel and unusual punishment. 1972, *Albany Law Review,* **36**, 428-438.
   Other case examples of damages paid to victims:
      Clappier v. Flynn, U.S. Dist. Ct., Laramie Co., Wyo. 1977. JB#860CS
      Doe v. Frank, Travis Co., Tex. 1977. JB#862CS
      Holda v. Kane County, Cir. Ct. Kane Co., Ill. 1977. JB#771CC.
6. Irwin, J. 1970. *The felon.* Englewood Cliffs, N.J.: Prentice Hall.
7. Cotton, D. J. 1981. Protocol for crisis intervention services to sexually assaulted male inmates in the San Francisco County Jails: Revised 1981. San Francisco Department of Public Health, Sexual Trauma Services, San Francisco, CA.

9
Rape of Men in the Community

Arthur Kaufman, M.D.

ABSTRACT

Fifteen male rape victims treated in a county hospital emergency room and outpatient clinic over a three-year period are compared with 100 randomly selected female victims treated over the same period. The male victims as a group sustained more physical trauma and were more likely to have been a victim of multiple assaults from multiple assailants. They were more reluctant to initially reveal the genital component of their assault and were more likely to use denial and control their emotions in reaction to the assault. Social and economic characteristics of this group demonstrated considerable instability in the lives of these victims. Proper diagnosis and treatment of male rape victims requires a high index of suspicion and sensitivity to the likelihood of major, hidden trauma.

INTRODUCTION

Increasingly, lay and professional literature is focusing attention on female victims of sexual assault (Burgess and Holmstrom, 1974; Metzger, 1976). The violent rather than sexual nature of the assault is emerging in public consciousness, law enforcement and legal services are becoming more sensitive to victim needs, and treatment and support services are broadly advertised throughout our communities. As a consequence, we have witnessed nationally a sharp increase in willingness to report sex assault by women victims.

Few male victims in the community report their assaults, and such victimization is scarcely reported in the medical literature. Many assume that male victims are usually children, the prey of child molesters. When adult male victims are cited, it is conceived either as an aberration of prison life, as a vicarious rape against women (Brownmiller, 1975), or as a violent outgrowth of the homosexual subculture. Such stigmatization, most likely, continues to hinder men's reporting their assaults today, as myths of victims' complicity with their assailants hindered women's reporting their assaults in the past. Nevertheless, there is a noticeable increase in the reporting of male victims of rape (Kaufman et al., 1980).

In this chapter we would like to explore the nature of sex assault against men presenting to a county hospital and a community clinic. To better characterize this victim population, comparisons will be made with data generated from female victims seen in the same medical facilities over a comparable period of time.

METHODS

Over the past six years, the University of New Mexico School of Medicine's Department of Family, Community and Emergency Medicine has sponsored a Sex Assault Response Team. The team is composed of medical, nursing, and pharmacy students, both men and women, supervised by faculty members from the department and from the School of Nursing. Team members provide 24-hour crisis care at the University of New Mexico Hospital, the county teaching hospital for the medical school, and follow-up care at the University's Family Practice Clinic (Kaufman et al., 1976). They take histories, orient the patients to the health care and legal options available, and offer follow-up services for the victims' family and friends. Increasingly, the training of team members has incorporated an understanding of the special problems and management of male victims.

Data sheets on each victim, seen both acutely and on follow-up, are filled out by the team members. The sheets include demographic information, specific information about the assault, emotional reactions of the victim, and degree of adjustment noted on follow-up visit (see Appendix). Background information on victims of all ages and both sexes was reviewed. Then information from this same source was compiled on a sample of 15 male victims, 15 years of age and older, who were assaulted in the community and treated at the University Hospital or Family Practice Clinic. All male victims cared for by the University Team within the state prisons or city jail were excluded from this study. However, two male victims assaulted in jail during a less-than-24-hour detention but who subsequently came to the University Clinic for care are included. Comparison data was gleaned from a sample of 100 female victims, of comparable age, seen over the same period of time.

RESULTS

Results of data collected during the first three years of the program showed that an increasing percentage of all victims were men (Kaufman et al., 1980). While in 1975 there were no male victims seen, by 1978 10% of victims were males. Yet there was a larger percentage of young victims in the male group as opposed to the sample of 100 randomly chosen female victims. Almost half the males were aged 14 or under, whereas only one-fifth of the females were 14 or under.

Of the sample of 15 male victims 15 years of age or over seen during the past three years, their ages ranged from 15 to 49, with a mean age of 26.6 years (Figure 9-1). One-third were Hispanic, approximately the same proportion of Hispanic victims among the female victims. The various settings of assault approximated those among the female group with the exception of the two male victims assaulted during several hours of the incarcerations in the city jail, subsequently treated at our clinic. All but two denied any prior homosexual contact.

A major difference in the nature of the assaults was found in the number of assailants. Nine of the victims (60%) were assaulted by more than one assailant. This can be compared to the female group in which only 23% were assaulted by more than one assailant. The level of brutality also seemed to be greater among male victims presenting for care. Coercion included the use of a knife on four occasions and a gun on two occasions. Eleven percent of the female victims sustained major physical trauma, compared to 53% of the male victims. Four males (27%) incurred stab wounds and eight (53%) sustained nongenital wounds. Fifteen (100%) were sodomized and six (40%) were forced to commit fellatio. Eight (53%) in this group sustained anogenital wounds. This degree of physical brutality was far in excess of that among the female cohorts in which 28% sustained genital trauma and 36%, nongenital trauma.

Typical emotional reactions of the male victims observed by team members in the initial encounter differed considerably from that observed among female victims. Five of the male victims failed at first to report the sexual component of their assault during the initial interview with the emergency department or clinic staff, preferring to reveal and seek treatment solely for their nongenital trauma. Although this specific information was not collected for females, team members and emergency department staff felt this to be a rare occurrence among female victims. Twelve of the male victims (80%) appeared quiet, embarrassed, stoical, withdrawn, or unconcerned upon first encounter. This compared to what team members estimated to be the more common initial reaction of female victims; well over half expressing strong emotions, for example, tearfulness, fright, or anger.

Social and economic characteristics of the male victims revealed a pattern of instability. Five were unemployed; five were without a stable home; four had prior, major psychiatric histories or learning disabilities; and two were alcoholics. Again, this proportion of social and economic instability among the male victims appeared to team members to be far in excess of that among female victims.

The following case vignettes illustrate the range of characteristics presented by male victims described in this report.

PATIENT	AGE	ETHNICITY	SETTING OF ASSAULT	NUMBER OF ASSAILANTS	SEX ACTS	INJURIES	ECONOMIC	SOCIAL
1	17	Anglo	Hitchhiking	1	Sodomy	None	Student	Learning disability, psychiatric history
2	22	Anglo	Hitchhiking	1	Sodomy	Anal laceration	Student	Lives at college
3	25	Hispanic	Hitchhiking	3	Sodomy	Anal contusion	Stable work	Stable family
4	18	Anglo	Street	3	Sodomy	Anal and body contusions	Student	Lives at home
5	20	Anglo	Store	2	Sodomy	None	Stable work	Lives at home
6	17	Hispanic	Another's house	1	Sodomy	None	Student	Learning disability Lives at home
7	31	Anglo	Jail	4	Sodomy Fellatio	None	Stable work	Stable family
8	21	Hispanic	Unknown	1	Sodomy	Anal and body contusions	Unemployed	Psychiatric history
9	18	Anglo	Jail	4	Sodomy Fellatio	None	Unemployed	Transient Frequent arrests
10	15	Hispanic	Car	1	Sodomy Fellatio	Stabbed in chest	Student	Lives at home
11	49	Anglo	Car	2	Sodomy Fellatio	Body abrasions and contusions	Unemployed	Homeless Psychiatric history
12	44	Anglo	Street, car	1	Sodomy	Stabbed in neck Subconjunctural hematoma Anal abrasion	Stable work	Stable family
13	16	Anglo	Another's house	2	Sodomy Fellatio	Stabbed in arm	Truant from school	Runaway
14	38	Hispanic	Unknown	3	Sodomy	Anal larceration Facial laceration	Unemployed	Alcoholism
15	49	Anglo	Car	4	Sodomy Fallatio	Orbital contusion Anal and body contusions	Unemployed	Alcoholism

Figure 9-1. Summary of data concerning 15 male victims of sexual assault presenting to a community clinic.

Case Vignettes

Case 1.   R. Q. is a 25-year-old married Hispanic man who picked up three male hitchhikers in downtown Albuquerque, ten o'clock at night, six hours before presenting to the emergency room. The three hitchhikers convinced him to buy some beer, which they all drank at roadside in a city barrio. Suddenly the three men turned on him, violently subdued him, dragged him out of the car, and pulled down his pants. While two of the assailants restrained him, the third produced a jar of lubricant, applied some to his anus and forced his penis into the patient's rectum, while the two restraining assailants laughed at him. The patient experienced severe anal pain during the assault. Afterwards, the assailants forced the patient to drive to another city location where he was told another man would have sex with him, but the patient managed to escape at a stoplight and notify the police.

In the emergency ward the patient's clothes were covered with dirt. He was sullen, and occasionally tearful in relating the history. Abnormal physical findings were confined to an anal contusion which was exquisitely tender to palpation. An evidence kit was collected, gonorrhea cultures taken, and pro-phylactic antibiotics prescribed. A follow-up appointment was not kept by the patient.

Case 2.   J.S., a 15-year-old high school student, was walking on a main street at night when a man drove up and asked if he wanted to "get high." J. S. accepted and got in the car, and they drove off. The driver had been drinking. They smoked marijuana while driving around and then stopped by a park. The driver produced a gun, which he played with, pretending he would shoot out the lights of a nearby church. He then pointed the gun at J. S. whom he commanded, "Give me a blow job, man." When the youth did not move, he shook the gun saying, "Time's running out." J. S. complied. The driver then ordered him to take down his pants, then sodomized him. The driver led J. S. from the car to a shack and stabbed him in the back. As J. S. turned, he was again stabbed, this time in the face. He escaped and ran to the emergency department of a nearby hospital. On initial presentation, J. S. complained only of the knife wound. Subsequently he admitted to having been sexually assaulted, and a team member was called.

Anal examination revealed a 3-centimeter laceration. Evidence was collected, and laboratory tests for venereal disease were done. Initially J. S. was reluctant to talk and was very shy and embarrassed. He was subsequently able to give a full history and to allow a physical examination, saying that it was "dumb" of him to go with the assailant. J. S. was hospitalized for treatment of stab wounds and was counseled while in the hospital and thereafter in the Family Practice Clinic.

Case 3. T. P., a 31-year-old married traveling salesman, was on a business trip to Los Angeles two weeks prior to being seen in the Family Practice Clinic. He rented a car that, unbeknownst to him, was stolen. The police apprehended him, and he spent eight hours in a Los Angeles jail until his innocence was ascertained. However, during his brief incarceration he was physically assaulted by six cell mates in his "holding tank." Four held him down while two sexually abused him. They both forced their penises into his rectum but were unsuccessful in trying to force him to commit fellatio. One assailant ejaculated and smeared sperm over the patient's mouth. After his release the patient described feelings of being foul and vile. He rinsed his mouth out with alcohol and gave himself a Fleet's enema. He told no one of his assault, fearing that his self-image would be tarnished if he told his wife or employer or pressed charges. Finally he called the Albuquerque Rape Crisis Center, without giving his name, to find out how he could receive prophylaxis against venereal disease. They referred him to the Family Practice Clinic, where cultures were collected and prophylactic antibiotics administered.

Case 4. Mr. C. was a 38-year-old man who was brought to the emergency department by the police. He initially complained of a laceration on his chin. Mr. C. said he had been walking home after a night of drinking when he was accosted by three men who dragged him into a basement and began beating him. A passerby saw this and called the police, who apprehended the men, one of whom was discovered in the act of sodomizing Mr. C. Mr. C. had little recollection of the events, but when informed that treatment for the sexual assault was available, he requested this also.

On examination, Mr. C. was disheveled and had a strong odor of alcohol on his breath. He had blood on his clothes, hands, and face. There was a 1-centimeter laceration on his chin. His perianal area was covered with sand, and there were two anal lacerations as well as three abrasions over the sacrum. Evidence was collected as well as specimens for venereal disease.

Mr. C. was seen in follow-up three days later, at which time he denied any complaints and seemed to be coping with the rape primarily by denial. Laboratory tests were negative. Mr. C. failed to return for further follow-up.

Follow-up health care needs of sex assault victims and their families and friends can be complex and require close attention by the health care team. In a study of 43 consecutive sex assault victims, mostly female, cared for in early follow-up at the University of New Mexico's Family Practice Clinic, 39 presented rape-related problems (e.g., gonorrhea, anal abrasion, neck sprain, anorexia, referral to Navajo Medicine Man), 20 presented nonrape-related problems (e.g., ovarian cyst, condyloma accuminatum, enuresis, need for social service), and in 22 of the cases, family members sought care (e.g., anxiety, school problems, need for sedation, mediation with law enforcement and court system) (Kaufman et al., 1976). The two following case studies illustrate the complexity of follow-up health care needs of many of these victims.

Case 5.   A teenage boy was brought to the Pediatric Clinic by his distraught mother after he had returned home from a mysterious two-week absence. It was discovered that the boy had been kept in the home of an old man. Though fed and clothed, he was repeatedly sodomized and forced to masturbate and commit fellatio on his abductor. Physical examination in the clinic revealed an anal abrasion and guaiac-positive stool. The boy was very withdrawn and depressed. His mother declined to bring the boy back for further clinic visits. Consequently, a team member initiated a series of telephone contacts and made several home visits. The boy began to reveal his feelings, discussing longings for his father who had recently died. The mother, 39 years old, was generally aloof and secretive during the home visits.

After three weeks, she told the team member she had "bad hemorrhoids" but was too embarrassed to have them examined. After much coaxing, she came to the Family Practice Clinic. In addition to having large painful external hemorrhoids, she was found to be six months pregnant. She had feared revelation of her condition, worrying that others would castigate her for having had sexual relations with a man soon after her husband's death. She also was found to be anemic (hematocrit reading 28%). She was enrolled in a prenatal program, given a topical hemorrhoid preparation, evaluated for anemia, begun on a regimen of iron given orally, and referred to a social service agency for financial assistance.

Case 6.   Mr. W. was an 18-year-old, mildly retarded man, who was a student living at home, supported by his parents. On a weekday evening he was walking through a city park when he was assaulted by three teenaged males. In front of onlookers, the patient was beaten and sodomized, after which the attackers fled. The patient notified his family and his mother brought him for treatment. He was found to have tenderness and contusions about the anal area and evidence of trauma on his trunk. He refused evidence collection but accepted venereal disease prophylaxis.

At a follow-up appointment three days later the patient was accompanied by both parents. He still had anal tenderness and feared playing in the same park. The mother was distraught over the possibility of future assaults on her son and had become agitated after a neighbor told her someone was taking photographs of her son's assault. The father was angry, impatient, and complaining of bureaucratic red tape delaying apprehension of the assailants. The health care provider noted that the parents now seemed more upset then the victim, who was now calm with anal contusion healing.

The patient returned in three weeks accompanied by his mother. At this time he came for treatment of diarrhea, nausea, and vomiting, felt by the doctor to be gastroenteritis. However, the mother revealed that she and her husband had had a fight the previous evening for which the police had to be called to mediate. She said they noted the home environment was unsafe for the mother's 4 1/2-year-old daughter, so the latter was sent to a relative's house for the night until family tensions could abate. Unbeknownst to the mother, the father picked up the child the morning of the visit and "disappeared." She implied the father may have been sexually molesting this child and said the police were now looking for them both. The family practice health worker immediately notified child protective services.

DISCUSSION

Until recently, reports on male rape victims in the community have been rare. A decade ago a U.S. Department of Justice (1972) survey of criminal victimization in a sample city during a one-year period identified no males among the 1100 reported rape victims. In a past review of 90 articles on rape listed in *Index Medicus* for 1975-1978, no articles appeared primarily concerned with male victims (Kaufman et al., 1980). Reference to males within these articles usually concerned children (Orr, 1978). Then, following a national surge of interest and research on female rape victims, there appeared a growing interest in their male counterparts (Josephson, 1979; Kaufman et al., 1980; Groth and Burgess, 1980; Schiff, 1980).

Two currents seemed to be merging. On the one hand, a heightened sensitivity to the magnitude of sexual violence was broadening researchers' concerns beyond the now familiar crime of female victimization into newer, more hidden sexual violence such as incest and rape within marriage. Male victimization, too, could now be scrutinized more carefully. Concurrently public awareness of publicized victim services appeared to facilitate victims' reporting. The small but growing number reports by male victims in Albuquerque appears to exemplify the value of public awareness of rape, a shift away from blaming the victim for the crime, and the well-publicized medical and legal services for such victims in the state. The institution of these services had been shown to substantially increase the reporting of rape among female victims (Kaufman et al., 1977).

Yet, the barriers against males who have been sexually victimized reporting their assaults remains high. Groth and Burgess (1980) summarize three important barriers as follows: (1) societal beliefs that a man is expected to be able to defend himself against sexual assault, (2) the victim's fear that his sexual preference may become suspect, and (3) the fact that telling is highly distressing. Thus, one might speculate that if only 10% to 20% of female assault victims report their assault (Federal Bureau of Investigation, 1970), a far smaller proportion of male victims report theirs. And if male victims do seek medical attention, they are more likely than female victims to seek help for secondary physical and emotional trauma without reporting the sexual component of the assault.

Burgess and Holmstrom (1974) described an acute and chronic reaction to rape among female rape victims, which they labeled the "rape trauma syndrome." The acute phase begins with "impact reactions," in which "the woman may experience an extremely wide range of emotions." These include feelings of shock or disbelief. Victims tended to exhibit one of two emotional styles: the "expressive" style — crying, sobbing, smiling, or restlessness — and the "controlled" style — calm, composed, or subdued affect. The reactions of female victims in their sample were divided roughly equally between these two styles. However, in our sample of males, 12 (80%) showed a "controlled" style. This preponderance of controlled emotional reactions may reflect a gender role expectation that it is unmanly for males to express emotion, even in the face of enormous physical and emotional trauma. One can postulate that this is an extension of the different socialization patterns of males and females in our society for reaction to illness. Boys are taught from an early age to remain more stoic in the face of discomfort (Mechanic, 1964; Nathanson, 1975). And yet despite the outer blunting of emotion, on careful interview, the underlying feelings expressed by male victims appear similar to those of females. Groth and Burgess (1980) recorded these narratives from male victims:

"I was terrified . . . thought he was going to do me in."

"I was flabbergasted and didn't know what to do."

"I don't think a lot of people believe it could happen. . . . I'm 6'2" and weigh 220 lbs."

Overall, male victims seen in the emergency department and clinic seemed to have sustained greater physical trauma than did their female counterparts. This may reflect the degree of force (either by number of assailants or weapons) marshaled to ensure the male victim's submission. Or it may well reflect the highly selective sampling out of the pool of all male victims, the likelihood of reporting rising with the degree of physical trauma.

The high rate of family disruption, unemployment, and social dysfunction in this group appears greater than among female sex assault victims. This high rate may also be a product of skewed sampling rather than a true representation of social disruption among all male sex assault victims. On the other hand, a disruptive life-style characterized by frequent mobility and little economic or social stability may place one at a higher risk for victimization of many kinds.

The concept of recidivism has traditionally been applied to the assailant in a crime. However, recent work in the field of victimology has evolved a concept of victim recidivism (Ziegenhagen, 1976). In a study of recidivism among female sex assault victims it was found that of 341 victims, 82 (24%) had been sex assault victims before (Miller et al., 1978). This subgroup of recidivist victims who appear more vulnerable to assault differed significantly from the group of one-time-only sex assault victims in having a higher unemployment rate (33% versus 18%), and in having more often received professional help for emotional problems (48% versus 21%). In many respects the group of male victims seen at the medical center exhibited many social and economic features akin to the subgroup of women who had been assaulted on more than one occasion. Unemployment was common, home life was unstable, and the incidence of emotional instability was high. Such a profile may well predispose an individual to victimization of all kinds including sexual.

Male victims of sex assault in our study seemed in general to be unaffiliated with the homosexual community. As in the case of female victims, sex assault of males appears to be an expression of anger, power, and dominance over another (Groth et al., 1977). A study by Sagarin (1976) of nine male prison sex assault aggressors revealed that none identified himself as homosexual, each stating that the sex assault on males was an acceptational practice of heterosexual males within the prison milieu. One wonders if the same gender-blind, "sexual" aggressiveness recognized in confinement does not also take place frequently in the community.

Because male rape victims are likely to report their assault infrequently, and because the nature of the assault is so often masked, identification of such victims requires a high index of suspicion. In light of recent data concerning the effect of rape on males, it appears that, despite the controlled reaction usually evident, male victims may experience major, hidden trauma.

Implications for Case Identification

In light of a great reluctance to reveal the sexual nature of their assault, a large percentage of male sex assault victims will be treated by physicians, nurses, psychologists, and social workers for somatic and emotional complaints with the root cause of these complaints hidden from the therapist. The health professional must therefore maintain a high index of suspicion that sexual assault might have occurred when a male patient presents in the following circumstances:

1. *The patient has been physically assaulted.* An old myth held that if a woman who claimed she was raped couldn't demonstrate evidence of resistance, that is, physical trauma, she probably wasn't raped. In reality most female victims we have cared for over the past six years have put up no struggle. A victim's first concern is preservation of life, and the fear of being killed is so overwhelming and paralyzing that when the threat of deadly force presents itself, most female victims comply with their assailant's demands. One can speculate that an identical set of responses occurs among male victims. In careful histories of our male victims, most complied with their assailants when deadly force, for example a gun, was used as a threat. In most cases beatings

occurred not because the victim was attempting to protect himself from rape but in the course of what appeared to the victim to be a spontaneous physical assault by one or more assailants. Thus, when a male patient presents to a trauma ward or outpatient clinic for repair or treatment of injuries from a physical assault, especially at the hands of multiple assailants or when a deadly weapon was used as a threat, the possibility of sexual assault should always be entertained by the health care team.

2. *The patient appears emotionally withdrawn.* Since the overwhelming majority of male sex assault victims exhibit a controlled emotional expression, sullen and withdrawn, the treatment staff must be alerted to the possibility of sexual assault when further history reveals the patient was recently the victim of a crime. There is no social stigma borne by the victim of residential burglary or robbery with a gun. For those of us who have interviewed male victims of such crimes, the victims are usually angry and animated in describing the crime. Thus an overly controlled reaction should raise a red flag for the interviewer to probe deeper into the nature of the crime.

3. *The patient presents a high-risk profile for victimization; economic, social, or emotional instability.* Demographic patterns of rape follow patterns of other violent and nonviolent crimes in terms of the location of crime and characteristics of victims. For example, an unemployed man might find housing only in a poor, high-crime area of a community. Without money to buy a car or purchase gasoline, he may have to rely on hitchhiking as his primary mode of transportation. Both place him at higher jeopardy for becoming a victim of any crime, including sexual assault. For this reason rape can also be included as a "class crime."

The high unemployment found in our small sample of male victims may also be indicative of a group of individuals less able, for social or psychological reasons, to obtain and keep a job. Less able to cope with everyday living demands, they may become easier prey for perpetrators of sexual assault.

A large percentage of the male victims (40%) appeared rootless — either as unemployed persons or as runaways. While the popular press has recently publicized the sexual victimization of male children who are runaways, similar risks can await older, rootless men, since they, too, must rely upon strangers for food and shelter.

The profile of male victims in our sample also seems to include a high risk for men who are emotionally impaired (note the frequency of alcoholism, psychiatric disturbance, and learning disabilities). These features may well increase their vulnerability to sexual assault. Ability to judge external danger may be grossly impaired either because of naive trust, influence of intoxication, or overwhelming dependency needs.

4. *Prior incarceration in jail or prison.* While rape of males is prevalent in jails and prisons, it is almost never reported to the guards or institutional health

staff for fear of reprisal. Many victims fear that if they are labeled with a "snitch jacket" by other inmates, they will be marked for murder. In this regard, much pent-up anguish can be vented only upon release from incarceration. The University of New Mexico Department of Family, Community and Emergency Medicine has run health clinics in a prison facility for the past six years. On only two occasions has an inmate revealed that he had been sexually assaulted. On the other hand, we have seen many more men in our emergency room and outpatient clinics in the safety of civilian life who have discussed their sexual assaults during prior incarceration. Again, the treating health worker should be alert to the possibility that a patient who was previously an inmate may well have been a sex assault victim. The majority of such victims will not spontaneously reveal that hidden, frightening part of their past.

When confronted with any of the above circumstances triggering a suspicion that sex assault of the male patient may have occurred, how should questions in the interview be framed? In the training of volunteers on the University of New Mexico Sex Assault Response Team and residents in Obstetrics and Gynecology, Family Medicine and Pediatrics, considerable effort is expended in ensuring that health workers caring for victims are skilled in framing questions that will facilitate revelation of embarrassing, frightening, or otherwise hidden information about the assault. In the past, male victims appeared so infrequently that when they presented for treatment at the emergency room the triage nurse was often uncertain which service he "belonged to." The skills in interviewing, which health care providers had carefully honed over the years in caring for the now-familiar female sex assault victim, seemed to evaporate when dealing with male victims. But with the surge in male victim reporting each in-service training at the university concerning interviewing sex assault victims always includes time devoted to the needs of male victims.

We emphasize the following points:

1. Questions must be framed in a nonjudgmental way. For example, questions that begin with "Tell me what you thought then . . ." are preferable to "Didn't you think that. . . ."
2. As with female victims there should be no implication in the questioning that the male victim was responsible for the assault. A poor question might be, "When you got drunk with them and they started calling you 'queer' didn't you know they were going to attack you?" A better comment might be "You must have been terrified when they suddenly became violent after you were all drinking, having a good time."
3. The interviewer should help the patient share information about very sensitive areas. Many men will not, for example, share information about fellatio if the question is put, "After he raped you anally then what did he do?" A question more conducive to revealing possible fellatio would

be, "Many rapists try to do all kinds of things to scare their victims. For instance, they often put their penis in their victim's mouth. Did that happen to you?" The patient need only nod his head slightly and you've obtained important information.

4. When information is elicited about the assault there should be no assumption that the male victim tried to fight off his attacker (Kaufman et al., 1976). A poor question might be, "Of course you tried to fight him off, didn't you?" A better one would be, "Most of us are paralyzed when confronted with the possibility of being killed. How did you react?"

5. There should be no implication that the victim is homosexual. A poor question would be, "Are you a homosexual?" A better statement would be, "Most men who are sexually assaulted are not homosexual. Many feel, however, that others will think they're homosexual. Have you had any fears like that?"

Questions concerning sensitive areas should be framed in terms the victim can understand and that clearly imply that you need complete information, not that you feel he is untruthful.

There will be some health care providers who simply have a difficult time caring for male victims because of personal experiences, conflicts, or insecurities. It is far better for that provider to defer to a counselor who is more at ease and skillful than to further traumatize the male victim with an insensitive, inept interaction.

Implications for Treatment

In light of the high potential for hidden trauma in male sex assault victims, it is imperative that males who present with physical or emotional trauma, and who are at high risk for sexual assault, receive a full physical examination, if they are willing. At that time a careful anogenital examination can be performed.

It is also imperative, in large institutions or in communities, that potential health care providers for adult male victims be identified, so that when the crisis occurs the victim feels cared for and not rejected or punted from doctor to doctor or service to service.

Because many providers of care for female sex assault victims have felt it was better for the victim to be cared for by other women, a number of rape crisis centers have assumed it would be better for male counselors and doctors to care for male victims. In our experience the gender of the advocate or health provider is of little consequence when compared to his or her sensitivity, caring, and skill. Those qualities are quickly apparent to the victim and set the tone for the rest of the encounter.

The physical examination of the male victim, evidence collection, and prophylaxis against venereal disease are conducted in an identical fashion to those for female victims. In New Mexico we use the exact same protocols.

Finally, we must pay careful attention to the follow-up needs of the victim and his family and friends. In light of the greater likelihood of masked trauma among male sex assault victims, follow-up needs may be greater and perhaps more diligence should be exercised. Because the victims who come to our attention seem a subgroup, with an inordinately large component of economic deprivation and psychological stress, a coordinated health care team should ideally be readily accessible to deal with the victim's physical, emotional, and social needs. It is also clear that follow-up must be initiated soon after the crisis care visit, certainly within three days, if the patient is to have a high likelihood of seeking return services for himself and his family (Kaufman et al., 1976).

REFERENCES

Brownmiller, S. 1975. *Against Our Will.* New York: Simon and Schuster.
Burgess, A. W., and Holmstrom, L. L. 1974. Rape trauma syndrome. *Am. J. Psychiatry,* 131:981–986.
Federal Bureau of Investigation. 1970. Uniform Crime Reports for the United States. Washington, D.C., U.S. Department of Justice.
Groth, A. N., and Burgess, A. W. 1980. Male rape: Offender and victims. *Am. J. Psychiatry,* 137:806–810.
Groth, N., Burgess, A. W., and Holmstrom, L. L. 1977. Rape: Power, anger, and sexuality. *Am. J. Psychiatry,* 134:1239–1243.
Josephson, G. W. 1979. The male rape victim: evaluation and treatment. *J.A.C.E.P.,* 8:13–15.
Kaufman, A., DiVasto, P., and Jackson, R. 1977. Impact of a community health approach to rape. *Am. J. Pub. Health,* 67:365–367.
Kaufman, A., DiVasto, P., Jackson, R., Voorhees, D., and Christy, J. 1980. Male rape victims: non-institutionalized assault. *Am. J. Psychiatry,* 137:221–223.
Kaufman, A., VanderMeer, J., and DiVasto, P. 1976. Follow-up of rape victims in a family practice setting. *South. Med. J.,* 69:1569–1571.
Mechanic, D. 1964. The influence of mothers on their children's health attitudes and behavior. *Pediatrics,* 33:444–453.
Metzger, D. 1976. It is always the woman who is raped. *Am. J. Psychiatry,* 133:405–408.
Miller, J., Moeller, D., Kaufman, A., DiVasto, P., Pathak, D., and Christy, J. 1978. Recidivism among sex assault victims. *Am. J. Psychiatry,* 135:1103–1104.
Nathanson, C. 1975. Illness and the feminine role. *Soc. Sci. Med.,* 9:57-62.
Orr, D. P. 1978. Limitations of emergency room evaluations of sexually abused children. *Am. J. Dis. Child.,* 132:873–875.
Sagarin, E. 1976. Prison homosexuality and its effect on post-prison sexual behavior. *Psychiatry,* 39:245–257.
Schiff, A. F. 1980. Examination and treatment of the male rape victim. *South. Med. J.,* 73:1498–1502.
U.S. Department of Justice Law Enforcement Administration. 1972. Criminal Victimization Survey in San Diego. Washington, D.C., U.S. Department of Justice.
Ziegenhagan, E. A. 1976. The recidivist victim of violent crime. *Victimology,* 1:538–550.

APPENDIX I
VICTIM DATA SHEET

DEMOGRAPHICS

____ 1. Sex of victim: 1. Female   2. Male
____ 2. Marital status:
       1. Single   2. Married   3. Divorced   4. Widowed   5. Separated
____ 3. Ethnic background:
       1. Anglo   2. Chicano/Mexican American   3. Indian   4. Black
       5. Other _____
____ 4. Victim's age: _____
____ 5. Site of initial visit:
       1. Emergency Room (ER)   2. Family Practice Clinic (FPC)
       3. Pediatrics (Peds)   4. Obstetrics/Gyn (Ob-Gyn   5. Other BCMC
       clinic   6. Other hospital   7. Other _____
____ 6. Date of visit to above: ___ / ___ / ___
____ 7. Hour of visit to above: (0000–2400 hours) From _____ until _____
____ 8. Living situation:
       1. Alone   2. W/parents 3. W/spouse   4. W/children   5. W/friends/
       SOP 6. Transient   7. Student housing   8. Institution (jail, etc.)
       9. Other _____
____ 9. How long at present address?
       1. Less than 1 month   2. 1–6 months   3. 6 months–1 year
       4. 1–3 years   5. More than 3 years
____ 10. How long in Albuquerque?
       1. Less than 6 months   2. 6 months–1 year   3. 1–3 years
       4. 3–6 years   5. More than 6 years   6. Not from Albuquerque
____ 11. Number of moves in last three years:
       1. One   2. Two   3. Three   4. Four   5. Five or more 6. No moves
____ 12. Predominant means of financial support:
       1. Self-sufficient   2. Chiefly supported by family   3. Completely
       supported by family   4. Chiefly supported by friends/SOP
       5. Completely supported by friends/SOP   6. Welfare   7. Social
       Security 8. Unemployment
____ 13. Level of occupation:
       1. Unemployed   2. Minimally employed   3. Student
       4. Homemaker   5. Unskilled   6. Semiskilled   7. Skilled, managerial
       8. Professional/administrative
____ 14. Level of occupation of head-of-household:
       1. Unemployed   2. Minimally employed   3. Student
       4. Homemaker   5. Unskilled   6. Semiskilled   7. Skilled, managerial
       8. Professional/administrative
____ 15. Education completed by patient:
       1. 1–6   2. 7–9   3. 10–12   4. Some college   5. Completed college
       6. Some graduate work   7. Completed graduate work

___ 16. Education level of head-of-household:
      1. 1-6 2. 7-9 3. 10-12 4. Some college 5. Completed college
      6. Some graduate work 7. Completed graduate work

HISTORY OF ASSAULT

___ 17. Date of assault: ___ / ___ / ___
___ 18. Day of the week of the assault:
      1. Mon 2. Tues 3. Wed 4. Thurs 5. Fri 6. Sat 7. Sun
___ 19. Time of the assault (0000–2400): From_____ until _____
___ 20. Where was patient accosted?
      1. Own home 2. Friend's home 3. Own vehicle 4. Assailant's
      home 5. Hitchhiking 6. Streets—lot, alley, etc. 7. Private social affair
      8. Public place 9. Bar 10. Other_____
___ 21. Site of the assault:
      1. Own home 2. Friend's home 3. Assailant's home 4. Own
      vehicle 5. Assailant's vehicle 6. Undeveloped areas/countryside
      7. Streets 8. Private social affair 9. Public gathering places
      10. Housing not belonging to patient or assailant
      11. Other _____
___ 22. Assailant's drug use before/during assault (per patient):
      1. Unknown 2. None 3. Alcohol 4. Marijuana 5. Stimulants
      6. Depressants 7. Heroin 8. Inhalants 9. Hallucinogens
      10. Other _____
___ 23. Patient's drug use before/during the assault:
      1. Unknown 2. None 3. Alcohol 4. Marijuana 5. Stimulants
      6. Depressants 7. Heroin 8. Inhalants 9. Hallucinogens
      10. Other _____
___ 24. Number and sex of assailant(s):
      1. One 2. Two 3. Three 4. Four 5. Five or more
      6. Male 7. Female 8. Male and Female 9. Unknown
___ 25. Number of patients:
      1. One 2. Two 3. Three 4. Four 5. Five or more
___ 26. Were there others besides patient(s) and assailant(s) present?
      1. No 2. Yes _____
___ 27. Assailant(s) threatened to use:
      1. No threats 2. Physical violence 3. Concealed weapon
      4. Visible weapon 5. Violence to others 6. Blackmail 7. Death
      if patient reported assault 8. Nonspecific threat of death
      9. Unknown 10. Other _____
___ 28. Assailant(s) actually used:
      1. No force 2. Restraints 3. Physical force – push, grab, throw
      to ground 4. Violent physical force – slap, punch, kick 5. Weapon
      6. Unknown 7. Other _____

___29. Assailant's relationship to victim (for multiple assailants, list all):
    1. Assailant(s) unknown   2. Acquaintance   3. Friend   4. Father
    5. Stepfather   6. Grandfather   7. Uncle/cousin   9. Stepbrother
    10. Husband   11. Ex-husband   12. Authority figure (teacher, bus
    driver, babysitter, etc.)   13. Other _____
___30. Can patient describe assailant(s)?   1. Yes   2. No
___31. Was anything stolen?
    1. No   2. Money   3. Purse   4. Clothes   5. Car   6. Household
    goods   7. Other _____
___32. Acts committed during assault:
    1. Vaginal-penile   2. Anal-penile   3. Oral sex on assailant(s)   4. Oral
    sex on victim   5. Vaginal penetration with fingers or object   6. Anal
    penetration with fingers or object   7. Fondling-molestation only
    8. Unknown   9. Other _____
___33. First person contacted after the assault:
    1. Spouse   2. Family   3. Friend   4. Neighbor   5. RCC   6. Police
    7. ER/FPC   8. Passerby   9. Other _____
___34. Patient brought to ER by:
    1. Spouse   2. Family   3. Friend   4. Neighbor   5. RCC   6. Police
    7. Passerby   8. Self   9. Other _____

PREVIOUS ASSAULT HISTORY

___35. Has the patient been a victim of a sexual assault before?
    1. No   2. Yes, once   3. Yes, more than once   4. Unknown
___36. What occurred during the most recent incident (if there are others,
    code them in SE)?
    1. No previous incident   2. Criminal sexual penetration   3. Exhibi-
    tionism   4. Fondling/molestation only   5. Heterosexual   6. Ho-
    mosexual   7. Other _____
___37. When did the most recent incident occur?
    1. No previous incident   2. Less than 6 months ago   3. 6 months to
    1 year   4. 1–5 years   5. 5–10 years   6. 10–15 years   7. 15–20
    years   8. 20 or more years
___38. In relation to the most recent incident, patient:
    1. No previous incident   2. Told no one   3. Told others only
    4. Told police   5. Received counseling   6. Received medical
    attention   7. Contacted SART/RCC
___39. If incest, was perpetrator of previous incident:
    1. Not incest   2. Parent   3. Stepparent   4. Sibling   5. Cousin
    6. Aunt/uncle   7. Grandparent   8. Other _____
___40. Is there history of incest?   1. No   2. Yes

COUNSELING HISTORY

___41. Has the patient been seen for emotional/psychiatric problems before?
    1. Yes   2. No   3. Unknown

____42. Has the patient been hospitalized for such problems?
    1. Yes, at _____   2. No   3. Unknown
____43. When was the patient seen?
    1. Not seen   2. Presently being seen   3. Stopped less than 6 months
    ago   4. Stopped 6 months–2 years ago   5. 2–5 years   6. More than
    5 years ago   7. Unknown
____44. How long was the patient in therapy?
    1. 1 month or less   2. 2–6 months   3. 6 months–1 year   4. 1–5
    years   5. More than 5 years   6. Not in therapy   7. Unknown
____45. Was the therapy:
    1. On a regular basis (weekly, bimonthly, etc.)   2. Intermittent,
    irregular   3. Single event   4. No therapy   5. Unknown
____46. With whom was the victim in therapy (explain further in SE)?
    1. No therapy 2. RCC 3. SART   4. BCMHC 5. Private practi-
    tioner   6. Other   _____   7. Unknown

| EXAMINATION FINDINGS |

____47. Type of genital trauma:
    1. None   2. Tenderness 3. Contusions 4. Abrasions 5. Lacera-
    tions   6. Penetrating wounds   7. Other   _____
____48. Area of genital trauma:
    1. None 2. Vulva   3. Fourchette 4. Introitus   5. Vagina
    6. Cervix 7. Perineum   8. Rectum   9. Other male trauma _____
    _____   10. Other   _____
____49. Type of nongenital trauma:
    1. None 2. Tenderness 3. Contusions 4. Abrasions 5. Lacera-
    tions   6. Penetrating wounds   7. Fractures/Dislocations
    8. Concussion 9. Other   _____
____50. Area of nongenital trauma:
    1. None 2. Head 3. Face   4. Neck 5. Arms 6. Breast
    7. Abdomen 8. Back and other trunk wounds   9. Legs
____51. Non-assault-related abnormalities:
    1. No   2. Yes,   _____
____52. Patient's observable affect when first encountered by SART member:
    1. Calm/composed   2. Tearful/sad 3. Anxious/agitated
    4. Fearful/withdrawn 5. Mute/flat 6. Stuporous   7. Inappro-
    priate 8. Histrionic
____53. Changes in affect:
    1. No change   2. Changed for the better   3. Changed for the
    worse (describe in SE)
____54. Patient's emotional state upon first encounter:
    1. Happy 2. Sad 3. Angry 4. Frightened 5. Guilt-ridden
    6. Other   _____

___ 55. Changes in patient's emotional state:
    1. No changes 2. Increased in level 3. Decreased in level
    4. Changed emotions, same level 5. Changed and increased in level
    6. Changed and decreased in level
___ 56. Patient's emotional state on discharge:
    1. No change 2. Changed for the better 3. Changed for the
    worse (describe in SE)
___ 57. Patient's demonstrated thought processes upon first encounter:
    1. Alert/coherent 2. Slow/impeded 3. Disorganized
    4. Delusional 5. Unconscious 6. Intoxicated
    7. Other _____
___ 58. Changes in thought processes: (describe changes in SE):
    1. Stayed the same 2. Improved 3. Deteriorated
___ 59. Did the patient appear intoxicated? If so, indicate level:
    1. Not intoxicated 2. Slightly (mild breath odor of ETOH or HX of
    drinking) 3. Speech slurred, uncoordinated movements, obvious
    odor of ETOH 4. Comatose
___ 60. Who was with the patient in the ER/clinic?
    1. No one 2. Parent(s) 3. Sibling(s)/other relative(s)
    4. Spouse 5. Police 6. SOP 7. Friend(s) 8. RCC advocate
    9. Neighbor(s) 10. Other _____
___ 61. Reactions of those in ER/clinic with patient:
    1. Not applicable 2. Agitated 3. Angry about incident 4. Hostile
    to staff 5. Worried/concerned 6. Supportive/empathetic
    7. Fearful 8. Histrionic 9. Sullen 10. Detached
    11. Other _____
___ 62. Assessment of support system in patient's life (quality):
    1. Good support 2. Tenuous support 3. Poor support 4. No
    support 5. Not known
___ 63. Support assessment (chief source):
    1. Parent(s)/sibling(s) 2. Spouse/SOP 3. Other relatives/
    children 4. Friends 5. No support 6. Unknown
    7. Other _____

LAB RESULTS

___ 64. Urine pregnancy test:
    1. Positive (+) 2. Negative (–) 3. Not done: reason _____
___ 65. Wet mount slide for sperm:
    1. Positive (+) 2. Negative (–) 3. Not done
___ 66. Sperm present on Pap smear:
    1. Positive (+) 2. Negative (–) 3. Not done
___ 67. Vaginal gonococcus test:
    1. Positive 2. Negative 3. Not done
___ 68. Pharyngeal gonococcus test:
    1. Positive 2. Negative 3. Not done

___ 69. Rectal gonococcus test:
    1. Positive   2. Negative   3. Not done
___ 70. Rapid Plasma Reagent (RPR) for syphilis:
    1. Positive   2. Negative   3. Not done
___ 71. Pap smear:
    1. Positive   2. Negative   3. "Suspected"   4. Other _____
    5. Not done
___ 72. Other tests done (blood alcohol, urine chemistry, etc.):
    1. No   2. Yes: Test(s) _____
                 Result(s) _____

| MEDICATIONS |

___ 73. Antipregnancy medication (APM) prescribed:
    1. DES   2. IUD   3. Other _____   4. None
___ 74. If no pregnancy preventative used, give reason:
    1. APM was used   2. Prepubertal   3. Postmenopausal 4. Birth
    control in use   5. Pregnancy unlikely at time of cycle, etc.
    6. Sterilization Hx (tubes ligated, hysterectomy, etc.)   7. Contra-
    indicated by other Hx (CA, emboli Hx)   8. Suspected pregnancy
    9. Patient refused, reason _____
    10. Other _____
___ 75. Antiemetic prescribed:
    1. No   2. Compazine   3. Tigan 4. Other _____
___ 76. Antibiotics administered:
    1. None, reason _____   2. Procaine penicillin
    (Wycillin) 3. Ampicillin   4. Tetracycline   5. Other _____
___ 77. Probenecid (Benemid) administered:
    1. No   2. Yes
___ 78. Tetanus toxoid administered:
    1. No   2. Yes, reason _____
___ 79. Other medications administered or prescribed:
    1. No   2. Yes _____

| FOLLOW UP |

___ 80. Patient's interest in follow-up, at initial contact:
    1. Refuses follow-up   2. Not interested   3. Ambivalent 4. Fairly
    interested   5. Very interested
___ 81. Support system's interest in follow-up:
    1. No support system at first contact   2. Refuse follow-up   3. Not
    interested   4. Ambivalent   5. Fairly interested   6. Very interested
___ 82. Was a follow-up appointment scheduled?
    1. Yes   2. No, reason _____

___83. Was the follow-up appointment kept?
    1. Yes (attach report)   2. No, plans _____
    3. No follow-up scheduled
___84. Where was initial follow-up appointment?
    1. No follow-up   2. FPC   3. Patient's home   4. Phone
    5. Other _____

EPILOGUE

___85. Which law agency was contacted?
    1. None   2. APD   3. BC sheriff   4. Other sheriff   5. APS security
    6. Tribal police, tribe or pueblo _____
    7. FBI   8. Other _____
___86. If present, was (were) law enforcement officer(s):
    1. Not present   2. Cooperative and understanding to patient
    3. Cooperative with patient and staff   4. Not cooperative
___87. Does patient wish to prosecute:
    1. Yes.   2. No, reasons _____
    3. Undecided
___88. Was evidence collected?
    1. Yes   2. No, reasons _____
___89. Evaluation of RCC advocate:
    1. Not called   2. Called, but not present   3. Helpful to patient
    4. Helpful to patient and staff   5. Not helpful to patient and staff
___90. Evaluation of ER/clinic staff:
    1. Cooperative and understanding to patient   2. Cooperative with
    patient and you   3. Not cooperative
___91. Examination done by:
    1. Ob-Gyn   2. FP   3. Peds   4. ER   5. Other _____
___92. Evaluation of doctor:
    1. Cooperative and understanding to patient   2. Cooperative with
    patient and you   3. Not cooperative

SUBJECTIVE EVALUATION

Name: _____   Date of Birth: _____
Hospital #: _____   Chart #: _____
Address: _____   Phone #: _____
Doctor: _____   Start: _____
RCC Advocate: _____
Additional Comments:

Please indicate on the graphs below any injuries found during examination:

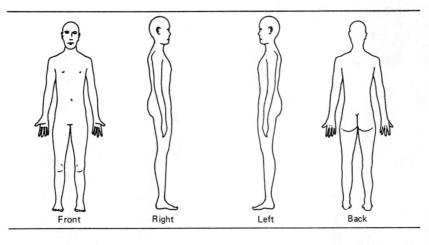

Front   Right   Left   Back

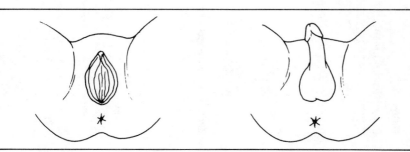

FOLLOW-UP REPORT

Name: _____

Date of Birth: _____

Subjective Comments: _____

Date of Follow-Up: _____

	1	2	3	4	5
Sleep Disorders	Sleeping well	Mild; episodic nightmares; broken sleep	Moderate; difficulty falling asleep; nightmares	Severe; 1-3 hours sleep per night; early morn awaking; stressful nightmares	No sleep; awake all night most nights; sleep-deprived state
Appetite	No noticeable change	Very little change; not quite as much food intake as before assault	Moderate change; eating less food less frequently	Severe; no appetite, eating out of habit	Hardly eating at all; prodded by others to eat
Phobias	Calm and relaxed	Mild suspicion; little change in life-style/habits	Moderate suspicion; some fears expressed, change in life-style moderate	Severe; fears dominating life; seeking help; anxiety immobilizing	Succumbed to fear; will not leave home, answer telephone, or talk with nonfamily

Score	Motor Behavior	Relations	Self-blame	Self-esteem	Somatic Reactions
1	Calm and relaxed	SOP(s) supportive, understanding, and patient	Free from guilt, accepts event	Feels good about self	No symptoms; none reported and symptoms denied when asked about a specific area
2	Mild restlessness; expressed desire to make changes in work or home life	Relationship(s) intact, strained but supportive	Mild guilt, feels it can be overcome	Occasionally doubts self-worth	Mild symptoms; minor discomfort reported; ability to talk about discomfort and feeling of control over symptom
3	Restlessness and dissatisfaction with indecisiveness, reduction in activities	Relationship(s) showing stress, nonsupportive, weakened	Moderate guilt, feels responsible	Disappointed with self; feels badly about self	Moderate symptoms; ability to function but some disturbance of life-style
4	Job or home change; reduction in activities; lack of interest, self-control	Severe tension, anxiety; relationship(s) disintegrating	Severe guilt; blames self, feels dirty, cheap	Disgusted with self	Severe symptoms; distressing symptoms described, life-style disrupted
5	Uprooting of life (job and home); no activities	Denial of or from SOP(s); broken relationship with family, partner, friend	Overcome with shame; feels cannot forgive self	Feels worthless or hates self; completely unsatisfied with self	Compounded symptoms directly related to the assault plus reactivation of symptoms connected to a previous condition; e.g., heavy drinking or drug use

10
Sexual Assault of the Older Woman

Dorothy J. Hicks, M.D.
Denise M. Moon, B.S.

ABSTRACT

The rape of the older woman is something that many people fail to understand and are unable to accept. Since the number of older rape victims is comparatively small, the assumption is made that this is not a significant problem. However, the impact of this experience on these victims is usually severe and requires longer and more intensive care from all persons involved. The medical treatment of the older victim is essentially the same as that of the younger patient, but the incidence of injury is increased. The physical and psychological impact of these injuries is intensified in the older patient and increases her feelings of helplessness and dependency. Crisis intervention therapy is the treatment method most commonly used with rape victims of all ages and is an acceptable method for the older patient. This is discussed and examples are given. Outreach services are essential for this age group because of physical, psychological, or financial problems.

> Right after the rape, I wouldn't leave the house. Even now, I don't go out of the house unless I go with my husband or the children or someone else. I won't walk anywhere. I'm always frightened. If we take the dog for a walk, I always look behind me. I don't think it will ever pass. It's horrible; it's like living a nightmare.

Pauline, a 60-year-old woman, was a rape victim. Like so many other women throughout the United States, the horror of that night remains with her. However, with Pauline, the nightmare has changed her life so drastically that even now, some three years later, she still suffers from it. She has moved twice and separated from her husband of 40 years. While she was still living with her husband, her sex life was minimal; now it is nonexistent. She has become almost totally dependent on her grown children, and this has created immense pressures within their respective families.

As her dependency increased and she required more support and care from her children, her feelings of guilt intensified. The relationships, nurtured for decades, started to deteriorate, and she was forced to face her own inadequacies and insecurities. Pauline's reactions are not unusual for the older rape victim.

Although emotional and medical reactions to sexual assault are always present, in the older age groups these reactions seems to be more prolonged and more severe. The seriousness of the problems faced by these victims has never been fully realized because underreporting is prevalent in this group, and the numbers are relatively small. Estimates on underreporting in this age group range from 30% to as high as 95%, or 19 out of 20 rapes are not reported. (Law Enforcement Assistance Administration, 1977). Older rape victims, because of their shame and embarrassment, are less likely to report the rape even if they report other facets of the incident.

Attempted sexual assaults are known to be much higher in this age group than statistics reveal, and rape-homocide data reflect that this victim has an increased probability of being murdered at the time of the rape. (Dade County, 1982).

Other statistics reveal that not only is the number of rapes in this population not realized, but also the intensity of the impact on this victim has not been appreciated. In our series, the majority of older victims were assaulted in their homes, and this invasion intensifies feelings of insecurity. Eighty-eight percent were assaulted by someone unknown to the victim; in the younger age group, only 36% were not acquainted with the attacker. Twenty-one percent of these older women were raped by multiple offenders; only 9% in the other groups were victims of gang rapes. Both of these factors aggravate the rape trauma.

This trauma is compounded by the widely accepted misconception that all rape victims are young and beautiful. In our series, 33% of the victims were between the ages of 19 and 25 years, but 30% were below the age of 16, and 5% were more than 50 years old. In this older age group, 1% were between 65 and 74 years, and 1% were 75 and older. The oldest patient was a 93-year-old woman.

The belief that older women do not get raped is still prevalent in our society, and it is a myth that has been passed on from generation to generation. Most people do not associate rape with anger, hostility, and sexual deviancy, but rather with sexual passion. It is difficult for the older population to understand the reasons behind their rape victimization because they do not see themselves as sex objects.

In the report, *Florida's Plan to Reduce Crime Against the Elderly* [L.E.A.A. 1980.], it was stated that the problems of crime against the elderly must not be measured by the frequency, but rather the effect upon the victim. In a L.E.A.A. study, *Rape Victimization in 26 American Cities* (1979), a completion index was used to illustrate this. This index is obtained by dividing the rate of completed rapes by the rate of attempted rapes. The resulting ratio indicates the relative risk of becoming a victim of a completed rape attack. Although the rate of victimization for the older group is quite low, the completion ratio was the highest of any age group (1.07). Because completed rape attacks are more serious than attempted rapes, the victimization suffered by the older victim is usually more severe.

Not only do older rape victims face a higher probability of a more severe rape victimization, but they face other problems because of their relative fraility. The difficulties experienced by these older victims are not unique but are intensified by such variables as age, their perception of the crime itself, and their overall fearfulness. The younger victim usually possesses the resiliency to overcome the attending psychic, financial, and physical hardships imposed,but the older victim may never recover from this experience without special attention and long-term support.

Older victims cannot conceive the crime to be an act of hostility because they are indoctrinated by society's myth that rape is an act of passion. When such a woman is raped the reality of the experience strikes her, and only through counseling does she begin to understand the dynamics of the crime and desexualize the act.

Another variable is the fearfulness characteristic of this generation. A recent survey from the national Criminal Justice Information and Statistics Services (L.E.A.A., 1980) indicated that there are four major problem areas:

1. Fear of attacks by adults
2. Fear of attacks by youths
3. Fear of property theft
4. Fear of vandalism

These fears may be part of the victim's environment prior to the attack and are intensified by the rape. Therefore, these concerns must be explored and dissipated during counseling.

In our society there are inherent values that incorporate a prototype of its older population. Davis and Brody (1979) state that "Surely, if the prevailing belief is that an older woman is physically weak, emotionally distressed, fearful and incompetent, she will be viewed by the rapist as an easy victim." Although this picture of the older population is not universal, these are characteristic traits associated with aging that may make it difficult for the older victim to react or resist an attack. These distinctive features are both psychological and physical. If he senses of sight and hearing are decreased, the older woman may not notice the intruder coming into her home. Skeletal and neuromuscular changes seen in the frail elderly impair their ability to move or turn quickly, and they do not have the agility and power required to fight off an assailant. Other characteristics of the aging process, such as hypertension, heart conditions, and arthritis, compound the problem.

For the purpose of this chapter, the victim population will consist of all women over 50 years of age. We have included the 50 to 65 age group because their feelings are more similar to those of the elderly than to those of premenopausal women.

MEDICAL ASPECTS

All rape victims, regardless of their age, should be offered medical examination and treatment as well as counseling as soon as possible after the attack. It should not be necessary to report the crime to the police for this care to be given. Ideally, this should be done in a quiet area adjacent to a hospital emergency room that is equipped to handle trauma of any degree. This is especially true for the older women because they are more likely than the younger victims to have injuries. In 1981, in our center, 63% of victims in the older age group had body trauma compared to the overall incidence of 19%. Thirty-eight percent had vaginal trauma; the overall incidence was only 5%.

Once the victim reaches the hospital she becomes a patient and merits all the confidentiality that term engenders. Everyone who comes into contact with her should be sensitive to the needs of a rape victim. She should be taken to an area that will ensure her privacy, but she should never be left alone (Halpern et al., 1978). The patient should be allowed to talk freely, but no pressure should be put on her. At this time only the required consent forms should be signed, and the information necessary to generate a chart extracted. (See Figure 10-1.) The older victim usually needs more reassurance that she is safe. If she wishes to have a friend with her during her examination, this should be allowed.

A nurse or counselor should be with the patient as much as possible and always during the examination. This staff person plays a supportive role only, but may explain to the patient the procedures during the examination. No patient should be forced to have an examination, but no treatment should be prescribed or given without one.

The physician should arrive as soon as possible after the patient is in the area (Hicks, 1980). If the police are there the examiner may wish to get some of the history from the officers, but at no time should the police, regardless of their sex, be allowed in the examining room. The examiner elicits only history necessary for the medical evaluation. Investigation of the crime is a job for law enforcement personnel, not medical people. Those facts not needed for the medical chart may jeopardize the case when it is prosecuted because details gathered immediately after the fact may be inaccurate.

The date, time, and place of the examination should be written on the chart. The date and time of the assault should be documented. The actual

RAPE TREATMENT CENTER

JACKSON MEMORIAL HOSPITAL   UNIVERSITY OF MIAMI SCHOOL OF MEDICINE

PATIENTS
ADDRESS _____

PLACE OF EXAM _____ DATE: _____

PERSONAL HISTORY   TIME: _____

PARA __ __ __ __ GR. _____

LMP DATE _____ NORMAL ABNORMAL

LAST COITUS: DATE _____ TIME: _____

CONTRACEPTION: YES NO TYPE: _____

DOUCHE BATH DEFECATE VOID SINCE ASSAULT

VENEREAL DISEASE: YES NO TYPE _____ RX _____

HEPATITIS YES NO WHEN _____ RX _____

HISTORY OF ASSAULT _____

DATE: _____ TIME: _____

LOCATION: _____

NO OF ASSAILANTS _____ RACE: B W L O UNK

ATTACKER: KNOWN _____ UNK _____ RELATIVE _____

THREATS: YES NO TYPE _____

RESTRAINTS: YES NO TYPE _____

WEAPON: YES NO TYPE _____

RESIST YES NO

           ORAL ANAL VAGINAL DIGITAL FOR. BODY
TYPE OF SEX: ____ ____ _____ _____ _____

PENETRATION: ____ ____ _____ _____ _____

EJACULATION: ____ ____ _____ _____ _____

COMMENTS: _____

BIRTHDATE _____ RACE ____ M S W D SEP

POLICE DEPT. _____ CASE # _____

OFFICER _____

GENERAL EXAM: (bruises, trauma, lacerations, marks)
NO HISTORY

PELVIC EXAM: (include signs of trauma, bleeding, foreign bodies)

VULVA _____

HYMEN _____

VAGINA _____

CERVIX _____

FUNDUS _____

ADNEXAE _____

RECTAL _____

| PAGE 1 | SEXUAL BATTERY FORM |

Figure 10-1A.

FILE COPY

RAPE TREATMENT CENTER
MIAMI, FLORIDA

JACKSON MEMORIAL HOSPITAL   UNIVERSITY OF MIAMI SCHOOL OF MEDICINE

PHYSICIAN_____NURSE_____COUNSELOR_____

TESTS   HEIGHT_____   WEIGHT_____   **TREATMENT**

GC CULTURE: ORAL ANAL CERVICAL OTHER_____   V.D. PROPHYLAXIS: YES NO TYPE_____

VDRL: YES NO (5cc venous blood - red top)   PREGNANCY PROPHYLAXIS: YES NO TYPE_____

PAP TEST: YES NO   TETANUS: YES NO OTHER MEDS:_____

EVIDENTIAL SPECIMENS, TESTING AND RECEIPT

RESULTS OF PRELIMINARY TESTS: A.P.: NEGATIVE WEAK MODERATE STRONG

SPERM: NONE 1-5   6-10   10 +   MOTILE   NON-MOTILE

SPECIMENS OBTAINED:	GIVEN TO POLICE	OTHER TREATMENT
10 cc VENOUS BLOOD (red top)_____	_____	X-RAY_____
FINGER NAIL SCRAPINGS _____	_____	SURGICAL CONSULT _____
PUBIC HAIR COMBINGS _____	_____	PSYCH. CONSULT_____
VAGINAL { SMEAR_____ SWAB_____	_____	OTHER: (Explain)_____ _____
CERVICAL { SMEAR_____ SWAB_____	_____	_____
VAGINAL ASPIRATE _____	_____	_____
RECTAL { SMEAR_____ SWAB_____	_____	_____
ORAL { SMEAR_____ SWAB_____	_____	_____
SALIVA SPECIMEN_____	_____	GIVEN TO POLICE

CLOTHING (number)_____ { TYPE_____
CONDITION_____

FOREIGN BODIES (number) _____ { TYPE_____
LOCATION_____

OTHER SPECIMENS_____   PHOTOGRAPHS: YES NO TAKEN BY_____

TOTAL NUMBER SPECIMENS   **TOTAL TO POLICE**

RECEIPT OF EVIDENCE: THE ABOVE EVIDENCE HAS BEEN RECEIVED BY ME ON (DATE) _____ AT

(TIME)_____   (OFFICER'S SIGNATURE)_____

PHYSICIANS SIGNATURE: _____

WITNESS SIGNATURE_____

JMH-02-2082-0
9-1-78

PAGE 2 | **SEXUAL BATTERY FORM**

Figure 10-1B.

location is not necessary, but the general area where the assault took place should be noted.

A past history is essential with the older patient. Does she have any chronic diseases or conditions for which she is taking medication? When was her last menstrual period? Has she undergone any gynecologic surgery recently or in the past? When was the date of her last consensual intercourse? It should never be assumed that the older patient is not sexually active. Has she ever had venereal disease; if so, what kind and was she treated for it? Has she had hepatitis?

The history of the attack should be taken by the physician, and the patient's own words used as much as possible. Was there violence? Was she restrained by being held or was she actually tied up? Older women often have increased capillary fragility and will bruise much more easily than the younger victims. It is common to find discolored areas from the pressure of the rapist's fingers on the woman's body, especially on the neck, arms, breasts, and inner thighs. Did the attacker have a weapon? Did she know him? How many men took part in the assault? It is important that the physician ask the patient exactly what the rapist did. Was there fellatio, sodomy, vaginal penetration? Did he ejaculate? Did he ejaculate on or wipe the penis on any part of her body? In many cases, the older patient will not tell the police that these things happened because she is too ashamed and embarrassed to admit it; she will tell the doctor.

A statement about the emotional condition of the patient may be made, but again, this should not be in detail. A blood screen for drugs or alcohol is not necessary unless requested by the police.

Although the woman who is only a few years postmenopausal is usually not difficult to examine, the elderly and especially the frail elderly can pose many problems. Most of these older women must be assisted onto the table and have difficulty lying there in a dorsal position unless the head of the table is elevated. The patient must be comfortable if the examination is to be successful.

A general inspection of the patient should be done in a good light so that any injuries can be seen easily. Any foreign materials, that is, sand, dirt, grass, etc., should be put in a clean envelope and sealed. Findings not related to the rape do not need documentation, and the mention of tattoos and old scars may prejudice a jury. Contusions, lacerations, abrasions, ecchymoses, etc., however, should be accurately described. At the present time, the size of any lesion should be documented in inches. American juries cannot visualize the size of a bruise if it is described in centimeters.

Bite marks are extremely important, and whenever possible a forensic dentist should be consulted. This science is now so precise that in some cases tooth marks can provide absolute identification of the offender.

If the attacker deposited semen on the victim's face or body, a Woods lamp should be available. Semen on the skin glistens pale yellow but when viewed under this filtered ultraviolet light will fluoresce. Specimens may be obtained by moistening cotton swabs with saline and carefully wiping the stains from the skin surface. These swabs should then be put into a container and sent to the forensic laboratory for testing.

Broken fingernails should be clipped and put into a clean envelope; it may be possible to match them with a fragments found at the scene of the crime. An orange stick may be used to take scrapings from under the nails. The material should be placed in a clean envelope and sealed.

The pubic hair should be combed for any foreign material. The comb and combings should be placed in a clean envelope and sealed. Several pubic hairs from the patient should be plucked and placed in a second envelope and sealed.

Examination of the pelvic area in the elderly age group is especially important because the elasticity of the tissues decreases with aging and the lack of estrogen, and injury to these tissues is common. This is especially true in those women who are virginal or who have never delivered a child vaginally. Many of these patients cannot abduct their thighs enough to allow them to use the stirrups on the pelvic table, and it is necessary to do the examination with patient in a lateral, rather than the lithotomy, position.

Since the primary emotion experienced by the rape victim is fear, there is usually no physiologic lubrication during a rape and these victims are sore. The pelvic examination should never be hurried. The perineal area should be inspected carefully and any erythema, abrasions, or lacerations described. A Pederson speculum should be moistened with water (lubricating jelly will interfere with the forensic tests) and carefully inserted into the vaginal canal. On occasion, it may be necessary to use a pediatric speculum.

Any secretions in the vagina should be described. The vaginal vault and sidewalls should be inspected. They often are lacerated during a rape because the elasticity of the vaginal epithelium is decreased. Swabs should be taken from the distal portion of the vagina and from the fornices. The endocervical canal should be avoided unless it has been at least a week since the last sexual exposure. Air-dried smears should be made, and the swabs placed in sterile tubes. These tubes must not be airtight or the specimens may be destroyed because moisture buildup within the tube allows overgrowth of bacteria and mold. An aspirate may be made of the vaginal secretions by injecting two cubic centimeters of normal saline into the vagina canal, retrieving it, and putting the liquid into a capped tube. This material may be examined immediately for the presence or absence of sperm, and motility may be determined. A culture for gonorrhea should be taken from the endocervical canal, plated on Thayer-Martin or similar media, placed in a carbon dioxide environment almost immediately, and incubated as soon as possible.

A bimanual pelvic examination should be done to be sure there is no preexisting pathology. Any tenderness in the lower abdomen that may be secondary to the rape should be noted.

If there was sodomy, the perirectal area should be examined. Since these tissues are also atrophying, injury is common. Any evidence of forced entry should be described. Swabs and smears may be made, but they must be free of feces. The tone of the rectal sphincter should be noted. A culture for gonorrhea should be taken. A finger examination of the rectum should be done, and when indicated, an anoscope should be used.

If fellatio was performed, swabs should be taken from the cheek pouches and the oral cavity and a culture for gonorrhea taken from the nasopharynx.

Blood samples should be drawn and placed in red-topped tubes. One sample is for a serology, and the second is sent to the forensic laboratory to be used for typing.

A specimen of saliva should be collected from the patient as a routine. This is sent to the forensic laboratory and may be used to determine the secretor status of the victim. A small square of clean cloth chewed by the victim and handled by no one except the victim may be used for this purpose.

A forensic laboratory should do the sophisticated testing, but preliminary examination of the vagina aspirate and the swabs can be done at the time of the examination. A wet mount made from the aspirate and looked at under the high power of a microscope will identify sperm and determine the presence or absence of motility.

If no sperm are seen, the swabs and the aspirate can be tested for the presence of acid phosphatase. Acid phosphatase (ACP) is an enzyme found in many body fluids but is in high concentration in seminal fluid. If a qualitative test is positive, this is generally accepted to mean that semen is present (Gomez et al., 1975).

It is not necessary to do all the procedures on every victim. The examination and tests should be tailored to the facts of the particular case.

The serology and the cultures for gonorrhea should be sent to the appropriate laboratory in the hospital as soon as possible.

The evidential specimens are properly labeled with the patient's name, date of collection, and initials of the examiner, and placed in a paper bag. This sack is then sealed, initialed, and handed directly to a police officer whenever possible. A property receipt should be obtained. Signatures are required each time the specimens are transferred from one person to another if the chain of evidence is to be preserved. This evidence will then be valid for trial.

Whenever possible, photographs of any significant physical findings should be taken by the police. There is then no question of a break in the chain, and the photographs are invaluable at a trial.

Any clothing that may be used as evidence should be initialed and placed in a paper sack, which should be sealed appropriately. Plastic bags should never be used because the overgrowth of bacteria will destroy seminal stains.

The physician must remember that rape is a legal term, not a medical diagnosis, and the doctor can say only that the results of the examination do or do not support the history.

Medical Treatment

Prevention of pregnancy is not an issue in treating the older woman who has been raped, but there is still the fear of venereal disease, and prophylaxis for syphilis and gonorrhea should be offered to these victims. No patient should be forced to take any treatment.

If the patient is not allergic to penicillin, Probenecid, one gram orally followed by 4.8 million units of aqueous procaine penicillin intramuscularly, will treat gonorrhea and incubating syphilis.

If the patient is allergic to penicillin, Spectinomycin, two grams intermuscularly, is specific for gonorrhea.

Oral medications may be used: Doxycycline, 300 milligrams orally followed in one hour by 300 milligrams orally; or Tetracycline, 1.5 grams orally followed by 500 milligrams four times a day for four days.

Tetanus toxoid should be offered to the victim when indicated.

The patient should be reexamined six weeks after the assault. At this time she should have a general examination and the serology and gonorrhea cultures should be repeated. This is also a good time to reassess her psychological adjustment if she has not taken advantage of the counseling sessions offered at the time of the initial examination.

PSYCHOLOGICAL ASPECTS

The emotional reaction of the older rape victim should be evaluated on several levels: the prerape level, the rape level, and the postrape level. It is critical to thoroughly explore and understand all the factors that may influence the reaction of the older rape victim. (See Figure 10-2.)

Prerape Factors	Rape Factors	Postrape Factors
Age	How did the rape happen?	Did the victim tell anyone?
Sex	Who did it?	Support services offered?
Race	What was done?	Support services received
Marital status	Amount of aggression	Family support
Self-esteem	Theft involvement	Legal intervention
Sexual Awareness	Where did it happen?	Financial assistance
Coping mechanisms	Physical harm	Ability to make changes in
Support	How long did it take?	environment
Financial status	When did it happen?	Overall mobility
Living environment		Physical recovery rate
Value system		

Fig. 10-2

Although the younger rape victim is influenced by the same prerape factors, the problems of the older woman are intensified because of her age, a significant factor. She will have a heightened reaction to the aggressive aspect of the rape and experience increased feelings of vulnerability because of her lessened effectiveness.

Another factor that appears to impact on the older victim's reaction is her decreased financial flexibility. She may have neither the resources nor the economic support from family members to change her immediate environment and may be forced to remain in the home where the rape occurred. This in itself creates many problems. If the victim feels threatened in this environment and relocation is impossible, it is important that she realizes that changes within this setting are essential if she is to deal with the fear of future victimization. The counselor should link her with agencies that may provide her with funds for securing her home, that is, changing locks, repairing broken windows, etc. The victim should be guided, not forced, to make these changes or it may only intensify her feelings of inadequacy.

The mores and values of this generation are other prerape factors that may increase the older victim's difficulties in adjusting to this experience. These values make it hard for the older woman to understand her own victimization, increasing the change that she will have adjustment problems. For example, a 65-year-old woman claimed that it was impossible for her to ventilate her feelings about the rape to her husband, nor could she discuss the sexual details of the assault; people in this generation do not speak of these things.

In most cases a woman in this age group represents the classical role of wife and mother in the family unit. Along with this model are inherent characteristics that may pose problems for the older victim. In this role her needs are secondary to those of her husband and children. It is difficult for the older woman to recognize that after a rape her own needs are the primary concern; therefore she experiences increased feelings of guilt and anxiety. A 68-year-old woman once related that although she was frightened to go to the market alone, she refused to ask for assistance from her husband or children; she did not want to burden them. As a counselor, it is essential in this situation to involve the complete family unit and explore these feelings.

The rape factors, the who, what, when, where, and how conditions of the act itself, create more severe reactions in the older victim. Sexual acts such as fellatio and sodomy may be foreign or even abhorrant to this age group and intensify her feeling dirty and spoiled. It is essential for the counselor to understand that these victims may have had a sexual relationship with only one man. This experience may disrupt a pleasant and nonthreatening memory of a former mate, or impose new problems on an existing sexual life-style. The older victim may not have the resiliency to accept these changes.

Some women in this age group have minimal emotional support, and the reason for their existence is the memory of a deceased loved one. If this is so, the rape exaggerates their feelings of emptiness and loneliness. Usually such a victim will need long-term treatment if she is to recover. Activities and social interaction must be encouraged or this woman will fail to improve.

If there is a present partner he should be evaluated to determine his need for counseling. Resistance from the partner is not uncommon, however, because he is usually of the same generation and also may have problems discussing sexual issues.

The postrape factors affect the older victim to a greater degree than the younger one. Whether or not she tells anyone about the assault, the care received, the level of acceptance by her family, the support from outside agencies, the recovery rate from physical injuries, and her overall ability to accept change are important elements. She may feel disgraced and hesitant to talk about the assault. Because of increased shame and humiliation, this victim may never tell anyone that she was assaulted. Even speaking the word *rape* is almost impossible for her.

Another factor that may be augmented by the rape and by the family's reaction to it is the victim's feelings of helplessness and lack of control. Generally when an older woman, especially a frail one, gets raped, she is forced to recognize her inability to control her life. This may impact on her self-concept, her socialization patterns, and her family dynamics. Previous conflicts of dependency, which are characteristic of a child or adolescent, are brought back. These feelings must be dealt with in counseling. Family members should understand these dependency issues and not attempt to control the victim in their efforts to "do what's best."

Crisis Intervention with the Older Victim

As soon as the needs of the older victim are identified at all three levels, it is necessary to develop a treatment plan and implement it. Treatment methods for the older victim do not differ significantly from those used with younger ones; however, the former need more intensive follow-up to help them recover.

The most common form of therapy used with victims of sexual assault is crisis intervention. Rape is a situational crisis that results from an unanticipated traumatic event (Hoff, 1978). The crisis model, in brief, consists of the impact stage, the recoil-turmoil stage, the adjustment stage, and the reconstruction stage. The rape trauma syndrome is similar to the crisis sequence and consists of the acute, the outward adjustment, and the resolution stages.

In the acute stage, the victim may experience hysteria, fear, and denial. In the outward adjustment stage, the victim usually appears to have coped with the crisis. The resolution stage is that period when the victim has the need to understand feelings that may have been dealt with only superficially during the other phases.

In the older woman, these stages are basically the same as in the younger victim. However, the older woman often does not have the emotional or the physical resources to recover as quickly as her younger counterpart and may take longer to move through these stages. Some older victims may never fully resolve this experience.

The predominant emotions experienced by these older victims during the acute reaction stage are denial and fear. Most women have problems believing that they have been a victim of rape: "It happens to other people." The older victim has had more years to reinforce th is belief, and the common misconception that rape only happens to attractive young women supports her feelings. Difficulties arise when the victim is forced to accept her own victimization. The older woman feels more comfortable believing that it was only a nightmare.

> Alice was a 72-year-old woman who lived alone and was raped in her home by a young male. During the medical examination, she was hysterical and kept repeating, "I can't believe this has happened to me" (Alice, 1978).

Alice, like so many older victims, continued to deny the rape experience. Repeated attempts to contact her only resulted in her adamant refusal to seek further assistance. After the attack, she did not leave her home and her physical and mental condition continued to deteriorate. She refused to admit anyone into her home to help her and eventually required hospitalization for malnutrition.

While in the hospital, Alice was contacted by the counseling staff, and she stated that if she acknowledged the rape, then she would be useless and out of control. When she realized that the rape was something that she could not forget, it was too late for her to do anything about it by herself, "I had lost control of my whole life" (Alice, 1978). Once she accepted counseling, she began to recover and is now functioning at a satisfactory level.

It is essential that the counselor develop a strong alliance with the older victim during the initial contact, which may be the only opportunity the counselor has to talk with her. Immediate bonding with the counselor is critical so that the older victim understands that she is not alone and that there are people willing to help her.

The counselor can be effective with this age victim by supporting her so that she will not feel threatened by the rape experience. This victim must realize that the nightmare will not go away, and she must face it. A method we find useful is to go with the victim and discuss the episode in her own home. This may be frightening to the older victim; however, it is essential for her to know that she can learn to control her feelings about the rape in her own environment.

Another feeling that surfaces during the acute stage is that of fear. Since most assaults of this age woman happen in her home she does not feel safe there, yet is afraid to leave. The older victim feels more vulnerable because of her lack of physical prowess to defend herself against future attacks. Trapped by her fear, she may withdraw and become a recluse. The mere presence of helping professionals in her immediate surroundings can ease this fear. Open discussions about the incident will increase the victim's awareness and may prevent future attacks.

Involving the older victim with agencies such as senior crime watch groups can give her a support system composed of people who usually have the same values, mores, and attitudes. This kind of agency linkage should be done during the acute phase of the victim's emotional recovery. The counselor may not have the opportunity to do this at a later date.

Ethel, a 58-year-old woman, came to the rape center for her first counseling appointment three days after the assault. At that time, she claimed that she "felt fine" and did not need further treatment. She stated that the day after the rape, she returned to work as a volunteer at a local hospital and felt like "nothing had happened" (Ethel, 1980).

For Ethel, the acute stage had lasted only one day and she had moved into the outward adjustment stage. She felt "wonderful." This victim appeared to have fully recovered from the rape. Unfortunately, this recovery was short-lived.

Because of the dynamics of her role in the family unit, the older victim feels compelled to go on with her life as if nothing had happened to her. She is the one in the family who has been designated by classical role modeling as the person who deals with and resolves everyone else's problems. She believes her feelings should be secondary to those of her husband and children. This kind of family structure can be detrimental as it frequently forces an older victim into the outward adjustment stage before the counselor can lay the groundwork for any discussions of her feelings. On the other hand, if the older victim is unable to move into the outward adjustment stage, her feelings may be compounded by the guilt of placing "unnecessary burdens" on her family, and her problems become intensified.

The role of the counselor in this second stage is supportive and educational. It is necessary that the victim understand that these feelings of relief may be only temporary, and she must be aware that negative feelings about the rape may surface in the future. This support should be given with the utmost sensitivity.

Ethel, who had felt "wonderful," returned for her medical reevaluation four weeks after the rape. At that time, the counselor had the opportunity to reassess her emotional state and found that she was having nightmares and was afraid to leave her home. She had resigned from her job and spent endless hours crying while sitting at home by herself. She requested additional help. Ethel had moved into the final period of her emotional recovery, the resolution stage.

During the resolution stage, the older victim feels that the rape has totally disrupted her life-style.

I just don't feel comfortable doing anything anymore, everyone frightens me and I can't sleep. My husband doesn't understand and I feel so guilty telling him about the rape and upsetting him even more. My family keeps telling me to forget about it, and I try to, but it keeps haunting me. I almost feel no desire to go on. [A 60-year-old rape victim, three months after the rape.]

In the resolution stage, the older victim complains of both physical and emotional difficulties; in contrast, the younger victim usually has few physical complaints. At this time, the older victim may experience muscular pain, urogenital difficulties, general malaise, and sleep disorders that demand medical attention. Psychologically, these are more dangerous to the older woman because they are a constant reminder of her lessened capability to remain independent. Because the rape experience may complicate preexisting medical problems, the older victim is a good candidate to surrender to her physical maladies. She may lose all desire to go on living.

Counseling the victim to seek further medical treatment and arranging appointments and transportation is important. The older victim may not seek this help on her own and often does not know whom to call.

I'm like an old house, falling apart at the seams. Each day it's an effort to even get up ... there's no reason to go on ... nobody cares and nobody needs me anymore. [A 72-year-old victim.]

When the counselor persists and encourages the victim to determine the real extent of her medical problems and to seek treatment for them, it reinforces feelings of being loved and cared for. Often her physician may be the only person that she believes is interested in her welfare. A telephone call to the physician, with her permission, can make him aware of the problems she may be having and give him the opportunity to become an active member of her support system. If she lacks another adequate support system, these relationships can give the older victim a reason for living. Linking her with the Visiting Nurse Association, Homemakers, and Meals-On-Wheels can offer her additional support from persons who care.

During this stage the older victim may also experience multiple emotional problems. She may be having nightmares about the rape which tend to reinforce her fears and feelings of vulnerability. It is important that the counselor ask about bad dreams; the older victim may not volunteer this information. If she is having nightmares, the content of these dreams may help the counselor identify problem areas.

If security measures for the home have not been discussed before, these prevention techniques can help the victim control the constant fears generated by the experience. Resources such as the police, community agencies, or Senior Crime Watch can offer aid and even financial resources to buy new locks for doors and windows. They may be able to arrange for relocation to a more secure setting.

I thought I had to live in that house feeling so scared. I knew I didn't have the money to buy new windows or locks for my doors and for a solid month I just stayed awake at night watching the door. It wasn't until those nice people from the police came and helped me did I realize that there was anything else I could do. [A 72-year-old victim, one month after the rape.]

After a rape, sexual issues are also a problem for the older victim. Although the general public believes that sexuality ends with menopause, this is not true. The older woman has sexual desires and needs much like those of the younger woman. After a rape these desires may cause conflicts. She may believe that wanting sex at her age is "naughty and wrong" and may view the rape as punishment for these feelings. It is very important for the counselor to educate the older woman so she can accept her sexual identity and understand that it is natural for her to have such desires.

Open discussion about these feelings may be embarrassing to her but critical if she is to understand them. It may be necessary for the counselor to raise this issue because the older victim is usually reluctant to admit these conflicts.

I have a boyfriend that once told me that I was good in bed. Now everytime he comes near me I freeze. He's very understanding, but I'm afraid that I'll lose him because of this. [A 75-year-old rape victim.]

Positive heterosexual social contacts both individually and in a group setting can be helpful in these areas.

The older rape victim does have severe reactions to the rape experience. It is essential for the counseling staff to provide social networking alternatives, problem-solving techniques, and the opportunity for open and judgment-free discussion if she is to fully recover. The older woman may never need these kinds of services more than after a rape experience.

SUMMARY

Although it is hard to accept, sexual assault of the older woman does exist. Most people believe that the incidence of sexual assault on the older woman is relatively low. However, underreporting is significantly higher in this age group compared to other groups. These victims have a tendency to retreat rather than report the incident, and even if they report the assault they do not report the rape.

Conflicts involving dependency, general anxiety, financial matters, and long-term physical and emotional recovery impact on the older victim's ability to resolve the trauma.

These patients need immediate and intensive counseling and more prolonged follow-up if they are to return to a functioning level.

REFERENCES

Dade County Medical Examiner's Office. 1982. Accepted for publication, *J. Forensics Science.*

Davis, Linda, and Brody, Elaine. 1979. *Rape and the Older Woman: A Guide to Prevention and Protection.* Washington, D.C.: D.H.E.W. Publication No. (ADM) 78-734.

Gomez, Rolando, et al. 1975. *Qualitative and Quantitative Determinations of Acid Phosphatase Activity in Vaginal Washings.* Miami, Fl.: University of Miami Medical School.

Halpern, S., Hicks, D. J., and Crenshaw, T. 1978. *Rape: Helping the Victim.* Oradell, N.J.: Medical Economics Book Company.

Hicks, D. J. 1980. Rape: Sexual assault. *Am. J. OB-GYN,* 137(8):932–935.

Hoff, Lee Ann. 1978. *People in Crisis: Understanding and Helping.* Menlo Park, Calif.: Addison-Wesley.

Law Enforcement Administration Assistance (L.E.A.A.). 1977. *Sourcebook of Criminal Justice Statistics.* Washington, D.C.: National Criminal Justice Information and Statistic Services.

Law Enforcement Administration Assistance (L.E.A.A.). 1979. *Rape Victimization in 26 American Cities.* Washington, D.C.: National Criminal Justice Information and Statistics Services.

Law Enforcement Administration Assistance (L.E.A.A.). 1980. *Florida's Plan to Reduce Crime Against the Elderly.* Washington, D.C.: National Criminal Justice Information and Statistics Services.

11
Marital and Sexual Dysfunction Following Rape: Identification and Treatment

William R. Miller, Ph.D.
Ann Marie Williams, Ph.D.

ABSTRACT

This chapter examines the long-term impact of rape on the victim and her male partner. The focus here is on the disturbances in the dyadic relationship that occur following rape. The primary relationship problems include communication disturbances, increased dependency, mutual resentment and emotional distance, and a variety of sexual dysfunctions. Case histories of couples seen in treatment are used to illustrate these problems. Treatment issues involved in marital and sex therapy with rape victim couples are explored. An eclectic treatment approach, using male/female cotherapy teams, and a blending of individual and conjoint sessions, is advocated.

It is well known that rape can leave deep and long-lasting scars on the psychological adjustment of the victim. Yet, the rape victims are not the only ones who are victimized by rape. The victims of rape include the spouses or lovers of the women who are raped. In recognition of this fact, this chapter discusses the identification and treatment of marital and sexual dysfunctions in rape victims and their male partners.

A rather consistent picture of the psychological impact of rape on the victim has emerged from a large number of clinical and research studies. The victim response patterns that have been identified typically include some reference to difficulties in interpersonal relationships, fear of men, and sexual concerns and conflicts. In spite of these findings, little attention has been given to the long-term impact of rape on the victim's marital relationship and on her male partner. It was as a consequence of the paucity of information on this topic that the authors initiated a systematic study to determine the nature of the effects that rape has on dyadic relationships and to assess the effectiveness of conjoint marital therapy in alleviating marital and sexual conflict in couples where the woman has been raped. The material in this chapter was developed from the results of this research study.

DESCRIPTION OF INDIVIDUAL AND RELATIONSHIP DISTURBANCES

One of the major aims of the research study, to identify the individual and couple response to rape, was accomplished with very interesting results. Through a variety of methods, including clinicians' ratings, therapists' notes and clinical summaries, and the couples' self-report, we were able to identify the common individual and relationship problems that follow a rape.

The Victim's Response to Rape

The victim is flooded with an existential uncertainty, resulting from the loss of her illusion of the world as a safe place. This illusion of absolute safety, although not reality-based, provides a sense of security and protection (Gould, 1977). The precipitous loss of this illusion leaves the victim feeling vulnerable and terrified. Many victims find it difficult or impossible to articulate the precise nature of these feelings, but the primary emotion reported by the victims is fear. The central fears are of death and physical injury which, in global terms, involve a fear of loss of control over one's life. Fears of objects, people, or situations that were features of the rape incident are usually present. Thus, we find fear of being alone, of sex, of men, and depending upon where the rape occurred, either fear of being at home or out-of-doors. Shame and guilt are also common emotional reactions.

The disruption of bodily functions characteristically associated with chronic anxiety and depression is also typical. Victims report changes in sleep patterns with disturbances in the quality and quantity of sleep, as well as recurrent nightmares. Loss of appetite is also a common response. The victims attempt to cope with their excessive anxiety through a variety of mechanisms. Some resort to alcohol or tranquilizing/sedative agents. Others develop a phobic avoidance of feared objects and situations. Sexual intercourse, discussion of sex, and sometimes even nonsexual physical affection and touching are avoided. Some women begin to view their own genitals with disgust and revulsion and as a reminder of the rape. A common response is the avoidance of routine gynecological examinations. If the rape occurred in the victim's home or neighborhood, she may change her place of residence. The need to relocate is so great that the victim frequently moves within days after the rape. All too often, however, changing the place of residence has mixed effects. Changing her surroundings may make the victim feel more safe and secure from retaliation by the rapist or rapists. However, since she is usually already terrified of being alone, the sudden separation from her friends and neighbors may increase her feelings of aloneness and isolation. Another response entails the use of compulsive mechanisms for reducing anxiety, such as the ritualistic checking of door and window locks (see Case 1 below).

The victim's fear often increases her feelings of dependency on her partner, an outcome that can have very damaging consequences for the relationship (see below). One final method of coping with the fear warrants mentioning. Many victims attempt to deal with the fear, as well as the entire memory of the rape, thorough denial and repression. They make major efforts to block thoughts of the incident from entering consciousness. Obviously, when this mechanism is used, there is also an avoidance of discussion of the rape and of feelings about it with the partner. In spite of attempts to avoid or escape memories of the rape, some victims obsessively ruminate about the assault.

The passage of time, with or without therapy, reduces the level of disorganization experienced by most victims. A variety of residual symptoms such as phobias, compulsive rituals, and excessive dependency may continue, however, to interfere with a complete return to the prerape adjustment. One favorable sign is the eventual emergence of anger. Some victims are able to break through their fear of loss of control and feelings of helplessness by mobilizing their anger. The venting of rage at an appropriate target can, in itself, have a cathartic effect. In addition, focused anger can energize and motivate the victim to once again take control of her life. With some victims, the experienced rage can lead the victim into potentially dangerous situations, for example, when the victim begins to search for the rapist in order to obtain retribution (see Cases 3 and 4). In most cases, however, the recognition of anger marks the transition from the incapacitating fear and excessive dependency to the development or resumption of greater self-determination and more independent functioning.

The Partner's Response to Rape

There has been very little documentation of the male response to the rape of his partner. One recent article suggested that boyfriends and husbands often have strong negative reactions toward the victim (Miller et al., 1982). Male partners were reported to be angry and resentful toward the victim. The males were seen as feeling personally wronged, since they typically endorsed the attitude that the woman was the male's exclusive property. This response has not, however, been typical of the male partners in our experience.

In fact, we have observed some strong similarities between the reactions of the victim and the reactions of her male partner. some of the men experience an immediate fear response, although the fear is usually short-lived. The male partners have not, after all, personally experienced a life-threatening situation. Shortly after it becomes clear that the victim is alive, will not suffer from permanent physical damage, and is not pregnant, the male's fear markedly decreases. He may, however, exhibit sleeping or eating disturbances for a few days or weeks. Since the male's level of fear is not chronically high, phobic avoidance patterns and compulsive behaviors do not emerge.

The men may feel a sense of responsibility for their wives' or girlfriends' having been raped. The men berate themselves for not having been at home or, if they were at home, for not having adequately protected the partner. Such guilt feelings usually subside as the rage response emerges. During the fear and guilt stage, the men often spend much more time with their partners than had been the case prior to the rape. Of course, the increased attention given to the victim is not solely a function of the man's internal state. He is also responding to the very real needs of the victim for support. Taking time off from work to be with the victim sometimes causes additional problems for the male. In two cases, the male partner actually lost his job due to lack of attention to his work responsibilities, an outcome which seriously aggravated the husband's feelings of powerlessness.

With the quick dissipation of fear, the most dramatic emotional response of the male emerges: *rage.* Many of the men in our sample become consumed by anger and rage. Their waking hours and their dreams are filled with fantasies of confronting the rapist and killing or maiming him. The manner in which the rage response is manifested depends largely upon the man's general personality style.

In cases where a suspect has not been caught, the male partner spends many hours either thinking of ways by which he could apprehend the rapist or actually searching for the attacker. The partner's inability to vent his anger on an appropriate target increases his feelings of powerlessness and helplessness, feelings that are also shared by the victim. To counter these feelings, many of the men attempt to reestablish control through indirect means. One such method is to take increased precautions for physical security, for example, by installing new door locks or by moving to safer neighborhoods. Sublimation of aggressive impulses also occurs, often with the male directing enormous amounts of energy into work, presumably to gain power through greater authority and a higher income. In cases where a suspect has been arrested, the boyfriend or husband often pressures the victim to prosecute, even when she is quite reluctant because of her fears of retaliation or dread of rekindling her nightmares.

It is important to examine the potential sources of the male's rage response. It could be argued that the rage response is consistent with Silverman's (1978) observation. That is the male's anger is at least partially directed at the victim and basically due to the feeling that the male's property has been damaged. We have, however, seen no evidence for this view in our sample of couples. Rather, our clinical observations indicate that the male identifies with his partner and, therefore, shares to some extent her pain and trauma. His rage derives from his sense of injustice and his powerlessness at altering the situation.

Our observations do not deny that some, or even many, male partners of rape victims react negatively toward the victim because of beliefs about her being his exclusive property or about her somehow being culpable. (Only one of the men in our sample exhibited this response.) Our experience has been that many couples terminate their relationship shortly after the rape, while other victims refuse couple counseling because their partner "just doesn't understand." It very well might be that it is for these couples that the negative reactions of the male partner to the victim are present.

The Couple's Response to Rape

To illustrate the impact of rape on the *relationship* of the victim and her partner, we shall first present four typical case histories.

Case 1.   Ellen, a 27-year-old white female, is a shy, retiring person who was raised by her grandparents in a "safe" rural area until she was 10 years old. During her adolescence, her parents were strict with her and her older sister. They were emotionally and physically distant from each other. She was told that she should not date until she was engaged. For her, sex education was nonexistent until she left home at 19 years old to marry John. They met when John spent a summer at a university-sponsored program near her parents' home.

John, a 28-year-old white male, is a college graduate who is endeavoring to set up his own business. Ellen is working for her bachelor's degree on a part-time basis and plans to work with John after her graduation. They have been married eight years and have a 1-year-old son.

One evening, while John was working, an unknown assailant broke into the couple's apartment. Ellen, who was alone with her son, was threatened, violently thrown to the floor, choked, and raped. After the rapist fled, Ellen's first response was to comfort her child, who had been crying throughout the assault. She then called John at work, and he came home immediately and took Ellen to the hospital emergency room.

Ellen's immediate responses to the rape were terror, shock, and disbelief. John was also frightened by the assault, but he was also feeling guilty, blaming himself for having left Ellen alone. John took a couple of weeks off from work to be with Ellen and to try to comfort her.

A number of dramatic changes soon occurred in John and Ellen's life. first, the couple moved to a new apartment in a neighboring city. Second, John lost his job, because of missing much time at work. The couple initiated counseling three months after the rape.

When the couple entered counseling, Ellen was terrified of being alone anywhere. In fact, her fear had triggered obsessive-compulsive rituals. When home alone, her fear would escalate to near panic proportions, at which time she would go through the house checking all the doors and windows. This behavior would reduce her level of fear, but only temporarily. In time, the fear would build again, and once more Ellen would initiate the checking ritual. This sequence would be repeated until John came home.

Another less dramatic consequence of this fear had a more disturbing influence on the marital relationship. The fear increased Ellen's feeling of dependency on John. Eventually, the excessive dependency generated resentment and hostility on the part of both Ellen and John.

Prior to the rape, Ellen's sexual adjustment was only marginal. She was timid and embarrassed by discussions of sex, and she rarely acknowledged her own sexual impulses or desires. The rape experience intensified her negative attitudes and fears of sex. The couple's frequency of sexual activity dropped to zero. All of the effects described above, combined with Ellen's intense feelings of shame and guilt, resulted in a disruption in the couple's communication.

John's primary reaction to the rape was one of self-blame. He irrationally held himself responsible for the rape. He would ruminate about "Why didn't I stay home that night? Why hadn't I checked the door locks more thoroughly?" This self-blaming response led John to spend almost all of his time with Ellen. He withdrew from work so much that he eventually lost his job.

John also failed to communicate effectively with Ellen. He too was afraid to talk about the rape or about his own sexual desires. John showed a displacement of anger onto male authority figures in Ellen's life, specifically some of her teachers in college. If Ellen did poorly in an exam, John had fantasies of physically hurting these men.

Case 2.   Alice is a 28-year-old black homemaker who is unemployed, but hopes one day to return to college to finish her bachelor's degree. When she was 14 and 15 years old, Alice was periodically raped by neighborhood gang members who were friends of her teenage boyfriend. She did not report the assaults because she felt her foster mother would blame her for "getting herself raped" and would force her to give up her boyfriend. When she was 16 years old, her fiance was killed in a fight among the gang members. When she was 18 years old, she married and had her first child. Her second child was born two years later. This relationship broke up when she was 23 years old. After her divorce, Alice began dating Ted, with whom she has now been living for three years. Her daughter by Ted is now almost 3 years old. All three of her children live with them.

Late one night three years ago, when Alice was walking home from a friend's apartment in the neighborhood, she was attacked by three young black males one of whom had a knife. Alice was immediately overpowered and could not resist or scream.

Two years later, after the trial of her assailants, she was still unable to leave her house without a stiff drink to calm her shaking and soothe her nerves. With the help and understanding of her boyfriend, she had managed to weather the immediate crisis and had gotten over the initial shock of the rape. Because her close friend had also been raped when she had let a man whom she did not know very well into her house, Alice did not feel that she was alone in her grief and fear. Again, she was not able to tell her foster mother since she feared she would be blamed or being in the wrong place at the wrong time.

Unlike our middle-class couples, Alice and Ted could not afford the luxury of moving to a "better" neighborhood. Since she cloistered herself at home, Ted became her primary companion, the source of her support and security. Her refusal to join Ted in any outside activities increased the emotional distance between them. For Ted, this burden was added to their financial hardships and his own struggle to get his high school equivalency diploma. The extra burden of her dependency frustrated him in trying to reach is own goals which would indirectly help both of them to improve their living situation. Her fears of the unpredictable and the seemingly uncontrollable attacks from strangers caused her to turn to him in anger: "Why can't you do something?!" They both hold in their resentment and frustration until at last they explode in severe clashes that threaten the survival of the relationship.

Case 3.   Sally is a 26-year-old white female high school graduate, married for three years, working, who was raped during the summer of 1977. The only child of working class parents, she had a fairly traditional Catholic upbringing. She met her husband through the boyfriend she was dating at the time; both men were attending the same drug treatment program.

Gene is also 26 years old. He has a history of drug abuse, drug-related arrests, and arrests and convictions for a number of minor criminal offenses. He describes himself as a "con-man," an apt description based on what he and his wife say about him.

Sally and her husband went together for three years prior to marriage. Her husband was in and out of trouble during that time and continued in that pattern after their marriage. In the months prior to the rape, Sally had become increasingly unhappy with their relationship. Finally, shortly before, the rape, they separated, Gene moving into a friend's apartment.

The rape occurred during the separation, and the couple began living together again shortly after the rape. The suspected rapist was known to Gene and had been to the apartment with Gene the afternoon of the rape. Knowing from his visit earlier in the day that the door lock to the apartment was broken, the rapist entered the apartment that evening while Sally was asleep, forced himself on her in the bedroom, but left apparently without actually penetrating her. This detail contributed to Sally's not reporting the rape to the police.

Sally's reaction to the rape has gone through two stages. At first, she was very fearful and afraid to be alone. Next, she wanted just to forge the whole experience. Initially, also, she became extremely distrustful of her husband and suspected his complicity in the rape, but she quickly accepted his protestation of innocence. Although she has continued to work, has continued her relationship with her friends, and functions reasonably well, she remains fearful of living alone and still occasionally has nightmares about the rape. She has resisted reporting the rape and pressing charges because she does not want to be reminded of the rape in any way. However, with Gene, she did seek out the rapist, told him she knew who he was, and warned him to stay away.

Gene's initial reaction was strong and single-mind. He wanted revenge, specifically, to kill the rapist. He spent much of this time thinking about and scheming how to accomplish this. He says he went so far as to interfere in a job possibility he knew the rapist was exploring to prod the rapist to come after him so that he could kill him in "self-defense." Seeing that his schemes were not working, he then put pressure on his wife to prosecute the rapist to get revenge; a step Sally was unwilling to take because of her emotional state. Gene has mostly abandoned these schemes since getting a new job but occasionally renews the suggestion that Sally should prosecute. He had admittedly shown little interest in or ability to listen to her fears, concerns, and conflicts about the rape, and does not respond to her needs for closeness, affection, attention, and understanding.

The rape has had a strong effect on Sally and her relationship with Gene. She has become much less trusting of anyone, especially her husband, although she has convinced herself that her husband was not at fault. Nevertheless, the experience has, first, reinforced the process of her questioning their relationship as it has been, a process already begun prior to the rape, and second, reinforced a belief that she needs and deserves more affection and caring than she had been receiving. She feels she needs him most, and she now wonders whether he will ever be responsive. She is in a quandary. She does not want to separate and return to live with her parents again, but she is afraid to live alone. At least with Gene she is not alone.

Case 4.   Martha is a 31-year-old white homemaker and mother of four school-age children. She and Tod, a 32-year-old white skilled machinist, have been living together in her home for the past nine months. Martha first married when she was 14 and divorced when she was 20, because her husband had been unfaithful. She remarried when she was 21 years old but was legally separated from her second husband because of his drunkenness and wife-battering. Tod is also married, but he has been separated from his wife for the past nine months. Both Martha and Tod are filing for divorces from their respective spouses.

In early fall, Martha began drinking heavily, which she attributed to the stress of the breakup of her second marriage. She became very depressed while drinking and was hospitalized for detoxification. While sober, her responsibilities had seemed overwhelming, since she had to support herself and four children on welfare payments.

One Saturday night, a teenage friend of her son asked for a ride to the bar where his father works. She agreed to take him there. While she was having a drink "on the house," the boy "borrowed" her car. While she waited for him to return, she danced and ordered another drink. Then she found that her purse had been stolen. Some of the people at the predominantly nonwhite bar began to taunt her and tell her to leave "their place." She went to a neighboring bar and tried to call her daughter. While she waited for her daughter to try to borrow her boyfriend's car, a man overheard her problem and offered to give her a ride home. She decided to wait for her daughter to call back to see if the daughter was able to borrow a car. While waiting she had a drink with the friendly stranger and danced with him. Finally, she got tired and the bar was closing. She had no car and no purse and was not familiar with that neighborhood, so she accepted the offer of a ride home.

The man, who had also been drinking, asked his friend to drive the car. The friend brought a supply of beer, and the three of them left the bar together.

Martha was driven to an abandoned house in another unfamiliar neighborhood. When they arrived, she was half asleep and half drunk. When she finally realized where she was and what they wanted, it was too late. They offered her a beer, but she wanted to go home. When she tried to scream, they beat her. By dawn the men were worn out from the violence and were sexually satisfied. As soon as she was certain they were both asleep, she fled. She was cold sober.

After she was released from the hospital, Martha was in almost continual contact with a Women Organized Against Rape (WOAR) crisis volunteer, a Center for Rape Concern (CRC) social worker, and/or one of the authors. She could not sleep for fear of horrid nightmares. Tod would sit up with her night after night until she would fall asleep the following dawn, exhausted. The three contact people worked with her by phone from 11 A.M. until midnight each day, while Tod got some sleep and took care of Martha's household responsibilities.

Tod's lack of sleep and absenteeism cost him his job. He had to go on unemployment compensation and gradually began to feel terrible about himself, since he did not contribute money to the household. He began to drink with Martha. During this period she became obsessed with castrating the primary rapist with a scissors. Several nights were spent roaming the area near the bar, but to no avail. Martha finally gave up her search, went home, and slept off and on for several days. She was determined to stop drinking so she and Tod returned to AA. When their lives had finally begun to settle down, it came time for her court appearance. After she spoke with the detectives at length, she went home and had another nightmare about the rape. Two days later, she asked to be admitted to a psychiatric unit in a nearby hospital. She was flooded with memories and knew she needed professional help. She had exploded and had beaten her children.

Meanwhile, Tod felt hurt and confused and alone. He had done everything he knew how to do, but it did not seem to be enough. She yelled and screamed to him to "do something." When he asked "Do what?" she either lashed out at him physically or dissolved in sobs.

The four case histories described above include the most common sequelae to rape. There is, of course, no standard, invariant response pattern for all couples. A variety of factors act to modify any particular couple's reaction to sexual assault. Nevertheless, we are able to identify specific responses to rape that seem to be typical.

Although there are some striking similarities in the response to rape of the male and female partners, both frequently lack an empathic understanding of each other. The two partners, both of whom are experiencing intense fear or rage, are seldom able to distance themselves enough from their own feelings to appropriately respond to the feelings of others. Another factor relates to the timing of the sequential emergence of emotions. Both partners may experience the same sequence, but the timing of the sequence is different. The male's stage of fear and guilt is much briefer than the female's. At the same time that the victim is fearful or anxious, the male has begun to experience the rage response. Thus, the main concern of the female is for safety and security, while the male's concern is for revenge and retribution.

Perhaps the most damaging consequence of rape for the couple is the disruption in the communication process that occurs. The victim clearly signals that she does not want to talk about the assault or even to think about it. The rape and even the victim's feeling response to the rape become taboo subjects. As a result, the victim does not ventilate her feelings, and her male partner is left to guess at what she is feeling and what she needs from him. At the same time, the husband or boyfriend is feeling confused and guilty. Yet, he knows that his partner is in pain and is concerned about burdening her with his feelings.

The victim becomes increasingly dependent on her partner. Although the male initially attempts to provide the support that is desired, his efforts are undermined by his own emotional trauma and by the external pressures of commitments to his job. Furthermore, the duration and intensity of her emotional reactions may wear down his resolve to be supportive for the indefinite future.

The male's rage response emerges, and is typically more intense than the female's. Now, the husband or boyfriend is even less able to fulfill his partner's dependency needs. The sometimes observed sublimation of aggression through greater work commitments also leaves the male with little energy to devote to his partner. Furthermore, the rage may increase the victim's anxiety. She fears that her partner will himself get into trouble, and the rage in some way may remind her of the violence of the rape itself. Finally, the lack of open communication and the victim's increased dependency on her partner lead to mutual resentment. Resentment develops in the woman for needing her partner so much and for her feeling that he is not totally fulfilling her needs. For the man, resentment is generated as a result of his being placed in a position where he can never be as supportive and protective as she requires.

When the victim's fear finally begins to decrease, the male starts to think of a return to their prerape style in interacting, including the resumption of sexual relations. Again, however, the communication process is disrupted. The male is concerned that his wife or girlfriend is not ready to resume sex. The victim herself is often starting to feel the desire to resume her sexual relationship, but she too is reluctant to initiate sex — her partner has not expressed interest. Once again, the communication disturbance prevents each partner from understanding the needs and desires of the other.

When sexual relations are resumed, performance problems may become evident. We have not observed sexual dysfunctions, other than loss of interest in sex, in any of the males. Some of the victims, however, have suffered from pain in intercourse (dyspareunia) or vaginismus, as well as loss of interest. Contraception is sometimes a problem, due to the victim's avoidance of gynecological exams. The failure of some couples to use reliable birth control measures only adds to the tension associated with sex.

TREATMENT ISSUES

Although it has been possible to describe a typical couple's response to rape, each couple has its own unique set of coping strategies, defenses, and dysfunctions. Also, as the case histories illustrate, the clinical picture may be complicated by preexisting conditions, for example, individual psychopathology, alcoholism, marital and family conflict, that not only affect the couple's reaction to the rape, but also continue as ongoing problems in their own right.

As a result of the complexity and variety of the couple's dynamics, there is no single "approach" to the treatment of all rape victim couples. Rather, the therapist needs to address the problems with what can be referred to as "informed eclecticism." That is, the therapist needs to make a careful assessment of needs of each couple and then to apply any of a wide variety of treatment approaches, techniques, and modalities to the issues at hand.

Almost invariably, the first therapeutic task is the establishment of rapport with the couple. For a few rape victim couples, this is not a serious problem —

some couples have been eagerly awaiting the chance to talk with someone who might help. For most couples, however, the establishment of rapport is a major hurdle that must be overcome if therapy is to be helpful. Many rape victims have developed a deep distrust of new people, especially those who are likely to be probing at feelings and issues that the victim has worked hard to repress and deny.

Advantages of Cotherapy

If the therapist happens to be a male, the establishment of a good therapeutic relationship with the victim is often made more difficult because of the victim's special fear of men. Male partners of rape victims may have particular difficulties with either male or female therapists. Problems arise with male therapists if the male partner is concerned that he did not adequately protect or "safe-keep" his wife. The husband then fears that the male therapist will judge him on the basis of this "fact." When the male partner has special difficulty with female therapists, the difficulty is usually the result of a concern that the female therapist will be more closely aligned to the victim and not understand the pain of the male partner.

Because of these complicated, gender-related concerns, our experience has been that male/female cotherapy teams represent a particularly useful mode of working with rape victim couples. With an awareness of the special, gender-related issues that may be present, the therapists can adjust the style of the cotherapy to deal with these concerns.

For example, if the victim is especially fearful of men, the female member of the cotherapy team will initially take primary responsibility for questioning and exploring issues with the victim. The male therapist is more active with the husband, while being supportive of the victim. As the rape victim begins to relax and to see the male therapist as less threatening, the male therapist starts to interact more actively with the victim.

Another helpful aspect of male/female cotherapy is that the cotherapists are modeling a way of communicating and interacting for the couple. As therapy progresses, the therapists can use their relationship as a vehicle not only for modeling but also for more directly demonstrating new communication patterns.

Individual versus Conjoint Sessions

Most marital and sexual therapy is conducted conjointly. With rape victim couples, however, our experience has been that there is more blending of individual and conjoint sessions than is usually the case in marital therapy. Individual sessions are held with each member of the couple and may be with either same- or opposite-sex therapist.

A major advantage of the individual session is the greater freedom to deal with the secrecy about certain thoughts and feelings that characteristically is found in many rape victim couples. The members of the couple experience a greater sense of safety and freedom in being able to "open up" with the therapist in the absence of the spouse. The therapist can also be somewhat more confrontive in exploring secrets in the individual session, since the partner does not need to worry about a negative reaction from a spouse who is listening.

When in the course of an individual session the therapist does uncover secrets that partners have been keeping, the therapist can freely explore and discuss the consequences of revealing versus keeping the secret. Often, the victim and/or her husband have erroneously concluded that revealing certain thoughts or feelings will elicit negative responses from the partner. In one case, both partners were keeping secret the fact that each was interested in resuming their sexual relationship. The husband made no sexual advances for fear that his wife was not ready and would feel pressured. The wife assumed that the absence of sexual initiatives by her husband indicated a lack of interest on his part, so she did not express her own desire for sex.

Partners' reactions to some secrets can, of course, be powerfully negative. The members of the couple, however, seldom adequately evaluate the costs of keeping the secret. Within the context of the individual session, the therapist assists with the analysis of these costs.

One cautionary note about individual sessions needs to be made. If too many individual sessions are held, or if there is not a balance between the number of individual and conjoint sessions, there is a danger that individual members of the couple and of the cotherapy team may form alliances with one another that interfere with the overall goals of therapy. This is a special concern in cases where the members of the couple are very angry at one another, in which case the formation of strong alliances can lead to a shift from empathic understanding of both positions to an adversarial posture.

General Treatment Strategy

As was mentioned above, the therapist needs to be familiar with a variety of treatment techniques and approaches. Consequently, a cataloging of treatment interventions does not seem appropriate here. What may be useful, though, is a description of how different techniques may be integrated into a course of treatment for a couple.

Suppose, for example, that a rape victim couple is having difficulty in discussing feelings with each other, as well as experiencing a decreased desire for sex. Suppose also that the victim is suffering from some generalized anxiety responses and that the male partner is having difficulty with anger directed at the rapist.

After establishing rapport with the couple, the therapy team might begin to work on the communication disturbances. The reason for starting here is that both partners are experiencing considerable emotional pain, and the therapists want to increase the capacity of each spouse to be supportive of the other. The communication disturbance thus interferes with the ability of each partner to empathically understand and support the other. Any of a large number of specific interventions for treating communication dysfunctions may be used, most relying on some form of specific instructions, behavioral rehearsal, and practice.

As the couple makes some progress in developing better communication skills, the therapists may have the couple focus their discussions on their own feelings, especially their fears and anger. In doing this, the therapists are assisting the couple in using their own relationship to be supportive of each partner's troubling feelings. Specific interventions, such as systematic desensitization for anxiety and cognitive therapy for both anxiety and anger, often need to be employed.

The treatment of sexual dysfunction is typically the last relationship problem to be dealt with. The sexual response is heavily influenced by the general status of the relationship and by the emotional life of the individuals. As a result, sexual problems are rarely amenable to treatment unless communication problems, nonsexual relationship conflicts or intense individual emotional states are first dealt with. In fact, the sexual problems of some rape victim couples spontaneously improve with the successful treatment of the nonsexual difficulties. In those cases where sexual dysfunctions persist, the use of behavioral sex therapy techniques usually leads to significant improvement in sexual functioning.

Finally, as was previously mentioned, many rape victim couples have preexisting individual psychopathology. Problems with regard to education, vocation, and financial planning are also common. Marital therapy can be of some value in addressing these additional problems, but special attention to these difficulties is often needed and is beyond the scope of marital therapy. Our experience suggests that marital therapy can be of enormous value in correcting the marital and sexual dysfunctions described above. When, however, additional life-planning problems and/or individual psychopathology are significant factors, the gains made through marital therapy typically are lost over time unless specific training in life-planning skills and individual psychotherapy are provided to one or both members of the couple.

REFERENCES

Gould, R. 1977. Evolution of adult consciousness. Paper for the Friend's Hospital Conference on Adult Development. Philadelphia, Pennsylvania.

Miller, W. R., Williams, A. M., and Bernstein, M. H. 1982. The effects of rape on marital and sexual adjustment. *Am. J. Family Therapy*, 10:51-58.

Silverman, D. 1978. Sharing the crisis of rape: Counseling the mates and families of victims. *Am. J. Orthopsychiatry*, 48:166-173.

12
Behavioral Treatment of Sexual Dysfunctions in Sexual Assault Survivors

Judith V. Becker, Ph.D.
Linda J. Skinner, Ph.D.

ABSTRACT

Many sexual assault survivors develop sexual problems as a consequence of their assaults, and these problems do not appear to dissipate with the passage of time. However, assault-related sexual dysfunctions are amenable to treatment. We have developed a time-limited, behaviorally oriented sexual dysfunction treatment package for use with sexual assault survivors. Based on the P-LI-SS-IT model, this treatment package incorporates components from a variety of approaches. The focus of the treatment is in helping a survivor regain control over her sexuality and learn to derive pleasure from it. Designed to be used across 10 one-hour therapy sessions, the package can be implemented in either an individual or a group therapy format and is appropriate for a wide variety of sexual dysfunctions. Built-in flexibility allows the program to be tailored to meet the specific needs of a survivor.

This chapter discusses how sexual dysfunctions can result from a sexual assault and the elements important in taking a sexual problem history. Following a brief discussion of the P-LI-SS-IT model, the sexual dysfunction treatment package is presented. This discussion explains the application of the therapy across 10 treatment sessions and notes frequent problems encountered in the different sessions. Finally, some special therapy issues are addressed. The case examples presented throughout the chapter were drawn from the histories of some of the sexual assault survivors evaluated at the Victim Treatment and Research Clinic at Columbia University in New York City.

[1] This research was funded in part by Research Grant MH-32982-03 from the National Institute of Mental Health. The authors want to thank Mary McCormack, Thomassina Hoeppel, Joan Cichon, Rosalind Axelrod, and New York Women Against Rape for their assistance with this research.

Behaviorally oriented therapy is frequently identified as the treatment of choice for sexual dysfunctions (Kaplan, 1974; Kilpatrick et al., 1978; Lazarus, 1963; LoPiccolo and Lobitz, 1972; Marks, 1981; Masters and Johnson, 1970; Rosen and Rosen, 1981; Segraves, 1976; Wolpe, 1958; Wright et al., 1977). Studies have assessed the efficacy of a variety of behavioral treatment packages when applied to specific categories of sexual dysfunctions (Kilmann, 1978; Munjack et al., 1976; Reynolds et al., 1981), when applied across categories (Leiblum and Ersner-Hershfield, 1977; Leiblum et al., 1976), or when treatment was aimed at alleviating the anxiety associated with specific sexual behaviors (Lazarus, 1963). Additionally, these interventions have been found effective at varying levels for couples and individuals with or without partners in individual, group, or self-treatment format across a broad range of treatment session intervals (Barbach, 1974; Carney et al., 1978; Ersner-Hershfield, 1978; Golden et al., 1978; Heiman and LoPiccolo, 1981; Leiblum and Ersner-Hershfield, 1977; Leiblum et al., 1976; Mathews, 1981; McMullen and Rosen, 1979).

In our work with sexually dysfunctional males and females, we have had good success with behavioral interventions. We have also found these interventions to be effective in treating sexually dysfunctional sexual assault survivors.[2]

SEXUAL DYSFUNCTIONS AND SEXUAL ASSAULT SURVIVORS

Disruption in sexual functioning is an all too frequent consequence of sexual assault. Certainly, a large number of women experience a lack of interest in or disdain for sex immediately following a sexual assault.

Cathy has been married about four years when she was raped. While she and her husband had enjoyed a mutually satisfying sexual relationship prior to the rape, Cathy experienced considerable dread when it was time for her to go to bed on the first night following the assault. She feared that her husband would want to comfort her physically and she felt that she was unable to tolerate being touched by anyone. When she did retire that night, she laid on top of the bedspread, fully dressed and wearing shoes. This behavior continued for several nights until she gradually resumed her preassault sleeping habits. Her lack of interest in being sexual continued, but her husband exerted no pressure on her to be sexual. With the passage of time, Cathy came to terms with her assault and found that her interest in sex began to return. At the time she was interviewed, Cathy reported that, through

---

[2] The term *survivor* rather than *victim* is used throughout this chapter in deference to the sensitivities of women who have already been made to suffer feelings of extreme helplessness. The authors do not want to risk, even remotely, contributing to the perpetuation of these feelings. The term is to be understood as having no implications whatsoever for probability of death associated with sexual assault.

mutual support and understanding, she and her husband had been able to resume their previously satisfactory sexual relationship.

Not only may sexual problems be experienced immediately subsequent to a sexual assault, but such problems may endure for many years (Bart, 1975; Becker et al., 1982, 1983a,b; Burgess and Holmstrom, 1979; Ellis et al., 1980; Feldman-Summers et al., 1979; Gager and Schurr, 1976; Hilberman, 1976; Holmstrom and Burgess, 1978; McGuire and Wagner, 1978; Skinner et al. 1982).

While she had never engaged in masturbation or penile-vaginal intercourse prior to her rape, Donna had enjoyed mutual petting and caressing and was aroused by these activities. About eight years after her rape, she was married. Early in the marriage, she enjoyed being sexual with her husband but was anorgasmic. Her inability to have an orgasm began to affect her sexual relationship with her husband, with the result that the frequency of their sexual interactions had diminished considerably and were often limited to Donna masturbating her husband to ejaculation. Throughout their 15 years of marriage, she never experienced an orgasm.

When interviewed, Donna reported that she was able to become very aroused when she and her husband were sexual but that she mentally withdrew from their interactions when she reached a high level of arousal. She indicated that she feared that the loss of control she associated with orgasm would be similar to the lack of control imposed on her by the rapist. With therapy, Donna was able to have an orgasm through masturbation and, eventually, during sexual interactions with her husband.

Sexual problems resulting from a sexual assault develop in accordance with a two-factor social learning theory. According to this classical conditioning model, the assault is an unconditioned stimulus that evokes fear and anxiety in a survivor. Similarly to other features of the assault, the sexual component can become a conditioned stimulus that evokes fear, anxiety, or some other negative reaction in the woman. For many assault survivors, these negative reactions generalize to specific or all sexual situations, behaviors, and/or interactions. A survivor may subsequently inhibit her sexual feelings or withdraw entirely from all sexual behavior in order to avoid the conditioned fear or anxiety, and as a result, these avoidance behaviors allow the negative responses to sex to endure.

Kelly was brutally raped just prior to her marriage. While she and her husband-to-be had enjoyed sex during their engagement, the rape caused significant problems. After the assault, she was sensitive to her husband's desire for sex but simultaneously dreaded the prospect of engaging in intercourse as such behavior caused her to relive the assault. When she was sexual,

Kelly began to withdraw mentally, distracting herself by planning the next day's meals or composing her shopping list. While such avoidance behaviors were effective temporarily, Kelly found that her anxiety and fear were no longer experienced just prior to and during their sexual interactions, but began generalizing to any sexual thoughts and the anticipation of sex. Consequently, if she picked up any cue from her husband in the morning that he would like to have intercourse that evening, she would purposely overwork herself that day to the point of physical exhaustion and save on task, such as the laundry, to be done when her husband was ready for bed. As a result of these extended avoidance behaviors, Kelly had eliminated sexual interactions almost entirely from her life.

For some women, aversion to particular sexual activities develop as a result of a sexual assault. In such cases, overall sexual pleasure may be satisfactory while one sexual behavior may be disturbed.

When Nina accepted a ride hitchhiking one afternoon, she was sexually assaulted by the driver. After fondling her breasts and genitals, he forced her to fellate him. Nina had never engaged in this activity before and was unable to perform to the assailant's satisfaction. Unhappy with her performance, the assailant threatened to rape her vaginally but did not.

A few years after the assault, Nina began dating a new partner and subsequently moved in with him. Her partner wanted her to perform fellatio on him, an activity from which Nina derived some pleasure. However, because of her assault experience, Nina was very anxious for him to ejaculate rapidly during fellatio as she feared that the activity would continue forever, as it had seemed to during the assault.

A SEXUAL DYSFUNCTION TREATMENT PACKAGE
FOR SEXUAL ASSAULT SURVIVORS

For many sexual assault survivors whose postassault sexual problems are transient in nature, no therapeutic intervention may be necessary. The passage of time may allow this group of survivors to resume satisfactory sexual interactions. However, some intervention may be necessary for assault survivors who report experiencing prolonged sexual problems.

From our earlier work with sexually dysfunctional women in general, as well as sexual assault survivors with sexual problems, we developed a time-limited, behaviorally oriented sexual dysfunction treatment package. Not only is this package appropriate for use in the treatment of a variety of sexual problems, but it also addresses problem areas specific to sexual assault survivors.

The basic goal of the treatment package is to help a woman regain control over her sexuality through gradual exposure to fear- or anxiety-producing sexual situations, behaviors, and interactions. As she increases her control, a woman learns to relabel her sexual feelings and be sexually assertive, a behavior that is incompatible with anxiety and fear. Through the restructuring of cognitions and modifying of behavior, a woman learns or relearns to view sex positively and enjoy her own sexuality.

Sexual Problem History

Before any therapeutic intervention is considered, a sexual problem history must be obtained. Guidelines for taking such a history from people in general (Annon, 1976) and specifically from sexual assault survivors are available in the literature. Briefly, a sexual problem history should cover five basic areas.

Description of the Current Problem.   The survivor should be asked to describe the problem she is experiencing. It is important that the description be clear and not confused by the use of labels.

Onset and Course of Problem.   Information about the age of the woman when the problem began, whether the problem appeared suddenly or gradually, and any changes in the course of the problem over time provides cues about the possible responsiveness of the sexual problem to therapeutic intervention.

Cause and Maintenance of Problem.   It is important to understand what the survivor perceives as causing and maintaining her problem so that erroneous conceptions can be corrected and to ensure that she will be receptive to therapeutic intervention.

Previous Treatment and Outcome.   Knowledge about previously attempted treatment, professional and self-administered, and outcome aids in the formulation of the current intervention.

Current Expectancies and Goals of Treatment.   It is important to understand what the survivor expects from therapy and to ensure that her goals are concrete and specific.

As can be seen, the sex problem history not only clarifies the problem that the survivor is experiencing, but also provides information about what she expects or wants from therapy and her possible receptiveness to treatment. Without such information, the treatment may not address the needs of the woman or may duplicate previously unsuccessful efforts and, consequently, further compound her problem.

Level of Intervention

The sexual dysfunction treatment package for sexual assault survivors is based upon the P-LI-SS-IT model, a framework of sex therapy involving a number of different levels of intervention (Annon, 1976). A woman's movement through the levels is determined by her needs.

For many sexually dysfunctional survivors, therapy may be limited to giving them permission (P) or, more important, helping them give themselves permission to engage in certain behaviors.

> Since her rape, Janet experienced rape flashbacks whenever she engaged in penile-vaginal intercourse. Realizing that this problem existed, her husband did not exert pressure on her to have intercourse. Instead, he was satisfied to limit their sexual interactions to caressing and kissing, behaviors that did not precipitate the flashbacks. However, Janet believed that such behaviors should only be preludes to intercourse and, therefore, was reluctant to engage in them. In the course of therapy, Janet was given permission to participate in kissing and caressing with her husband without having intercourse. When therapy was completed, Janet reported that her frequency of nonintercourse sexual behaviors had increased considerably.

Other women may need limited information (LI) or facts relevant to their particular problems.

> Fern had been sexually assaulted repeatedly as a child by her uncle and, consequently, developed a fear of sex. Until she was married, she had few sexual experiences, none of which included sexual intercourse. While she had made some progress in controlling the anxiety she experienced when she was being sexual, she continued to feel an uncomfortable amount. This problem was compounded by her husband's comments that other women did not experience muscular tension when aroused and that her tension was inhibiting her enjoyment. Fern was told that women respond differently when sexually aroused and that muscular tension was quite normal for many women. Provided with this information, Fern was able to relabel this aspect of her response appropriately, as well as share these facts with her husband.

Specific suggestions (SS) are used when a survivor is not utilizing behaviors in her behavioral repertoire or when a specific change in behavior will resolve her sexual problem.

> Rachel had a history of childhood molestations involving groups of older boys who would either physically overpower her or threaten her with physical

violence. When she was 23, she married a man with whom she had previously enjoyed a good sexual relationship. After their marriage, her husband became abusive and beat and raped her regularly over a two-year period. As his violence escalated, Rachel became afraid that she would be killed and was able to leave her husband.

Subsequently, whenever Rachel would meet a new potential partner, she was able to become aroused but experienced extreme anxiety whenever she attempted to engage in intercourse. The weight of her partner's body on top of her caused feelings of loss of control and helplessness and precipitated fears that her partner would become violent. Consequently, she began to avoid sexual situations, and, if sexual, would withdraw her awareness during the interaction.

Rachel was encouraged to assume the female superior position and to control the insertion of the penis. By modifying her behavior in this manner, she was able to engage in behaviors she had previously avoided. Rachel reported decreased anxiety, and greater satisfaction when being sexual after completion of therapy.

The final level of intervention of the P-LI-SS-IT model, intensive therapy (IT), is not included in the treatment package. Sexual assault survivors whose problems were not resolved by the other three levels or are associated with serious relationship or emotional problems may require intensive therapy. Only a minority of cases should require this level of intervention.

Basics of the Treatment Package

Components from a variety of other treatment programs (Masters and Johnson, 1970; Barbach, 1975; Deutsch, 1968; Dodson, 1974; Heiman et al., 1976; Kegel, 1952; Lobitz and LoPiccolo, 1972; Zeiss et al., 1978) were incorporated within the P-LI-SS-IT model in the development of the treatment package for sexual assault survivors. While the package was designed to be applied across 10 one-hour therapy sessions, the number or length of sessions can be modified to meet the needs of the woman. In addition to the treatment sessions, a major emphasis is placed on exercises and assignments that a dysfunctional survivor performs at home. The therapy is conducted with the woman only since a number of survivors may not have a regular sexual partner or wish to share with her partner or partners the fact that she was sexually assaulted. A lack of a partner will hinder addressing some sexual problems, such as becoming orgasmic through penile-vaginal intercourse. However, most of the sexual problems experienced by sexual assault survivors can be treated without a partner. Finally, the treatment package can be implemented in either an individual or a group therapy format.

The Focus of the Treatment Sessions

Generally, the progression of the treatment package parallels the P-LI-SS-IT model of intervention. Initially, the therapy focuses on giving a woman permission to enjoy sex once again and helping her to learn about her own sexuality. As treatment progresses, specific suggestions predominate and the focus of therapy expands to sexual interactions with others.

The discussion below outlines the treatment package when applied across 10 therapy sessions. The recommended focus of each session can be modified as necessary. Thus, additional time can be spent on sexual areas presenting particular problems or less time can be allocated for an issue that is not relevant.

Session 1. It is not unusual for a sexual assault survivor to believe that she is the only woman to experience sexual problems after an assault. Such an erroneous cognition can result in a woman believing that something is particularly wrong with her and foster guilt feelings that may compound her sexual problem. The frequency with which survivors believe that they are alone in having assault-related sexual problems is most probably a function of both the hesitancy of some women to discuss their sexual assaults and/or sexual behavior with others and the current trend that stresses the aggressive component of a sexual assault while deemphasizing or ignoring completely the sexual component of such assaults. Thus, it is very important to help a woman understand that many women develop sexual problems subsequent to an assault and to delineate the relationship between an assault and sexual problems.

One of the goals of the first session of therapy is to discuss the development of postassault sexual problems in accordance with the two-factor social learning theory. This discussion helps absolve any guilt a woman may be experiencing due to the development of such problems and also helps her understand how her current behavior helps to maintain the problems.

> In her early adolescence, Tina had been sexually assaulted, with the rape involving anal penetration. Tina felt that the assault had had no significant impact on her sexual behavior as her subsequent sexual experiences both pre- and post-marriage has been good. However, after 10 years of marriage, she suddenly began thinking of her assault and simultaneously experienced a loss of all desire for sex. She was feeling guilty about her lack of desire and worried about its impact on her relationship with her husband.
>
> As the development of postassault problems was discussed, Tina commented that just prior to the onset of her sexual problems, her husband had forced anal penetration on her, during which she experienced the same emotions and thoughts she had had during the rape. Tina came to understand that her fear that her husband would force anal sex again caused her to inhibit her sexual feelings entirely.

The second focus of this session is the determination of treatment goals. While it is important that a woman be allowed to determine her own goals, the goals must be specific, concrete, and realistic. Expressing the goals behaviorally helps to ensure that treatment progress can be evaluated.

Susan originally identified only one treatment goal — to enjoy sex more. Since that goal was so nebulous, much time was spent helping her be more concrete and specific. Following further questioning, Susan indicated that she would like to be orgasmic during penile-vaginal intercourse. While this revised goal was more concrete and specific, it was not realistic in this case. Susan was participating in a 10-session treatment program and had no sexual partner. Additionally, she indicated that she was not dating anyone and thought it highly unlikely that she would have a sexual partner in 10 weeks. However, as work on identifying her goal continued, Susan revealed that her orgasmic problem was not restricted to intercourse but also present during masturbation and that being orgasmic during self-stimulation was very important to her since this was frequently her primary source of sexual pleasure. Consequently, she revised her treatment goal to having orgasms when masturbating, a goal that was concrete, specific, and realistic.

As this case example illustrates, the identification of treatment goals can be problematic. The most frequent difficulty is the listing of global goals. One technique that aids a woman in making such goals more concrete and specific is to ask what she would like to be able to do upon the completion of treatment that she is unable to do now. Inclusion of the phrase "upon completion of treatment" is important in order to ensure that the goals are realistic within the framework of a time-limited treatment package.

While the onus of determining treatment goals falls on the woman, a therapist is not absolved from the responsibility of helping a woman identify and revise her goals when necessary. Goal specification aids a therapist in planning appropriate treatment and helps protect a woman from inevitable failure.

Session 2.   Many women in our society have been socialized to dislike their bodies. Conditioned to use the centerfold or Hollywood standards of beauty as the criteria by which they judge their bodies, many women feel inferior and continually focus on the various ways they believe that they fall short of these standards.

In a group of five sexually dysfunctional sexual assault survivors, the women were asked to identify what they liked about their bodies. In turn each woman listed her complaints, being too tall, being overweight, having small breasts or large feet. Not one of the women listed a positive feature. When the women were again asked to identify at least one positive, not negative, feature of their bodies, each drew a blank and, subsequently, was surprised when other group members began identifying something positive about her.

Feeling good about one's body and sexual enjoyment are closely related because a poor body image may inhibit a person sexually. Not only is appreciation of the external body important, but feeling good about the body's capabilities is necessary. For example, appreciating strong arms that allow the lifting of one's child or performing work is as important as liking one's body shape.

A sexual assault may have a significant impact on a survivor's body image. Since such an assault is directed at her breasts and/or her genitals, a survivor may develop particularly negative feelings about her body's sexual features.

Marianne, an attractive woman in her mid-50s, was sexually assaulted in her home by a man who had gained entrance through a fire escape window. During the rape, her assailant told her repeatedly "what a fine body she had for a woman her age." He particularly admired her breasts, and spent a great deal of time orally and manually stimulating them while verbally praising their beauty.

Prior to the assault, Marianne had taken pride in her body and enjoyed the pleasure it gave her sexually. After the assault, she gained 25 pounds and consciously began dressing in a manner designed to conceal her figure, especially her breasts. She avoided looking at her body altogether since that caused her anxiety. When she did engage in sexual relations with her husband, she would not permit him to stimulate her breasts, especially the left breast, which had been the primary target of the rapist. Marianne's changed attitude toward her body reflected her feelings that her body, which she had previously valued and enjoyed, had somehow betrayed her by being attractive to her assailant.

The focus of the second session is on obtaining mastery over one's body. The socialization of women to be viewed as objects and to dislike their bodies is discussed, as is the impact of a sexual assault on body image. Body image exercises are given as a homework assignment. The survivor is asked to find at least 30 minutes sometime before the next treatment session during which she will be free from outside interruptions. She is to use this time to examine carefully her nude body, from head to feet, before a large mirror. During this examination, she is to focus on the positive, noting the good of each feature.

Session 3.   A major focus of this session is the continued enhancement of body image. Discussion of the last session's homework assignment frequently reveals that the survivor noted some positives about her body but continues to focus predominantly on the negative aspects.

When discussing the body image exercises, Cynthia reported that she studied her body for at least two hours and was able to find "a couple of good things." However, she continued to feel overwhelmed by all of the things she disliked. In fact, she felt that the exercises had sensitized her to the negative features. When she passed a mirror or store window and glanced at herself, she saw only the things she disliked. During this session, Cynthia was unable to remember the positive things about her body.

Cynthia's response to the homework assignment is not atypical, and several techniques can be taught to a woman reporting similar problems. A woman who has difficulty remembering the positive features of her body can be instructed to write them down and review the list at least five times each day until she can recall them easily. The importance of the functional abilities of the body can be stressed for a woman who adamantly denies appreciating the physical aspects. Thought stopping (Geisinger, 1969) is a good technique for a woman who continues to focus on the negative. Additionally, the procedure of following any negative thought with a positive comment can also be taught. Increased sensitivity to the negative aspects of one's body does not necessarily mean that the exercises have failed. With the above techniques, such sensitivity can be used to increase the likelihood of replacing negative self-statements with positive statements.

Enhancement of body image also includes increasing the appreciation of the sexual pleasure one's body can provide. The basis of this appreciation is understanding how the body is pleasurable. A lack of knowledge of how one's body provides sexual pleasure is particularly common among women assaulted as children.

Virginia, an incest survivor, was unhappy about the way her husband fondled her breasts. When she asked him not to squeeze so hard, he responded that all women find such pressure arousing. His statement caused Virginia to think that something was wrong with her sexually, and these thoughts were interfering with her sexual interactions. While she knew she disliked his squeezing of her breasts, she did not know what type of fondling would be arousing.

Many women fail to realize that they should be the experts about what is arousing to them. Rather than accepting the responsibility for knowing how their bodies provide pleasure and communicating what is arousing to them to their partners, some women assume that their partners know or believe their partners' assertions that what is being done is arousing, as did Virginia. It is important to stress that each woman should know how her body provides sexual pleasure and that she must share this information with her partner.

The second focus of this session is to help the survivor learn what is arousing to her. The homework assignment is the incorporation of touch in the body image exercises. Once again, the woman is instructed to find at least a 30-minute interval that will be free from interruptions. In this exercise she is to explore her body tactually from head to toe. This examination should not be restricted to her breasts or genital area but rather should include all parts of her body. By varying her touch and the amount of pressure exerted and by focusing on the sensations experienced, the woman will learn what is arousing to her.

Session 4.   A problem experienced by many sexual assault survivors is difficulty in maintaining their focus on their behavior when being sexual. Instead, they allow their minds to wander to other topics or suffer from assault flashbacks. Thus, focus training may be necessary, and a goal of this session is to help the woman learn to increase her ability to focus on her sexual behavior. Two procedures, alone or in combination, can be used to achieve this goal.

> Since her rape, Cheryl had experienced some difficulty in achieving an orgasm during both intercourse with her partner and masturbation. Frequently she would feel increasing arousal and then begin to worry that she may not have an orgasm. This fear would then dominate her thoughts, resulting in a loss of arousal. With each similar occurrence, Cheryl found herself less interested in being sexual.

To enable Cheryl to control her intruding thoughts, she was instructed to refocus consciously her attention on her current behavior and sensations whenever her attention strayed. This refocusing could be accomplished by describing to herself or her partner her pleasurable physical sensations. Such conscious mental activity would decrease the likelihood of unwanted thoughts.

Sexual fantasies may also be used as a tool to prevent intruding thoughts while simultaneously enhancing sexual pleasure.

> In a group of sexually dysfunctional sexual assault survivors, one woman, Debbie, indicated that she felt it was okay to use fantasies when masturbating but inappropriate when she was with a sexual partner. Debbie believed that if she failed to focus her undivided attention on her partner she was being unfaithful to him. However, when she did not use fantasies, she had difficulty becoming aroused.

A second group member, Ellen, had no hesitation employing fantasies when she and her husband were being sexual. However, she was concerned that her arousal to lesbian fantasies meant that she was, in fact, a lesbian and, therefore, should not be married.

Part of this session focuses on the use of sexual fantasies. Some women may benefit from learning that the use of sexual fantasies is very normal and that most people use such fantasies. Other women may need to be given permission to use sexual fantasies whenever they are sexual, alone or with a partner. Women such as Debbie may need help in constructing fantasies that they consider appropriate for use when with a partner. For example, Debbie was encouraged to develop fantasies that included her partner and their sexual behavior but took place in exotic locations or during particular time periods. The use of such fantasies allowed Debbie to maintain her arousal while simultaneously remaining "faithful" to her partner. Finally, some women need to know that arousal to a wide variety of fantasy material is normal and does not necessarily indicate future behavior.

One of the homework assignments for this session includes the reading of fantasy material. It is helpful if the therapist provides this material. Numerous books (Friday, 1973, 1975; Cedar and Melly, 1979) containing sexual fantasies are available. The fantasy material provided should cover a broad spectrum of behavior. However, since some sexual assault survivors may be upset by fantasies containing physical force, it is advised that the provided fantasies be screened.

During this session, homework assignments for specific sexual dysfunctions are explained when appropriate. These techniques include the Kegel exercise (Deutsch, 1968; Kegel, 1952) for women with arousal or orgasmic problems, masturbatory training (Barbach, 1975; Dodson, 1974; Lobitz and LoPiccolo, 1972; Kaplan, 1974) for nonorgasmic women, and the use of dilators (Annon, 1976; Haslam, 1965) for women with vaginismus and dyspareunia. Since these techniques are standard treatment procedures and described in detail in sexual dysfunction therapy literature, they are not discussed in this chapter.

Session 5.   This session continues to focus on the use of sexual fantasies. Problems with the use or development of such fantasies are discussed.

Prior to her rape, all of Meagan's sexual fantasies included the use of physical force. She relied entirely on such fantasies when sexual and had been unable to become aroused to other fantasy content. However, since her assault Meagan was very uncomfortable with these fantasies, and consequently, refused to use any fantasies to augment her arousal level. While she had tried to change her fantasies by eliminating all references to force, she reported that these attempts were unsuccessful in that she felt no arousal with the new fantasies.

A desire to modify fantasy content is shared by some sexual assault survivors. However, like Meagan, most of these women report that their radical changes are ineffective. For these women, masturbatory conditioning (Abel et al., 1973; Annon, 1971; Davison, 1968a; Lazarus, 1968a; Marguis, 1970; Marshall, 1973; McGuire et al., 1965; Thorpe et al., 1963), a procedure by which fantasy content is gradually changed in the desired direction, is useful and very effective.

A few assault survivors who may never have used sexual fantasies previously may report that they did become aroused to some of the fantasies provided at the last treatment session but that they have great difficulty creating their own fantasies. These women can take some of the fantasies they liked and modify them in order to practice developing their own fantasies. With this procedure, the women gain experience in creating fantasies and, with practice, learn to develop original fantasies.

A final point that should be explained to a survivor is the importance of having a library of sexual fantasies for use. She can prevent diminution of the arousal-producing capacity of a fantasy by continually rotating or modifying fantasies.

Writing an original sexual fantasy and using a fantasy when being sexual are included in the homework assignments for this session. Additionally, a woman who is doing any of the specific sexual dysfunction exercises is instructed to continue them.

Session 6.   Some women may be unclear about the physiological responses to sexual stimulation, as well as the physical and emotional components of orgasm. Such lack of knowledge may be particularly common in women who were assaulted as children and subsequently repressed all sexual feelings and behaviors. The importance of discussing physiological and emotional responses may be apparent at the beginning of therapy or as treatment progresses.

> Sexually assaulted as a child, Tanya had never engaged in masturbation or sexual activity with a partner prior to her marriage. In her mid-20s, Tanya was married. While she reported that throughout five years of marriage she derived some pleasure when sexual with her husband, she had never experienced an orgasm.
>
> As part of her therapy, she was instructed to practice the Kegel exercises and begin masturbatory training. After a few weeks of doing the homework assignments, Tanya reported that she thought she had had an orgasm but was unsure. The experience had felt good but had not been like what she had imagined. Following a discussion of the physical components of orgasm, Tanya was delighted to discover she had, in fact, had an orgasm.

A focus of this session includes a discussion of the physiological components of sexual arousal and orgasm. Since, in our society, many people do not receive an adequate sex education and sexual assault survivors may be particularly hesitant to discuss sex with others, it should not be assumed that a survivor does not need to discuss these elements. Whenever possible, visual aids should be used to augment this discussion.

Cognitive restructuring is the second focus of this session. As a result of an assault, a woman may have developed a negative perception of sexual behavior or response and consequently may need to learn to replace such negative labels.

> As a result of her ongoing assaults by her father, Jenny felt that she had had all control over her sexuality destroyed. Having been sexual since her mid-teens, she felt she had recovered some sense of control. However, she had never allowed herself to have an orgasm for fear that she would once again lose all sense of control. Thus, whether masturbating or being sexual with a partner, she would allow herself to become aroused and then mentally turn off so that she could maintain her control.
> In the course of therapy, Jenny was helped to relabel orgasm as a pleasure she deserved and something she could allow herself to enjoy rather than as a loss of control over her sexuality.

Gradual steps should be taken to help a survivor alter her cognitions. In a case like Jenny, for example, a woman can first be asked to imagine what it would feel like emotionally and behaviorally to have an orgasm. Second, she is instructed to practice being orgasmic in private. This exercise entails having a woman act out what she anticipates her behavior would be during an orgasm. She is then told to engage in self-stimulation to experience an orgasm. Finally, she is instructed to be sexual with a partner. Through these steps a woman has the opportunity to test the inaccuracies of her misconceptions and subsequently change her cognitions.

The homework assignments for this session include practicing the cognitive restructuring exercises and continuing the specific sexual dysfunction exercises.

Session 7. As a result of her assault, a sexual assault survivor may experience a great degree of anxiety in specific sexual situations or, perhaps, whenever being sexual. Since this anxiety is incompatible with sexual pleasure, learning to reduce anxiety is the focus of this session.

> Nicole had been forced to perform oral sex during her assault and subsequently was very anxious when she attempted to do so with her sexual partner. Her concern about her partner's ability to ejaculate as a result of her oral stimulation increased her anxiety and prevented her from enjoying this activity.
> Nicole was encouraged to use sexual fantasies while fellating her husband in order to maintain her arousal. Additionally, it was pointed out to Nicole

that her partner may be very satisfied if she limited fellatio to a means of becoming aroused but used penile-vaginal intercourse to reach orgasm.

For some women, use of alternative behaviors in an anxiety-producing situation may reduce experienced anxiety. Thus, Nicole was able to enjoy fellatio when she realized that other behaviors could be used to achieve orgasm.

However, some women may experience such intense generalized anxiety that the use of alternative behaviors is not an adequate method for controlling anxiety. Systematic desensitization (Brady, 1966; Ince, 1973; Kraft and Al Issa, 1967; Lazarus, 1961, 1963, 1968b; Lazarus and Rachman, 1960; Wolpe, 1958; Wolpe and Lazarus, 1966) is an alternative therapeutic technique.

The homework for this session is to continue specific sexual dysfunction exercises. Additionally, systematic desensitization can be practiced for women who require it.

Session 8.   In the previous sessions, the primary focus has been on helping a survivor understand her own sexuality and regain a sense of control over it. However, unless she is able to communicate her sexual needs and desires to her partner, she may continue to experience dysfunctional interactions with her partner. Thus, an essential component of sexual dysfunction therapy is the teaching of sexual communication and sexual assertion skills.

Since her rape, Laureen found that she required an increasing amount of sexual stimulation in order to enjoy intercourse. Additionally, she had developed an intense dislike when her body was touched in particular places. Laureen was frequently disappointed in her sexual partner as he failed to stimulate her sufficiently and continued to fondle her body where she disliked it.

Laureen indicated that she had not talked to her partner about these problems as she believed he should know already. Rather than communicating to him that rubbing of her neck was not only not arousing but actually disturbing, she would continually reposition her body in hopes of helping her partner avoid the areas she disliked. This behavior was not effective, and Laureen's partner began to complain about her acrobatics.

In a case such as Laureen, it is important to stress that, rather than assume that her partner knows or should know her needs and desires, it is a woman's responsibility to communicate them to her partner.

In our society many women have been socialized to be unassertive in general, with this lack of assertiveness particularly apparent in their sexual interactions and compounded by a history of sexual assault. Thus, women frequently are very uncomfortable communicating their sexual likes and dislikes to their partners. During this session, the importance of good communication with a sexual partner is stressed. Successful communication enables a woman to avoid stressful sexual situations, experience increased sexual pleasure by having her needs and desires met, and improve overall sexual enjoyment for both parties.

Much of this session is spent helping a woman improve her communication skills through behavioral rehearsal (Lazarus, 1966). For example, Laureen was initially asked to identify her sexual desires and needs and then practice expressing them by role playing with the therapist. When she had difficulty expressing particular needs, the therapist demonstrated various ways those needs could be communicated effectively. Finally, Laureen was encouraged to practice alone the messages she wished to convey.

Effective communication can be either verbal, nonverbal, or a combination. Since Laureen disliked having her neck rubbed but was very aroused when her stomach was, she could tell her partner that she really enjoyed having her stomach rubbed, gently guide her partner's hand to her stomach, or guide her partner's hand while indicating that that touch felt very good. Some survivors have reported that the nonverbal or combination approaches are the easiest to utilize initially.

A frequently overlooked component of sexual assertiveness is being able to say no to being sexual altogether or to engaging in specific sexual behaviors. Some sexual assault survivors indicate that they are fearful of their partners' reactions should an overture be turned down.

> Helen's father had forced cunnilingus on her when she was a child, and as a consequence, she had developed an intense dislike for this behavior. With the passage of time, she felt she had recovered from the incest and did enjoy sex very much.
>
> Helen married in her mid-20s and reported that her sexual interactions with her husband were very satisfying. However, two years into the marriage, her husband expressed a desire to perform cunnilingus. Believing that he was trying to show her how much he cared for her and fearful that he would feel rejected if she refused, Helen acquiesced. Throughout this behavior, she experienced terrifying flashbacks about her incestuous assaults but pretended to her husband that she was enjoying it. Happy with her apparent responsiveness, Helen's husband began initiating cunnilingus routinely, resulting in Helen's losing interest in sex in general.

Helen identified as a treatment goal learning to say no to cunnilingus. The therapist helped clarify the relationship between the cunnilingus and Helen's subsequent loss of arousal and gave her permission to say no. With the help of the therapist, Helen then practiced explaining to her husband that his love and its expression were very important to her and particularly appreciated when they engaged in other sexual activities. By stressing the pleasure she derived from their sexual interactions in general, Helen was able to express her desire to forego cunnilingus.

During this session, sensate focus exercises (Masters and Johnson, 1970) are introduced as a means to improving sexual communication. Additionally, readings on sexual assertiveness (Phelps and Austin, 1975) are provided. The homework assignments include doing the sensate focus exercises and continuing the specific sexual dysfunction exercises.

Session 9.   Assertiveness continues to be discussed during this session. A primary focus is the response of a sexual partner to a woman's newly demonstrated assertiveness. It is very common for some women to have difficulty when first asserting themselves sexually. A frequent problem is that some women overstep the assertiveness boundaries when expressing their desires.

> Following the discussion of assertiveness, Lila tried to assert herself some when she and her partner were next sexual. Lila began by telling her husband to give her a message. When he first attempted intromission, she told him to stop and to fondle her breasts more. She then continued to tell him what to do step by step. The interaction was not enjoyable to either party, leaving Lila feeling unsuccessful.

As can be seen, Lila was not being assertive but actually was giving her partner orders. Her concern about communicating her desires clouded her ability to identify assertive communications. For women with similar problems, it is recommended that they use their own feelings as guidelines. Specifically, it is suggested that they determine how they would like to have a particular message communicated to them and then use such a communication with their partners.

If the sexual situation is particularly stressful, a woman can be encouraged to talk about her needs at a time when she and her partner are not being sexual. For example, Lila felt more comfortable discussing her desires with her husband when they were sitting alone in a local park as part of one of their evening walks. By initially holding such discussions in a "safe" location, Lila was able to gain security in asserting herself sexually.

A second problem that some women report is that they have difficulty enacting with their partners the scenes they had role played during the last session. having liked a specific way of expressing a need or desire, a woman may try to repeat the suggestion verbatim to her partner, only to discover that she becomes confused. It is important to stress the need of using words with which a woman is comfortable in her communications with her partner. Additionally, the value of practice should be noted. Just as most people practice other important communications, such as requesting a raise at work, a woman can practice how she wants to explain her needs and desires.

Finally, when working toward changing her partner's behavior in order to meet her sexual needs, a woman should be encouraged to aim for gradual changes rather than immediate global changes. This approach is more likely to meet with success.

The homework assignment for this session is to have a woman assert herself sexually at least one time before her next session. Additionally, work on the specific sexual dysfunction exercises is to be continued.

Session 10. In this final session, treatment goals are reviewed and progress on each is evaluated. Since many sexual assault survivors may be attempting to change chronic behavioral patterns, some of which involve a partner, achieving each goal completely within the 10 weeks of therapy may not be possible, and it is important that his message be communicated. Delayed progress may be particularly true for women who did not have a sexual partner while in therapy. However, a woman can learn the therapeutic techniques and implement them after therapy. We have found that therapeutic progress frequently continues after the termination of treatment.

SPECIAL THERAPY ISSUES

An issue that has never been addressed adequately is the use of male therapists in the treatment of sexual assault survivors. Some concern has been expressed about the possible additional trauma a survivor may experience as a result of interaction with males immediately subsequent to an assault (Silverman, 1977). This concern may be increased in the treatment of sexually dysfunctional survivors.

Our experience indicates that, in fact, the majority of survivors have a preference for a same-sex therapist and sometimes will not even consider a male therapist. However, other survivors have reported that the sex of a therapist is not the critical issue. Instead, these women are more concerned that a therapist be warm, understanding, and empathetic. Still a smaller group of survivors express a preference for a male therapist. This preference appears to be based either on a belief that interacting with a male therapist will be therapeutic in and of itself or a preassault history of having strong, close relationships with males. Thus, it appears that a male therapist can be effective when treating sexually dysfunctional survivors and that a survivor's preference should be a determining factor whenever possible.

A second important issue is the possible manifestation of additional problems as therapy progresses. For example, memories and fears associated with an assault may be rekindled. We have found that incest survivors frequently become depressed during therapy. It is important that both the therapist and the survivor realize that the manifestation of additional problems is not indicative of ineffective therapy. Rather, these new problems result from work on assault-related sexual problems and can be resolved.

Resolution of such problems may occur through the clarification of any misperception she might have developed about the assault, the addition of appropriate therapeutic interventions to the sexual dysfunction treatment package, or referral to appropriate treatment agents. An excellent source for further treatment may be survivor support groups run by local rape crisis centers. Regardless of the approach taken, it is important that both the therapist and the survivor realize that these additional problems must be resolved, not avoided or ignored.

Finally, our experience indicates that, while many sexual assault survivors do seek professional help for their assault-related problem, the impact of an assault on a survivor's sexual functioning is too frequently ignored. Consequently, postassault sexual problems may endure for many years. We have found that the treatment package outlined above has been effective in treating both acute and chronic sexual problems. Additionally, the package can be implemented even when a woman is concurrently in therapy elsewhere.

SUMMARY

As a result of a sexual assault, up to 40% of survivors may develop a chronic sexual problem (Skinner et al., 1982). The sexual dysfunction treatment package discussed in this chapter has been found to be effective in treating these assault-related problems (Becker et al., 1982). The package can be applied across a variety of sexual problems and can be modified to meet the specific needs of a survivor.

REFERENCES

Abel, G. G., Barlow, D. H., and Blanchard, E. B. 1973. Developing heterosexual arousal by altering masturbatory fantasies: A controlled study. Paper presented to the annual meeting of the Association for the Advancement of Behavior Therapy, Miami, December.

Annon, J. S. 1971. *The therapeutic use of masturbation in the treatment of sexual disorders.* Paper presented at the annual meeting of the Association for the Advancement of Behavior Therapy. Washington, D.C., September 1971.

Annon, J. S. 1976. *Behavioral Treatment of Sexual Problems: Brief Therapy.* New York: Harper & Row.

Barbach, L. G. 1974. Group treatment of preorgasmic women. *J. Sex and Marital Therapy,* 1:139–145.

Barbach, L. G. 1975. *For Yourself: The Fulfillment of Female Sexuality.* Garden City, N.Y.: Doubleday.

Bart, P. 1975. Rape doesn't end with a kiss. Unpublished manuscript.

Becker, J. V., Skinner, L. J., and Abel, G. G. 1983a. Sexual dysfunctions in sexual assault survivors. In D. S. Milman and A. D. Goldman (eds). *New Perspectives in Sexual Dysfunctions*. Dubuque: Kendall-Hunt, in press.

Becker, J. V., Skinner, L. J., and Abel, G. G. 1983b. Sequellae of sexual assault: The survivor's perspective. In I. R. Stuart and J. G. Greer (eds). *Sexual Aggression: Current Perspectives in Treatment*. New York: Van Nostrand Reinhold, in press.

Becker, J. V., Skinner, L. J., Abel, G. G., and Cichon, J. 1982. Time limited therapy with sexually dysfunctional sexual assault survivors. Paper presented at the annual meeting of the American Psychological Association, Washington, D.C., August 1982.

Becker, J. V., Skinner, L. J., Abel, G. G., and Treacy, E. 1982. Incidence and types of sexual dysfunctions in rape and incest victims. *J. Sex and Marital Therapy*, 8:65–74.

Brady, J. P. 1966. Brevital-relaxation treatment of frigidity. *Behavior Research and Therapy*, 4:71–77.

Burgess, A. W., and Holmstrom, L. L. 1979. Rape: Sexual disruption and recovery. *A. J. Orthopsychiatry*, 49:648–657.

Carney, A., Bancroft, J., and Mathews, A. 1978. Combination of hormonal and psychological treatment for female sexual unresponsiveness. *British J. Psychiatry*, 132:339–346.

Cedar and Melly (eds). 1979. *A Women's Touch: An Anthology of Lesbian Eroticisim and Sensuality*. New York: Womenshare Books.

Davison, G. 1968a. Elimination of a sadistic fantasy by client-controlled counter-conditioning. *J. Abnormal Psychology*, 73:84–90.

Deutsch, R. M. 1968. *The Key to Feminine Response in Marriage*. New York: Random House.

Dodson, B. 1974. *Liberating Masturbation*. New York: Body Sex Designs.

Ellis, E. M., Calhoun, K. S., and Atkeson, B. M. 1980. Sexual dysfunction in victims of rape: Victims may experience a loss of sexual arousal and frightening flashbacks even one year after the assault. *Women and Health*, 5:39–47.

Ersner-Hershfield, R. 1978. The effects of couples vs. women group treatment for female orgasmic dysfunction. Paper presented at the annual meeting of the Association of Sex Therapists and Counselors, Memphis, April 1978.

Feldman-Summers, S., Gordon, P. E., and Meagher, J. R. 1979. The impact of rape on sexual satisfaction. *J. Abnormal Psychology*, 88:101–105.

Friday, N. 1973. *My Secret Garden: Women's Sexual Fantasies*. New York: Pocket Books.

Friday, N. 1975. *Forbidden Flowers: More Women's Sexual Fantasies*. New York: Pocket Books.

Gager, N., and Schurr, C. 1976. *Sexual Assault: Confronting Rape in America*. New York: Grosset & Dunlap.

Geisinger, D. L. 1969. Controlling sexual interpersonal anxieties. In J. D. Krumboltz and C. E. Thoreson (eds). *Behavioral Counseling: Cases and Techniques*. New York: Holt, Rinehart and Winston.

Golden, J. S., Price, S., Heinrich, A. G., and Lobitz, W. C. 1978. Group vs. couple treatment of sexual dysfunctions. *Archives of Sexual Behavior*, 7:593–602.

Haslam, M. T. 1965. The treatment of psychogenic dyspareunia by reciprocal inhibition. *British J. Psychiatry*, 111:280–282.

Heiman, J. R., and LoPiccolo, J. 1981. Clinical outcome of sex therapy: Effects of daily vs. weekly treatment. Paper presented at the annual meeting of the American Psychological Association, Los Angeles, August 1981.

Heiman, J., LoPiccolo, J., and LoPiccolo, L. 1976. *Becoming Orgasmic: Sexual Growth Program for Women*. Englewood Cliffs, N.J.: Prentice-Hall.

Hilberman, E. 1976. *The Rape Victim*. New York: Basic Books.

Holmstrom, L., and Burgess, A. 1978. Sexual behavior of assailant and victim during rape. Paper presented at the annual meeting of the American Sociological Association, San Francisco, September 1978.

Ince, L. P. 1973. Behavior modification of sexual disorders. *Am. J. Psychotherapy* **17**:446–451.

Kaplan, H. S. 1974. *The New Sex Therapy: Active Treatment of Sexual Dysfunctions*. New York: Brunner/Mazel.

Kegel, A. H. 1952. Sexual functions of the pubococcygeus muscle. *Western J. Surgery*, **60**:521–524.

Kilmann, P. R. 1978. The treatment of primary and secondary orgasmic dysfunctions: A methodological review of the literature since 1970. *J. Sex and Marital Therapy*, **4**:155–176.

Kilpatrick, D., Best, C., and Veronen, L. 1978. The adolescent rape victim: Psychological responses to sexual assault and treatment approaches. In A. K. Kreuther and D. Hollingsworth (eds). *Adolescent Obstetrics and Gynecology*. Chicago: Year Book Medical Publishers.

Kraft, T., and Al Issa, I. 1967. Behavior therapy and the treatment of fridigity. *Am. J. Psychotherapy*, **21**:116–120.

Lazarus, A. A. 1961. Group therapy in phobic disorders by systematic desensitization. *J. Abnormal Social Psychology*, **63**:504–510.

Lazarus, A. A. 1963. The treatment of chronic frigidity by systematic desensitization. *J. Nervous and Mental Disorders*, **136**:272–278.

Lazarus, A. A. 1966. Behavioral rehearsal vs. non-directive therapy vs. advice in effecting behaviour change. *Behavior Research and Therapy*, **4**:209–212.

Lazarus, A. 1968a. A case of pseudonecrophilia treated by behavior therapy. *J. Clinical Psychology*, **24**:113–115.

Lazarus, A. A. 1968b. Behavior therapy in groups. In G. M. Gazda (ed). *Basic Approaches to Group Psychotherapy and Group Counseling*. Springfield, Ill: Thomas.

Lazarus, A. A., and Rachman, C. 1960. The use of systematic desensitization in psychotherapy. In H. J. Eysenck (ed). *Behaviour Therapy and the Neuroses*. New York: Pergamon.

Leiblum, S. R., and Ersner-Hershfield, R. 1977. Sexual enhancement groups for dysfunctional women: An evaluation. *J. Sex and Marital Therapy*, **3**:139–152.

Leiblum, S. R., Rosen, R. C., and Pierce, D. 1976. Group treatment format: Mixed sexual dysfunctions. *Archives of Sexual Behavior*, **5**:269–274.

Lobitz, W., and LoPiccolo, J. 1972. New methods in the behavioral treatment of sexual dysfunctions. *J. Behavior Therapy and Experimental Psychiatry*, **3**:266–271.

LoPiccolo, J., and Lobitz, W. C. 1972. The role of masturbation in the treatment of orgasmic dysfunction. *Archives of Sexual Behavior*, **2**:163–172.

Marguis, J. N. 1970. Orgasmic reconditioning: Changing sexual object choice through controlling masturbation fantasies. *J. Behavior Therapy and Experimental Psychiatry*, **1**:263–271.

Marks, I. M. 1981. Review of behavioral psychotherapy II: Sexual disorders. *Am. J. Psychiatry*, **138**:750–756.

Marshall, W. L. 1973. The modification of sexual fantasies: A combined treatment approach to the reduction of deviant sexual behavior. *Behavior Research and Therapy*, **11**:557–564.

Masters, W., and Johnson, V. E. 1970. *Human Sexual Inadequacy*. Boston: Little, Brown.

Mathews, A. M. 1981. Treatment of sex dysfunctions: Psychological and hormone factors. In J. C. Boulougouris (ed). *Learning Theory Applications in Psychiatry*. New York: Wiley.

McGuire, L., and Wagner, N. 1978. Sexual dysfunctions in women who were molested as children: One response pattern and suggestions for treatment. *J. Sex and Marital Therapy,* 4:11–15.

McGuire, R. J., Carlise, J. M., and Young, B. G. 1965. Sexual deviation as conditioned behavior. *Behavior Research and Therapy,* 2:185–190.

McMullen, S., and Rosen, R. C. 1979. The use of self-administered masturbation training in the treatment of primary orgasmic dysfunction. *J. Consulting and Clinical Psychology,* 47:912–918.

Munjack, D., Cristol, A., Goldstein, A., Phillips, D., Goldberg, A., Whipple, K., Staples, F., and Kanno, P. 1976. Behavioral treatment of orgasmic dysfunction: A controlled study. *British J. Psychiatry,* 129:497–502.

Phelps, S., and Austin, N. 1975. *The Assertive Woman.* California: Impact Publishers.

Reynolds, B. S., Price, S. C., and Heinrich, A. G. 1981. The effectiveness of group treatment formats for the sexual dysfunctions. Paper presented at the annual meeting of the American Psychological Association, Los Angeles, August 1981.

Rosen, R., and Rosen, L. R. 1981. *Human Sexuality.* New York: Knopf.

Segraves, R. T. 1976. Primary orgasmic dysfunction: Essential treatment components. *J. Sex and Marital Therapy,* 2:115–123.

Silverman, D. 1977. First do no more harm: Female rape victims and the male counselor. *Am. J. Orthopsychiatry,* 47:91–96.

Skinner, L. J., Becker, J. V., Abel, G. G., and Cichon, J. 1982. Sexual dysfunctions in rape and incest survivors. Paper presented at the annual meeting of the American Psychological Association, Washington, D.C., August 1982.

Thorpe, J. Schmidt, E., and Costell, D. 1963. A comparison of positive and negative (aversive) conditioning in the treatment of homosexuality. *Behavior Research and Therapy,* 1:357–362.

Wolpe, J. 1958. *Psychotherapy by Reciprocal Inhibition.* Stanford: Stanford University Press.

Wolpe, J., and Lazarus, A. A. 1966. *Behavior Therapy Techniques: A Guide to the Treatment of Neuroses.* New York: Pergamon.

Wright, J., Perreault, R., and Mathieu, M. 1977. The treatment of sexual dysfunction: A review. *Archives of General Psychiatry,* 34:881–890.

Zeiss, A., Rosen, G. and Zeiss, R. 1978. Orgasm during intercourse: A treatment strategy for women. In J. LoPiccolo and L. LoPiccolo (eds). *Handbook of Sex Therapy.* New York: Plenum.

13
Rape and the College Student: Multiple Crises in Late Adolescence

Edward L. Rowan, M.D.
Judith B. Rowan, Ph.D.

ABSTRACT

Rape is a crisis for anyone and especially so for a college student struggling with the developmental tasks of late adolescence. Issues of parental differentiation, mature sexuality, intimacy, role choice, and values clarification must be resolved in order to achieve a strong adult identity. The rape trauma syndrome consists of an acute phase of fear, anxiety, and disorganization followed by a period of superficial "normality" characterized by denial and suppression. The third and final phase is resolution and integration of the experience into the victim's life. At each phase of the syndrome, emotional support, here-and-now behavioral tasks, and psychodynamic exploration are essential. The rape counselor must be able to deal with his or her own stereotypes, fantasies, and feelings about rape so that the victim can explore her own more fully. Because of the high risk of rape in a college population, all institutions should take responsibility for preventive measures as well as treatment of student victims.

I lived in a cooperative dorm on campus. The cat had had kittens and I left the door open so she could come in and out. . . . I woke up about four in the morning and a man was standing at the foot of the bed. He said he wanted to feel me and he took out a gun. First he did oral sex, then he put down his gun so he could take down his pants. Somehow I had the presence of mind to pick up the gun but I couldn't scream. He grabbed the gun back and ran. I ran across the hall screaming, but he was gone. I was shaking, scared to death. . . . The campus police took me to the infirmary. The doctor gave me a mild tranquilizer and a friend stayed there with me that night. . . . The police were actually pretty good about it. They had me look through mug books but I don't know what they did later. . . . Some of the girls I lived with didn't believe it happened; they thought I made it up. Some people treated it as a joke. . . . My parents and I had just argued about my living off campus. In response to my telling them about the rape, my mother said, "Be strong," and my father wouldn't talk about it. . . . My reaction at first was to blank it out, "Hey, I'm tough; I can handle it," but I went through the last two months of school in a fog. I was angry at the school but I couldn't be terrified for myself. I couldn't feel how vulnerable I was. . . . Periodically, the fear still comes up. Maybe some of the risks I took were attempts to deal with how scared I felt. . . . I gained a lot of weight after the rape. When I was thin I got raped. I had sexual relationships but they didn't involve any emotional gratification and now I haven't been sexual in a long, long time. When I think about having sex now I get terrified, thinking I will just fall apart. . . . In my work now I deal with an incredible number of rapists, wife abusers, violent people. At some level I can't help feeling it's good for me to do that. After the rape I became much more interested in feminism; women raising their consciousnesses and being supportive of each other. I need to feel closer to other women. I need to feel safe with them. . . . I've just started in therapy for other reasons, but I think the rape is tied in. . . .

Rape is stressful. This victim's response pattern closely follows the crisis pattern outlined by Sutherland and Scherl (1970) and called the *rape trauma syndrome* by Burgess and Holmstrom (1974). The acute stage of fear, anxiety, and emotional turmoil is followed by a period of denial and suppression with resumption of "normal" behavior. The final stage of working through and resolution may take months or years to complete.

No rape victim escapes the kaleidoscopic emotions that accompany that traumatic event; however, in our clinical experience, the degree of personal stability prior to rape in part determines the extent of disability that follows. Individuals struggling with other issues at the time of rape are at a higher risk of difficulty in resolving the additional stress. Adolescence is a time of concentrated struggle. Biological developments of physiologic growth and mental maturation, interpersonal changes of shifting relationships, social upheaval of changing role demands, and ethical dilemmas inherent in the development of a personal value system all overlap and weigh heavily upon the individual attempting to maintain that equilibrium which is "mental health." We feel that to superimpose rape upon that adolescent identity struggle may result in a prolongation of a state of disequilibrium.

A significant number of late adolescents attend an institute of higher education or college. The educational model, with its emphasis on the acquisition of information and skills, differentiates it from the nonacademic setting. Special authority roles and relationships, standards of performance and behavior, a sense of tradition, the geographic setting, and characteristics of the peer group create a special atmosphere. The goal is to increase individual potential whether for personal growth, education for its own sake, or vocational development. The adolescent is stimulated intellectually, encouraged to internalize values, and given time for adaptation.

DEVELOPMENTAL TASKS

The adolescent must typically accomplish five major tasks before moving into adulthood: differentiation from parents with resolution of dependency issues, development of mature sexuality, establishment of intimate relationships, acquisition of a vocational role choice, and clarification of a personal value system. Although there is some overlap in these developmental tasks, there are quite specific concerns in each area.

The differentiation from parents implies a shift from dependency to independence. This shift is a difficult one because the parental model of interaction is the one in which the adolescent is currently enmeshed. From this enmeshed perspective it is often difficult for the adolescent to appreciate that the rest of the world might be different or that there might be alternative models for living. As a necessary intermediate step, peer identification provides support, and although transient, is often seen from within as a final solution rather than as a step toward true independence. Attendance at college prolongs the stage of control by authority, and in addition, dependence on parental financial support during this time reinforces the difficulty in separating. While constructive rebellion is limited in time and scope and results in a lessening of parental dependence while retaining parental love, destructive rebellion may lead to permanent alienation (Erikson, 1968).

"Sexual unfolding" is described by the Sarrels (1979) as a process by which the adolescent becomes aware of himself or herself as a sexual being, male or female, who relates sexually to others in a characteristic way. This includes the acquisition of a nondistorted body image and the resolution of confusion about sexual orientation. Early guilt and/or shame about sexual thoughts is modulated, and erotic stimuli are clearly recognized for what they are. The adolescent finds a place and value for sex in life and develops a satisfying (not dysfunctional or compulsive) and responsible (nonexploitive) sexual life.

Intimacy is different from sexuality but often confused with it as, for example, "If this is a sexual relationship, then I must be emotionally involved." Intimacy includes the emotional component of caring based on trust, affection, and commitment to another person, and an intellectual component based on learning from and with that other person's experiences, feelings, and beliefs. As a result, the growth process of both partners is enhanced. Issues of power and dominance are worked out. Adolescence is a time of practice relationships where intimate communication patterns are learned and rehearsed.

Role choice includes both vocational options and incorporation of sex role stereotypes. If a woman perceives marriage as her primary adult role, then her vocational options may be quite limited, and, in an equally restrictive way, an early vocational commitment may limit marital options. Work provides both security and self-esteem. The response to the questions, "What do you want to be when you grow up?" is one of the most public decisions the adolescent must make. A college atmosphere may demonstrate a wide range of role options and expose women to nontraditional choices and models.

The acquisition of a personal value system may be the most difficult task of late adolescence. While educators stress excellence and a make-the-most-of-yourself philosophy, society in general (as represented by peer groups and the mass media) stresses mediocrity. One common reaction to the world as perceived by the adolescent is apathy: the physical, intellectual, and emotional slump which indicates both an inability and an unwillingness to achieve an adult identity. Questions like "Why bother?" and "Is that all there is?" are common. Resolution of these complex questions is essential if the adolescent is to emerge with a truly adult identity.

THE COLLEGE SETTING

Not only does college concentrate the stresses of development, it also concentrates the factors that predispose to rape. The most common rape victim is a single woman aged 17 to 24 — the student age group. Men can be and are raped (Sarrels, 1979); however, the vast majority of victims are women, and they are the focus of this discussion. The campus is an obvious hunting ground for the rapist (both the blitz and confidence types of Burgess and Holmstrom, 1974) and also a common setting for acts that are often not recognized as rape. Rape is "forced penetration without consent" and includes events called acquaintence rape or date rape. In these instances the victim knew and agreed to some relationship with her date but was unable to control the course of events which led to nonconsensual sexual activity. These assaults probably occur with higher frequency and lower reporting than attacks by strangers. In addition to the sequelae of fear, the consequences of shattered trust accompany an experience of acquaintence rape.

The college campus also focuses attention on the sociopolitical predispositions to and consequences of rape, and may stress these to the exclusion of the personal, psychodynamic meaning of the attack. Both aspects must be considered.

RAPE TRAUMA SYNDROME

Based on the patterns of behavior observed and codified as the rape trauma syndrome, there are two distinct periods requiring therapeutic intervention: the acute, crisis phase and the working through or resolution phase. We believe that the better and more complete the crisis work, the less the likelihood of serious sequelae.

Regardless of the phase, there are important considerations for the rape counselor. Many, if not most, counselors are women, and as such are likely to identify closely with female victims. McCombie and Arons (1980) caution counselors to consider their own anxiety, vulnerability, and risk ("It could have been me") and not to avoid that issue by focusing blame on the victim through such attitudes as "I would not have had such poor judgment." The sadistic and masochistic feelings associated with the act of rape must also be identified so that the counselor does not identify too closely with victimization and/or hostility toward the rapist with resultant blame or rejection of the victim or collusion in nondiscussion of the act itself. Discomfort or fantasy about details might also preclude this discussion. Burgess and Holmstrom (1974) also caution against rescue fantasies, false reassurances, and advice giving. Male counselors must be aware of the role that their maleness plays in the relationship with the victim. The counselor as well as the victim must take responsibility for conflicts and feelings about rape.

The sociopolitical aspects of rape have been discussed widely (e.g., Morrison, 1980, and Brownmiller, 1975). Rape is an unusual circumstance wherein the victim is threatened, violated, and then socially condemned. The woman is somehow seen as at fault: "She asked for it" by provocative dress or action or by being alone at night; "boys will be boys, good girls don't get raped, bad girls shouldn't complain." This implies a societal role of woman as function, not as person. Rape is not a sexual act but an act of power or anger expressed sexually. The stereotypic responses of members of society must be understood by the counselor as they are often major concerns of the victim.

Acute Phase

A crisis is defined by Bassuk (1980) as a point of disequilibrium where the usual problem-solving mechanisms are ineffective. Crisis intervention facilitates working through this trauma. There are four areas of concern: medical/legal evaluation and treatment, availability of a social network for support, behavioral considerations so that a normal life-style is maintained, and psychological considerations about the experience and emotional responses to it. All this should occur in the context of emotional support.

Medical and legal responses to rape are often intertwined. Many hospitals have developed treatment plans and a rape protocol which take the crisis dynamics of rape into account and attempt to deal with anxiety, fear, loss of control, and physical damage. The victim is made comfortable in the company of friends or a crisis team and engaged in participation in her care in order to regain a sense of control over her life. The physical exam documents the assault (physical signs, evidence of semen) and initiates treatment (VD and pregnancy prophylaxis). It must not be another rape and should be performed in such a way that the victim will be willing to return in four to six weeks for testing for syphilis and pregnancy if appropriate.

Police must be sensitive to the victim. Their interview should document that there was forced penetration without consent and gather information about the identification of the rapist. It is essential that the counselor be aware of inconsistent reports, police frustration, and the delays and paperwork of the legal system, if charges are pressed, in order to help the victim confront these problems.

The social network may consist of family and friends, or if these are unavailable, a rape crisis center. Such a group can provide support, escort service, information, and further referrals.

The rape experience is a very powerful example of one-trial learning, with fear and anxiety classically conditioned by it and generalized to other stimuli present at that time. It may be necessary to begin shaping behavior toward a normal life-style within the bounds of safety. This includes determining travel routes, home changes, and security measures.

A conceptual framework for psychotherapeutic intervention is vital to the successful working through of issues related to rape. The five developmental tasks can provide this, and each should be explored with the victim.

Rape is a crisis for the family as well as for the victim. They often feel a need to blame, be it the situation (e.g., security), the assailant, society, the victim, or themselves. Too often there is an implication of moral disapproval of the victim's behavior, whatever it was. Issues in family dynamics should be discussed and put into perspective.

Doubts and fears about present and future sexual relationships are common. Burgess and Holmstrom (1979) found that more than two-thirds of victims decreased their frequency of sexual intercourse after a rape and many had sexual dysfunctions. Current lovers are most helpful if they can display sympathetic understanding. Predicting sexual reluctance and eventual recovery of interest is a reasonable intervention strategy.

Intimacy or trust issues are paramount in acquaintance rape. Many young women have previously interacted only with caring male family members and immature high school dates and have difficulty understanding rape behavior.

Role choice issues are not commonly thought through at this stage, nor are value clarifications. Clearly this is not a "just world" to the victim. An exploration and ventilation of feelings in a supportive environment is helpful, but working through may be a more reflective process and occur later.

In the acute phase, crisis intervention may occur in many settings, such as emergency room, crisis center, or student health service, and is often counselor-initiated, especially when a silent victim needs to be drawn out. The victim experiences a loss of control, helplessness, and especially, fear. Anxiety symptoms may take the form of free-floating anxiety, phobias, sleep disturbances, mood swings, recurrent thoughts of rape, depression, nonspecific physical complaints such as headaches or gastrointestinal disturbances, or trauma-specific symptoms such as inability to swallow or pelvic pain.

The goals of therapeutic intervention are to establish an alliance, determine victim concerns, identify and support strengths, evaluate the meaning of rape, and formulate a plan for resolution (McCombie and Arons, 1980).

The counselor should take a complete history, not only the factual but also the emotional aspects of each event. A flexible and nondirective approach is adopted during the history taking to help build rapport. The counselor attempts to elicit details of the assault itself so that it is not seen as too shameful and disgusting to discuss. Circumstances of the assault, a description of the assailant, threats and conversations, emotional and sexual response should be ascertained. Behavior after the assault should be identified: time until help sought; from whom and why; attempts at clean-up; and encounters with hospital, police, friends, and family. Finally an assessment of family and/or social support should be made and plans for the immediate future should be developed. Information obtained at this stage can ultimately be related to earlier, dynamically important events.

The counselor's goal at this stage of intervention is to help the victim master the emotional crisis. The observation that, "Whatever you did at the time was right because you're still alive," is appropriate and not false reassurance. The victim has survived a life-threatening situation. If the initial contact occurs immediately after the rape, then it is appropriate to discuss plans for notifying family and friends, arrangements for immediate safety, and decisions about medical exam and follow-up, police reports, and criminal charges. Intervention somewhat later would examine emotional responses to what has already happened and plans for what the next steps should be. The acute phase may last from four to six weeks, and regular counseling support may be necessary.

The patient whose history appears at the beginning of this chapter had no therapeutic intervention during the acute phase. Although the medicolegal responses appear to have been appropriately supportive and substantive, there was no peer group or parental support. A counselor able to reframe the peer disbelief or joke in terms of denial might have helped the patient see that peers could not deal with her experience and might have helped her either to confront them with the truth about the risk they all shared, or at least to feel secure in seeing their response as common and not specific to her. Acceptance of parental denial in the context of their inability to deal with rape might have been equally helpful.

Another example is that of an older, married student, a basically well-adjusted individual with an excellent support system. Meryl had taken a year off from work in order to finish her master's degree. She and her husband were living in an apartment in a neighborhood described as transitional, with fairly low rent and increasingly high crime. They had already been robbed earlier in the year. Meryl said she thought she was raped because she happened to be home at the time that her apartment was burgled. "He didn't hurt me; it was a pretty benign experience [for a rape.]" She called her husband right away. He was not able to come immediately, but asked his father to help her. Meryl felt very close to her father-in-law and was pleased to have his support at that time. The police were called; however, one of the officers was a black man, as was the rapist, and Meryl found herself unable to answer questions as long as he was there. The police called in a female member of the rape squad and she was able to establish rapport and get the necessary information. Neither Meryl's husband nor her father-in-law blamed her in any way for what had happened. They showed concern for her welfare and dealt with the rape as an aspect of living in a high-crime area. Meryl was taken to a gynecologist who was very gentle and helpful to her. He expressed anger about the fact that there were awful men around who raped women, and he helped her to separate the rapist from other men in her life who were supportive and loving. Meryl and her husband had intercourse a few days later because they wanted to feel close and because "it's like falling off a horse; you don't want to develop a mental block against it [intercourse]." She felt that her close relationship with her husband helped her through the experience. Her feeling of emotional closeness with her father-in-law increased because of his caring involvement during the postrape period. She did not require additional counseling to deal with the rape experience.

A third case demonstrates a great deal of difficulty during the acute phase. Diane, a nursing student, appeared at the hospital emergency room looking disheveled and frightened. The staff was not successful in gathering any information because she was unable to talk. She was also hyperventilating and unable to swallow when given a glass of water. She was observed in this state for several hours. After several attempts were made to elicit identifying information from her, she began to speak with difficulty but could not remember her name or address. She seemed tense and unable to relax. An aide was assigned to stay with her, and it was to her that Diane finally related the story of her rape. She was leaving the hospital after working the evening shift and was followed to her car by someone she thought to be a fellow worker. As she was about to enter her car, however, he pulled a knife and told her to get down behind the door and perform fellatio on him. He threatened that if she bit him, he would kill her. When she was free to go, she felt in a daze and did not remember how she got to the emergency room.

Following receipt of this information, the rape crisis team was called in to assist. School authorities and counseling staff were not notified because of Diane's fear that their involvement might lead to her being dropped from the nursing program. The rape crisis worker supported Diane during the police interview and reassured her that she had done the right thing in following the rapist's instructions. They also discussed safety issues at length and identified a support network for Diane. The worker offered her continued support and allayed Diane's anxiety about university involvement with reassurance that the counseling services were confidential and that she could utilize that resource if she so desired.

During the following week, Diane appeared twice more at the emergency room looking frightened and having difficulty in talking, swallowing, and recalling who she was. The staff checked out her physical health and sent her home. Diane refused a psychiatric consultation for her "hysterical symptoms." A week later Diane did finally make contact with the university counseling service where she was seen by a female psychologist. After establishing rapport and obtaining a history of the trauma, the therapist utilized a behavioral approach of progressive relaxation and desensitization. The hierarchy ended with Diane able to walk to her parked car without panic. After Diane regained control over this aspect of her life, the focus of therapy shifted to a consideration of control in other areas.

A final example is Beth, a freshman found wandering near fraternity row early on an autumn morning. Campus police brought her to the emergency room where she remained curled up and mute upon the examining table. Sexual assault was suspected because of the circumstances, and a student volunteer was summoned to sit with the patient. The volunteer was instructed simply to introduce herself and offer to be there with Beth. Beth passively accepted. An older male counselor arrived about an hour later. He quietly introduced himself, reassured Beth that she was now safe, asked her to tell what had happened, and waited. There was no response for several minutes, but Beth then began to sob uncontrollably and told of being at a fraternity party where she had too much to drink and was "gang-banged" by the brothers. She reluctantly agreed to gynecologic examination by a female physician and was encouraged to stay at the health center rather than return to her dorm. Other volunteers were contacted so that ongoing support would be provided.

Despite this support, Beth called her parents and asked to be taken home. A very angry father then appeared in the dean's office. He threatened legal action against the school and fraternity and demanded that charges be pressed. His daughter, however, was ambivalent about this as she blamed herself for drinking too much and wasn't sure she could identify her assailants. The father insisted that the school and fraternity were to blame. The counselor spent several hours with Beth, her parents, and the family together. Attempts were made to clarify the circumstances and calm and support the participants. The police investigator pointed out that without positive identification, it would be difficult to prosecute individuals; however, the dean's office was anxious to impose sanctions upon the identified fraternity. The parents insisted that Beth return home with them.

She subsequently enrolled in a smaller college near her home town. The status of her long-term adjustment is unknown.

Superficial Adjustment

A return to superficial normality can be anticipated. The first patient's "I'm tough, I can handle it" is a good example of this. The victim should be encouraged to continue contact through this phase and to seek further counseling if there is difficulty in integration and/or resolution. Availability, however, may be the only role possible for the therapist. Contact may be maintained by phone. This method is quick, easy, inexpensive, and nonintrusive; gives the victim some control; reaffirms concern; and gives opportunity for ventilation, clarification, and support (Burgess and Holmstrom, 1974.) Denial and suppression are the mechanisms in use at this time, but problematic issues may resurface at a later time.

Jennifer made and broke two appointments with a counselor at the student health service before keeping the third. At that time she expressed a desire to improve her utilization of time. She said that she had a heavy academic load and wanted to do well in her courses in order to get into graduate school. The major difficulty in exerting control over her daily schedule seemed to be her relationship with her boyfriend. She resisted any of the counselor's attempts to deal with deeper emotional issues that might be involved, so the counselor worked with her on asserting her needs and working out conflicts around scheduling events that involved her boyfriend. During a subsequent session, Jennifer made a vague reference to being used and controlled by men. The counselor followed up. After gentle probing, Jennifer revealed that she had been raped while out jogging over a year before; however, she quickly asserted that that experience had been satisfactorily dealt with at that time and that she was now more concerned with other matters in her life. While accepting this view at face value, the counselor urged Jennifer to further consider her attitudes toward men. It appeared that she had intellectualized her anger toward the rapist, generalized that feeling to all men, and utilized information from her women's history course to justify her position. While appreciating the validity of that position, the counselor encouraged Jennifer to explore what happened to her at a personal level. Her awareness of male violence in our culture was explored, as was her experience with males throughout her life. As Jennifer continued to prefer her global and rhetoric-based interpretation of events and continued to deny her feelings in general, the counselor assessed that she was not amenable to treatment at that time. The counselor then provided information about the stages of rape trauma response, related Jennifer's intellectualized feelings of anger to the rape, and encouraged her to return for further counseling. Hopefully, she could be helped to deal with her feelings of anger and helplessness and to become confident and in control of her life.

Resolution Phase

The resolution phase may be conceptualized as a posttraumatic stress disorder. According to DSM III (American Psychiatric Association, 1980) this includes: (a) existence of a recognizable stressor; (b) reexperiencing of the trauma (recurrent recollections or dreams or the sudden feeling or reoccurrence based on an association to an environmental or ideational stimulus); (c) numbed responsiveness to or reduced involvement with the external world (diminished interest in activities, detachment, constricted affect); (d) new symptoms such as hyperalertness or exaggerated startle, sleep disturbance, guilt for survival, memory impairment, avoidance activities that arouse recollection, or intensified symptoms when exposed to such activities. Such reactions occur not only in rape and assault victims, but also in those individuals exposed to battlefield experiences, accidents, and man-made as well as natural disasters.

Therapeutic intervention at this stage requires consideration of both the posttraumatic symptoms and the dynamic issues that give the rape an idiosyncratic meaning to the victim. A recovery model (Evans, 1978) which allows for regressions when stressed again and for subsequent readaptations takes into account the victim's associations to "environmental or ideational stimuli" as well as normal "depressive" responses associated with loss of control.

Most victims appear to have long-term symptoms (Kilpatrick et al., 1979), although no group has been able to do a complete retrospective or prospective analysis, as at least half of all victims are lost to follow-up in the best studies (e.g., Burgess and Holmstrom, 1979, and Nadelson et al., 1982). In addition to those who have moved or unlisted their phones, many women lost to follow-up are probably marginally functional or recidivist victims (Rabkin, 1979) who have significant characterologic and/or psychotic difficulties, or those victims who continue to deny difficulty at the time of follow-up.

In their recent work, Nadelson et al. (1982) found 76% of available follow-up victims still suspicious of others from one to two and one-half years after the attack, 61% restricted going out, 51% had sexual problems, 49% were afraid to be alone, and 41% were "depressed."

Again, the framework of developmental tasks is helpful in working through the effects of rape.

The principal issue with regard to the task of parental differentiation is a concern for the adequacy of the present level of independence. Regression to parental dependence (if it occurred) could refocus on previously unresolved issues. Substitute dependent relationships could develop. An exploration of dynamics is combined with behavioral tasks (e.g., shopping alone) to regain independence. A supportive therapist frequently evokes dependency transfer-ence, especially at termination of treatment, and this must be worked through.

Sexual dysfunction is extremely common, as has already been noted. Reac-tions and associations to penetration of body space result in abstinence or decreased frequency of sexual activity; "flashbacks;" avoidance of particular sexual activities and physical responses such as pain, discomfort, vaginismus, and anorgasmia. If problems are not alleviated by psychotherapeutic work in the strengthening of personal boundaries or reconditioning of behavior over time in a natural setting, then referral for sex therapy will be appropriate.

Intimacy issues are critical because loss of trust may lead to arrest of the developmental task of relationship building. Exploration of this issue is essential in order to prevent a premature closure of self-discovery made possible through relationships.

Role issues include present changes in life-style (such as moving, travel route changes, and job changes) which must be explored in terms of real safety precau-tions versus circumstance-specific "phobias," which might be dealt with behavior-ally or psychotherapeutically. Beyond the personal political issue of power relationships between men and women lies the societal issue where each victim must choose her own level of concern, involvement, or activity. Revalidation as a person might require speaking out about the experience of rape. Such political activism might validate the self and one's role in the community.

The most important issue of all is restoration of personal value, that is, autonomy and self-worth. "Depression" following rape is normal, as a loss of self-esteem, competence, and confidence has occurred. One aspect of this is a devaluation of the self if the rapist is not caught and punished in compensation for his assault. Another aspect is the need to express anger. Compassion for the rapist ("he's sick") makes it difficult to be angry. A feeling of guilt or shame precludes the expression of anger at the rapist because it interferes with a realistic perspective of the victim's passive role in the assault. Self-blame may inhibit restoration of personal value by focusing on one's inability to set limits (confusing power and sex), past rape fantasies (universal, not causal), or a belief that she deserved what happened because of her actions (societal stereotypes or risk-taking behavior which would require clarification.) A realistic integration of personal factors and their role in the assault is essential in the restoration of self-worth in rape survivors. Final resolution involves symptom relief, restora-tion of previous level of functioning, acquisition of new coping skills, and awareness of earlier conflicts in an individual's reaction to the rape experience.

Sandra appeared at the college health service requesting an abortion. During physical examination and initial interviews with a physician and social worker, she seemed uncertain about this decision and cried frequently. She said that she did not want to murder her baby. In light of her unsettled emotional state and her conflict about the abortion, she was referred to the counseling office for help in making her decision.

Sandra was seen by a female counselor who established a warm, supportive atmosphere appropriate for relating to someone in emotional crisis. During the first interview Sandra cried frequently and at times looked frightened, her eyes darting back and forth while she pursed her lips and talked of where she had gone wrong. History revealed that she had been in a relationship with a fellow student for over a year. During that time they had had unprotected intercourse several times. She had not wanted to have sex but had gone ahead anyway in order to please him. She said that the last time, six weeks previously, she had made up her mind not to have intercourse with him and had told him so. They discussed her feelings of guilt, and once again he persuaded her to go ahead with intercourse. While she did not want to follow through, she again felt caught between her own feelings and a wish to please him. Later that month she discovered that she was pregnant. The boyfriend immediately suggested that she have an abortion. While recognizing that his view was sensible in many respects, she was also angry about his lack of consideration for her religious views and also for what her family might think if they found out she were pregnant. She felt he had betrayed her by talking her into doing something she had not wanted to do and then was not helpful to her in dealing with the consequences.

During the week that followed, the counselor met with Sandra daily in order to help her regain a sense of control over her life. They focused on helping her relax, setting priorities about her daily activities, dealing with the rupture in her relationship with her boyfriend, and articulating other stresses in her life. She revealed a great deal of conflict in her life as a result of a change in her relationship with her mother, who had become hostile to her continuing to attend school. Previously the mother had been supportive of her desire to learn and to make the most of her life. Related to the family conflict was a conflict in values that Sandra felt between her ethnic, working-class background and the upper-middle-class academic environment in which she now found herself.

Because of the medical concern about time involved in an abortion decision, the following week was spent on the process of making that choice. In addition to a discussion and clarification of her values, the sessions also included more ventilation of her feelings about what the counselor labeled as acquaintance rape. This label seemed to fit Sandra's view of what had happened. By viewing the event as a rape, she was able to more fully vent her anger toward her boyfriend and also herself for not being more responsible for her own actions. Once she was able to get beyond her own passivity and take responsibility for what had happened, she could make the decision to go ahead with the abortion.

Appointments were tapered off to twice a week following the abortion. These sessions provided support for daily living in a stressful academic environment, expression of ongoing feelings related to the abortion, and exploration of her role in the rape. Later, weekly sessions dealt with family conflicts, especially the mother-daughter relationship. Sandra realized that she needed to be more assertive in her world and act more responsibly on her own behalf than she had done up to that point. This led to an exploration of how she might integrate her family background with her academic interests in choosing a vocational direction. As a result of the attention to her medical problems, values, family relationships, and vocational goals, Sandra was able to emerge from her crisis feeling more confident about who she was as a maturing adult.

The case material that opened this chapter includes some of Gail's recollections of her rape experience over eight years prior to the beginning of her therapy. Gail described herself as a very competent person who had achieved much of what she wanted in life and now had taken time off from her job to pursue advanced graduate study. While enjoying her return to academia, she was also more aware of conflicts and unfinished business from her previous student years. The fact that she was turning 30, had never married, and had not had a significant, intimate male relationship in years was very much on her mind. In describing the essential difficulties in intimacy, Gail highlighted her terror at having sex with a man. She recalled the rape experience and the fears she continued to have. Although appearing to be a self-confident, high-achieving individual, she reported postrape symptoms of depression, anxiety, worry, suspicion,and mistrust as well as continued fear of being attacked again.

In therapy Gail reported an increasing awareness of negative feelings stemming from the rape. She felt very angry with her mother for her response: "Look at how strong my daughter is . . . look at what she withstood." Gail felt that her mother's response did not give her permission to be scared, vulnerable, and helpless. The implicit message for her was to be strong, not fall apart, not get depressed or feel terrified; in short, not to feel anything. As a result she had drawn away from her mother following the rape and now had a rather distant relationship with her. By ventilating some of her anger toward her mother, Gail was able to complete the past work, see mother as the aging parent she now was, and consider a closer relationship with her. She could then generalize that trust to other people, and more significantly, acknowledge the validity of her own feelings.

As Gail thought of having a close male relationship that included sex, she experienced flashbacks to the rape experience. These frightened her greatly. The therapist pointed out that these vivid memory pictures were an understandable, learned response, and together they developed techniques by which Gail could pull herself back to present reality when these associations occurred.

Gail also wanted to lose weight. From her history it appeared that her weight protected her from sexual relationships. By interpreting the weight as something positive, the therapist conveyed respect for the body's ability to take care of itself. Over time, Gail was encouraged to respect her body and realistically integrate it into her self-concept. This was done following the steps developed by Barbach (1975) to help women become orgasmic. This approach appealed to

Gail because of its positive attitude about health and sexuality. After developing a better feeling about her body, Gail was successful in a weight reduction program. She then felt more open to potential relationships.

A final example demonstrates the use of dreamwork as a monitoring device. Carol was in treatment for "depression," which was attributed to her feeling worthless after an earlier rape experience. Both Carol and her counselor were aware that the primary dream process might alter the theme of sexual assault. In early sessions Carol spoke of recurrent dreams wherein she was constantly reaching out for something that was always just beyond her grasp. As she gained self-confidence and some measure of control, these dreams decreased in frequency. A later dream in which she knitted a sweater and wrote a book was interpreted as evidence of mastery of skills she had, in reality, never had. This theme of competence paralleled her increasing feelings of self-worth and of her mastery of her own emotions about the rape.

COLLEGE ROLE

The role of a college in the prevention and treatment of rape is multifaceted. The educational process can provide knowledge and skills to work through developmental tasks. Because rape is potentially a major problem on any campus, organized prevention and treatment are essential. Estabrook et al. (1978) outlined a program of preventive education and awareness with both community and campus programs. This included films, values clarification exercises, and small-group discussions about safety, the problems of victims, and societal myths and values. An extension of this might include workshops about violent crime (including rape), security (rooms and grounds), and self-defense. More than simple awareness is necessary. Female students may need help in developing assertiveness in dealing with sexual harassment. Administration should be receptive to student complaints and willing to deal swiftly and effectively with them, whether they be about faculty or staff demanding favors or residential groups behaving irresponsibly. Male consciousness should also be raised about "date rape" and their role in it. Men seldom get the opportunity to discuss sex outside the "locker room" context, and a discussion about responsible sexuality may be a major breakthrough.

The Estabrook group trains "counselor-advocates" to assist victims at the crisis stage. If such a group does not exist on campus, the student health service should establish liaison with a community-based rape crisis center. Such centers are also helpful in that victims may not wish to use an institution-based program, and other options should be open to them. In training counselor-advocates it should be borne in mind that volunteers for advocacy programs often have a history of rape or assault. In addition to empathy for other victims, volunteers often have unresolved feelings about their own experience. As a result, training should not be limited to factual presentations alone, but should also include opportunities for volunteers to deal with their own feelings and experiences associated with rape.

Betty was a graduate student volunteer who was the subject of a conversation between the emergency room head nurse and the rape crisis center volunteer coordinator. Betty had been observed to be "overly involved" with assault victims, that is, verbally and physically comforting and protective of them when dealing with staff. She was also overtly hostile to the examining physician, pointing out that he wasn't "caring enough." The coordinator and counselor/ advisor met with Betty and shared the concerns of emergency room personnel. Initially Betty angrily denied that there was a problem with her behavior and insisted that the emergency room was "cold and inhuman" and that "everyone knew" that the physician was an "unfeeling chauvinist." The counselor pointed out that volunteers might "relive" some of their own experiences when dealing with other rape victims and wondered if this might not be happening with Betty. Betty did indicate that she felt particularly alone and vulnerable at the time she was assaulted and she wished someone had been there to hold and comfort her. She had also had an impersonal and apparently reluctant exam by a physician who had been called early in the morning to see her. The counselor suggested that Betty had not fully dealt with her own experiences, and all agreed that she should not accept another volunteer assignment until she had done so.

Give the extent of the problem and the major potential sequelae, it is important for every institution of higher education to become aware of the factors that predispose to rape and to provide the opportunity for prevention and treatment.

We have discussed the experience of rape among late-adolescent college students and the important developmental tasks facing this age group. By focusing on all the issues confronting individuals at this life stage, helping professionals will be able to assist victims to achieve a strong adult identity.

REFERENCES

American Psychiatric Association. 1980. *Diagnostic and Statistical Manual III.* Washington, D.C.

Barbach L. 1975. *For Yourself.* Garden City, N.Y.: Doubleday.

Bassuk, E. 1980. A crisis theory perspective on rape. In S. McCombie, ed., *The Rape Crisis Intervention Handbook.* New York: Plenum.

Brownmiller, S. 1975. *Against Our Will: Men, Women, and Rape.* New York: Simon & Schuster.

Burgess, A., and Holmstrom, L. 1974. *Rape: Victims of Crisis.* Bowie, Md.: Brady.

Burgess, A., and Holmstrom, L. 1979. Rape: Sexual disruption and recovery. *Am. J. Orthopsychiatry,* 49(4):648.

Erikson, E. 1968. *Identity: Youth and Crisis.* New York: Norton.

Estabrook, B., et al. 1978. Rape on campus: Community education and services for victims. *J. Am. College Health Assoc.,* 27(2):72.

Evans, H. 1978. Psychotherapy for the rape victim: Some treatment models. *Hosp. and Comm. Psychiatry,* 29(5):309.

Kilpatrick, D., et al. 1979. The aftermath of rape: Recent empirical findings. *Am. J. Orthopsychiatry,* 49(4):658.

McCombie, S., and Arons, J. 1980. Counseling rape victims. In S. McCombie, ed., *The Rape Crisis Intervention Handbook.* New York: Plenum.

Morrison, C. 1980. A cultural perspective on rape. In S. McCombie, ed., *The Rape Crisis Intervention Handbook.* New York: Plenum.

Nadleson, C., et al. 1982. A follow-up study of rape victims. *Am. J. Psychiatry,* 139(10): 1266.

Rabkin, J. 1979. The epidemiology of forcible rape. *Am. J. Orthopsychiatry,* 49(4):634.

Sarrel, L., and Sarrel, P. 1979. *Sexual Unfolding: Sexual Development and Sexual Therapies in Late Adolescence.* Boston: Little, Brown.

Sarrel, L., and Sarrel, P. 1981. Can a man be raped by a woman? *Redbook Magazine,* May, p. 92.

Sutherland, S., and Scherl, D. 1970. Patterns of response among victims of rape. *Am. J. Orthopsychiatry,* 40(3):503.

14
Treatment of Prostitute Victims of Sexual Assault

Mimi H. Silbert, Ph.D.

ABSTRACT

A study of 200 women street prostitutes documents serious problems of juvenile sexual exploitation, with physical and emotional abuse in their backgrounds. Almost two-thirds of the sample were victims of incest and child sexual abuse from the ages of 3 to 16 (average age of victimization was 10). Virtually every woman who was abused reported extremely negative emotional and physical impact from the abuse. Additionally, 73% of these women had been raped totally unrelated to the work situation. Almost all of the subjects stated that they needed and would make use of such services as a 24-hour switchboard, group and individual counseling, advocacy, social support systems, and legal and shelter care services.

These services were offered by the Delancey Street Foundation, along with intensive residential treatment. Outreach services were well utilized, clients returned at a high rate of repeat usage, and their satisfaction with all the services was high. An in-depth study of the mediating effects of the counseling model was made on 53 of the prostitutes. According to both clients and their counselors, the treatment services had a highly significant effect on reducing subjects' sexual trauma in terms of emotional, mental, and behavioral impact, as well as increasing positive self-concepts.

Although there are a number of problems in treating prostitute victims of sexual assault, the Delancey Street model has been successful in treating prostitutes on an outreach basis, and also in a tightly structured residential center where hundreds of prostitutes not only have dealt with their problems of sexual abuse, but also have rebuilt their lives.

Recently I asked 100 people in the helping professions to list those clients whom they found the most difficult to treat. Prostitutes headed the list. The comments did not vary greatly and were typified by the psychologist who stated, "They are generally unamenable to treatment"; and the probation officer who wrote, "They take every positive opportunity you give them and throw it back in your face. They just don't want to change no matter what they say."

As president of the Delancey Street Foundation, a self-help residential center that successfully treats prostitutes, ex-convicts, and substance abusers through multidimensional services including individual and group treatment and vocational and educational training, I have worked with well over 1000 prostitutes in a clinical capacity over the past 12 years. I understand the frustrations of working with people who have self-destructive patterns such that they work against their own desire to change and destroy positive options. I also understand that this cycle of self-hate, guilt, fear of success, and self-destruction can effectively be overcome.

Because I found a consistent pattern of sexual abuse in the backgrounds of women street prostitutes, I designed and directed a three-year study for the National Institute of Mental Health of sexual assault of prostitutes, to explore the nature and extent of the problem, and to delineate the needs for services requested by the prostitutes. The study then implemented and evaluated the intervention services as a demonstration project for prostitute victims of sexual assault.

The results of the study[1] confirmed the clinical data that the problem of sexual assault is a serious one for the woman street prostitute, both prior to and since her work in prostitution. The study results confirmed the clinical experience that many prostitutes need treatment services and, with specific focus on their areas of concern, will respond well to treatment.

Two hundred women street prostitutes in the Bay Area were the subjects of the study. Seventy percent of the subjects currently prostituting were under 21; almost 60% were 16 years or under, with some being 10 and 11 years old. Seventy-eight percent of the sample report that they started prostitution as juveniles, and 68% were 16 or younger when they started prostituting. Sixty-nine percent of the prostitutes who participated in the study were white, 18% were black, 11% were Hispanic, 2% were American Indian, and 1% Asian. Despite the fact that two-thirds of the women were from families with average or higher income, the

---

[1] Three reports document the complete study results and are available from the Delancey Street Foundation or the National Institute of Mental Health (Grant Number 1 RO1 MH-32782-01): Silbert et al., Sexual assault of prostitutes, phase one final report November 1980; Silbert et al., Sexual assault of prostitutes final report, phase II, August 1982; and Silbert, Sexual assault of prostitutes, summary final report, September 1982. See also: Silbert and Pines, Occupational hazards of street prostitutes *Criminal Justice and Behavior,* 8(4); December 1981. Silbert Mimi, Prostitution and sexual assault, *Biosocial: The Journal of Behavioral Ecology,* Spring 1982. Silbert and Pines, Sexual child abuse as an antecedent to prostitution, *Child Abuse and Neglect,* 5, 1981. Silbert et al., Substance abuse and prostitution, *J. Psychoactive Drugs,* Spring 1982. Silbert and Pines, Pornography and sexual abuse of women, *Sex Roles,* forthcoming. Silbert and Pines, Juvenile sexual exploitation in the background of street prostitutes, *Social Work,* forthcoming. Silbert and Pines, The endless cycle of victimization of street prostitutes, *Victimology,* forthcoming. Silbert and Pines, Entrance into prostitution, *Youth and Society,* 13:471–500, June 1982.

vast majority of those currently prostituting (88%) described themselves as "very poor" or "just making it" at the time of the study.

While the majority of women came from middle-class, educated families, where they were given a religious upbringing (76% attended church regularly or attended a church school), there were extreme family problems existing beneath the surface. More than half of the women reported that one or more of their parents drank excessively while they were growing up; well over half had immediate family members abusing drugs regularly; in 51% of the families, the subject saw her father hit her mother violently; and 62% of the subjects were themselves beaten by their families while they were growing up. Only 19% of the subjects reported that they had a positive relationship with their fathers, and less than a third reported having positive relationships with their mothers. On the whole, the average number of home problems mentioned for each woman was 7.3; the majority of these were physical, emotional, and sexual abuse.

Almost two-thirds of the sample (61%) were victims of incest and child sexual abuse, from the ages of 3 to 16 (average age of victimization was 10). Seventy percent of the cases involved repeated abuse by the same person. Two-thirds of the victims were abused by natural, step, or foster fathers; 10% were molested by strangers.

Virtually every woman who was abused reported extremely negative emotional and physical impacts from the abuse, and over 90% of the victims lost their virginity through such child sexual abuse. Yet, in 91% of the cases, the victim felt there was nothing she could do, no one she could tell. Only 3% of the cases were reported to police. Only 1% was brought to the attention of professionals. Seventy percent of the women reported that the sexual exploitation affected their decision to become prostitutes.

Almost all the juvenile prostitutes (96%) were runaways before they began prostituting. The vast majority of the prostitutes studied stated that they had no other options when they began prostitution.

Victimization of prostitutes as part of their work is very high. Seventy percent were victimized by customer rapes or clients similarly going beyond the work contract an average of 31 times each woman. The majority were victimized by such things as nonpayment, robbery, and violence. Seventy-eight percent reported being victimized by perversion an average of 17 times each; two-thirds of them reported having been physically abused and beaten many times by customers; and two-thirds reported having been physically abused and beaten regularly by their pimps.

Contrary to the popular belief that "prostitutes can't be raped," 73% of these women have been raped in a situation totally unrelated to the work situation. (An additional 6% were victims of attempted rapes.) The vast majority of the rapes were committed by total strangers; most were violent; almost all of the victims reported serious physical injuries as a result of the rape; and *all* reported extremely negative emotional impact. Yet, in only 7% of the rapes did victims seek out services for any kind of assistance, support, counseling, or advocacy; only 7% of the rape cases were reported to the authorities.

The emotional trauma experienced by sexual assault victims in general[2] appears to be compounded by two factors: (1) The informal street code of the prostitute precludes the display of hurt or emotional upset or leaning on personal or social supports for assistance in resisting such emotional trauma. Most prostitutes felt they could not break that code and therefore dealt with their feelings alone, and/or attempted to suppress them. (2) The helplessness generally experienced as a result of rape[3] is exacerbated by a general feeling of powerlessness over their lives. The strongest sense of power these women experience derives from a sense of control over their sexual activity. The majority of street prostitutes who are residents at Delancey Street are poor and unskilled; two-thirds are Third World women. With no options or control over other areas of their lives, they place a disproportionate amount of energy on the independence afforded them as prostitutes and the ability to control their sexual activities. The impact of rape is thus compounded by the fact that it takes this important sense of control from them.

The pattern reported by the prostitutes in the study reflects the picture of the women street prostitutes treated at Delancey Street. Subjected to continuous abuse and victimization about which they have no understanding, and over which they have no control, these women have developed what I have termed a sense of *psychological paralysis* which prohibits their ability to do anything about further victimization. As learned helplessness grows into psychological paralysis, these women street prostitutes become totally passive, unable to change destructive behavior, debilitated, self-deprecating, and entrapped in helplessness and hopelessness. I believe this sense of psychological paralysis is directly linked to the exasperation expressed by helpers working with prostitutes.

The difficulties in treating prostitute victims of sexual assault fall into four categories. The first issue centers on the reticence of prostitutes to avail themselves of any services, particularly those they view as designed for the "straight world." Upon entering treatment, prostitutes face a second problem which revolves around the dual nature of their roles as victims of sexual abuse, on the one hand, and as perpetrators of illegal activities on the other hand. In the

---

[2] See, for example, Factor, M., Women's psychological reaction to attempted rape, *Psychoanalytic Quarterly*, 23:243–244, 1954; Halleck, S., Emotional effects of victimization, in R. Slovenko, ed., *Sexual Behavior and the Law*, Springfield, Illinois: Thomas, 1965; Sutherland, S., and Scherl, D., "Patterns of Response Among Victims of Rape," *American Journal of Orthopsychiatry*, 40(3):503–511, 1970; and Symonds, M., "Victims of Violence," *American Journal of Psychoanalysis*, 35:19–26, 1975.

[3] Brownmiller, Susan, *Against Our Will: Men, Women and Rape*, New York, Simon and Schuster, 1975.

course of treatment, a third area needing special attention arises which concerns the syndrome of psychological paralysis. Finally, as an outgrowth of the treatment of the specific presenting problems of sexual assault, a fourth area of concern emerges for those prostitutes who want to leave prostitution and require in-depth training to acquire needed life skills.

1. ENTERING TREATMENT

The first problem is the most obvious to note in the development of treatment services for prostitute victims of sexual assault, and also one of the most difficult to effect; prostitutes do not generally avail themselves of services, particularly those they view as designed for the "straight world." Feeling they are cut off from conventional society, prostitutes often reject their rejectors, which takes the form of repudiation of the conventional world. Anyone interested in designing treatment programs for prostitute victims of sexual assault must take into account the sense in which prostitutes feel removed from, and alien to, traditional organizations. Services should show special understanding of prostitutes' unique problems, and attempts should be made to publicize the services in areas where prostitutes are known to congregate.

In the study, we asked all the subjects what services they would recommend for prostitutes who were victims of sexual assault. Ninety-eight percent of the women studied stated they wanted a 24-hour switchboard, 97% selected group counseling, 99% chose individual counseling, 98% requested advocacy and social support, 97% chose rap groups, and 98% selected legal services. All the women emphasized as well the importance of having services provided by women who were former prostitutes or women who would not be judgmental of their lives and work.

On the basis of these data, Delancey Street offered the following outreach services:

Twenty-four-hour switchboard: A 24-hour switchboard was in operation seven days a week. Women were encouraged to call if they needed help of any kind. The switchboard was well publicized through announcements in the media, leaflets or billboards in areas where prostitutes were known to congregate, and cards distributed informally on the street. The phone counselors were trained former prostitute volunteers who took appointments for the services offered as well as provided information, made referrals, and provided phone crisis intervention.

Individual counseling: Each client received an intake interview by the counselor-on-duty (O.D.P.) when she first entered the program. By the end of the first counseling group, each client had been exposed to two or three of the four counselors, and she was asked to select the counselor she most wanted to see individually. Individual sessions between the counselor and client were held at

least once weekly. Sessions were primarily held at the Delancey Street Foundation in a small, comfortably decorated room, and lasted about an hour per
session.

Group counseling: Each woman who was a rape victim, a victim of juvenile
sexual exploitation, or a victim of some other sexual abuse, and who wanted
group counseling, was assigned to the static counseling group. The groups
ranged in size from 10 to 15 young women with two counselors, and met
regularly. The first group was started in the first quarter of the year, with new
groups added regularly, and proceeded until the end of the year without problems or significant attrition.

Social support services: Because peer support is very important to adolescents
in general, and particularly important to those undergoing crisis or change, a
strong component of the program was the provision of a social support network
for the victims. This aspect of services proved the most difficult to implement.
As noted earlier, the prostitutes studied tended to be extremely isolated, helpless,
and without resources. While they responded to the services provided by the
Delancey Street Foundation, and to the project staff, they were slow to reach
out in mutual support of one another. Only in the second half of the year did
several elements of social support develop. These included a leaderless peer group
exploring legal and legitimate social outlets, a vocational support group of
juvenile prostitutes who were working to learn other skills and supporting one
another's new goals, and an "abuse anonymous" group in which a series of
women traded phone numbers and called one another for support to deal
with physical or sexual abuse. At the clients' request, because of the anonymous
nature of this last group, no records were kept of meetings or client satisfaction.
However, participants verbally praised the services.

The DSF house was open a minimum of two days and nights weekly at
specified hours for social support gatherings. While this component was planned
as a feature to draw clients to more formal counseling, in fact it worked as a
separate element of services. Those who utilized social support services did not
tend to cross over to other services in significant numbers. Clients were extremely responsive to counseling services at the outset and more reticent to participate
in social events. Delancey Street rules specify no alcohol or drugs, and participants were asked to observe these rules. Staff maintained strict compliance
which discouraged involvement.

These events ended up primarily serving juveniles and as such served an
important function not only in providing some social support for one another,
but also in teaching these young women the rudiments of social interaction.
Towards the latter half of the year, participants not only became involved, but
also requested many more activities, particularly those in which they met
regularly in a group.

Rap groups: These groups were held two nights weekly (two hours each).
Clients, who were rape victims and victims of juvenile sexual abuse, dropped in

for any of these sessions and joined whichever group they liked on each visit. There were always at least two groups going on at one time. While counselors were available to enter any of the groups if requested, they were primarily leaderless rap groups.

Legal/social services advocacy: There are numerous aspects of the prostitutes' lives that could lead to the need for legal and/or other social services. When clients decided to report a prior or current sexual assault they needed legal counsel. Often they also needed immediate shelter and some type of financial assistance, particularly if they chose to leave the prostitution life, or file charges on a pimp. These services were primarily utilized by referrals from the switchboard to appropriate social agencies.

Our experience confirms the supposition that the need is great for such services for prostitute victims of sexual abuse, and that prostitutes will indeed use these services when designed to meet their specific situations and when well publicized in their own circles.

The services described were well utilized. Clients returned at a high rate of repeat usage, and their satisfaction was high. For example, over 3000 clients utilized the 24-hour switchboard, with 56% requesting information, 46% needing referrals, and 32% given crisis intervention by former prostitutes who had been trained to operate the hotline phones. Over 100 clients utilized the individual counseling, with the vast majority (over 86%) coming repeatedly, and giving positive ratings to the sessions. Over 150 clients utilized the continuous weekly counseling groups, with 84% being repeat participants, and 88% providing positive ratings.

Although the social support sessions drew the fewest number of clients, they drew the largest number of repeat participants. Forty-five clients utilized these services, with 96% repeaters. Only 1% gave negative responses to these services. Emerging from the general support services, a peer support group was held for six months, with meetings twice monthly, for 31 clients.

Two hundred fifty-eight clients participated in rap groups over the year. Because these were not static groups and were open to new drop-ins on a regular basis, the number of repeaters was the lowest of the services provided, about three-quarters being repeaters. Client satisfaction was high, with only 1% giving negative responses to the services.

Thirty-five clients utilized the legal advocacy services, with 60% utilizing legal services, 40% utilizing advocacy services, and 37% utilizing shelter services. (These tally more than 100% because many clients made use of multiple services.)

In summary, all of the services offered were well utilized, and clients benefited from each. However, despite the large numbers of clients who availed themselves of the services, it is clear that numbers of young women on the streets require actual street work to encourage them to ask for any kind of help. Plans are under way now to develop some street workers at bus stops, near the Hall of Justice, and other places where young runaways are solicited for prostitution, or prostitutes are vulnerable. Street workers will be available to talk with the young women, and encourage them to seek help in whatever areas they are having difficulties.

An in-depth study of the mediating effects of the individual and group treatment model was made on 53 of these prostitute victims who participated in the outreach services. Fifty-seven percent of this group utilized individual counseling; 43% utilized group counseling. Clients and counselors were given an in-depth case study interview administered three times, including an initial interview, a midpoint interview, and a final interview.

A series of counseling impact questionnaires was designed, pretested, and standardized by the staff of the study (Appendix A_1, A_2). The comparisons (t tests) between the initial interview and the final interview indicate the changes in the client from the beginning to the end of intervention services, and thus reflect the impact of the intervention model.

The group counseling contract was for ten months, with the midpoint questionnaire being administered after clients completed five months of groups. The average individual counseling contract was for six months, and the questionnaires were administered in approximate three-month intervals. All these interviews explored the impact of the sexual assault on the victims and the effects of the intervention model on lessening the negative impact.

According to both clients and their counselors, the treatment services had a highly significant effect on reducing subjects' sexual assault trauma in terms of emotional, mental, and behavioral impacts, as well as self-concept and availability of social support networks. Table 14-1 presents the specific outcomes of the services as reported by the clients. The difference between T_1 and T_2 reflects the midpoint changes, and T_1-T_3, the changes from beginning to end. Counselors' responses were very similar to clients' own responses. On completing an average of six months of individual and ten months of group therapy, subjects reported significantly fewer emotional problems related to sexual assault: fear, helplessness, hopelessness, anger, shock, unhappiness, shame, guilt. In terms of mental impact, after completing therapy, subjects experienced significantly more positive attitudes toward themselves, men, sex, emotional relationships, friendships, their lives, and their futures. In terms of behavioral changes, subjects reported, after completing therapy, using significantly fewer tranquilizers, alcohol, cigarettes, and illegal drugs.

The intervention model had statistically significant positive impacts on every single dimension of the subjects' self-concept that was examined: feelings about themselves in general, about people, about life; their sense of control over life; their feelings about being able to "make it" in society; their skills to "make it;" their future; their self-confidence; their sense of self-pride; their motivation to "make it;" their ability to communicate; their ability to change problems in their lives; their energy to change; and their feelings of entrapment.

TABLE 14-1. Client Questionnaire: Rape/Assault Impact

VARIABLES	T_1	T_2	T_3	T_1-T_2	T_2-T_3	T_1-T_3
		MEANS			T-TESTS	
Total number of problems	2.0	0.7	0.1	5.8***	4.7***	8.6***
Emotional impact						
Fear	4.5	2.7	1.7	10.3***	8.4***	18.9***
Helplessness	4.6	2.5	1.7	14.6***	7.0***	23.3***
Hopelessness	4.3	2.5	1.7	12.1***	5.5***	15.8***
Anger	3.8	3.5	2.8	1.2(N.S.)	3.6(.001)	4.4***
Shock	3.7	2.0	1.3	7.2***	3.9***	10.4***
Unhappiness	4.2	2.6	1.9	8.6***	6.0***	15.0***
Relief to be alive	2.6	2.6	2.0	0.2(N.S.)	2.2(.039)	2.7(.010)
Hatred (men)	3.8	2.9	2.2	4.2***	5.0***	7.5***
Numbness; nothing	3.0	2.0	1.8	4.7***	5.6***	7.2***
Shame	4.3	2.8	2.0	7.7***	5.0***	12.1***
Guilt	4.0	2.9	1.9	4.9***	10.6***	7.7***
Mental impact						
Self	1.3	2.5	3.2	-10.2***	-5.3***	-15.4***
Men	1.4	2.2	2.6	-7.1***	-3.4(.001)	-10.5***
Sex	1.3	2.2	2.6	-6.3***	-4.0***	-12.1***
Behavioral impacts						
Tranquilizers	3.3	2.3	1.9	4.6***	3.4(.001)	5.6***
Alcohol	3.8	2.5	1.8	6.2***	4.6***	8.1***
Cigarettes	3.6	2.4	2.1	5.9***	2.3(.027)	5.7***
Illegal drugs	4.0	2.4	1.7	7.2***	4.1***	9.0***
Total number of behavioral changes	1.5	0.8	0.6	2.7(.010)	0.7(N.S.)	3.2(.002)
Emotional relationships	1.4	2.6	3.2	-10.7***	-5.0***	-14.3***
Friendships	1.7	2.8	3.3	-9.2***	-5.2***	-11.6***
Life	1.6	2.9	3.2	-11.4***	-3.8***	-13.1***
Future	1.6	2.9	3.2	-9.1***	-2.7(.009)	-11.8***
Self-concept						
In general	1.7	3.1	4.0	-7.1***	-6.1***	-14.1***
Right now	1.6	3.4	4.3	-12.3***	-7.0***	-16.3***
Feelings about people	1.5	3.4	4.0	-12.3***	-5.7***	-20.5***
Feelings about life	1.5	3.4	4.0	-11.9***	-5.8***	-18.2***
*Control of life	1.4	3.2	3.9	-12.9***	-5.8***	-18.3***
*"Making it"	1.7	3.3	3.9	-9.5***	-5.8***	-11.7***
Skills to "make it"	1.8	3.2	3.7	-9.6***	-4.5***	-11.9***
Future	1.7	3.4	4.2	-10.7***	-6.1***	-17.6***
Self-confidence	1.3	3.0	3.6	-10.9***	-4.2***	-14.6***
Self-pride	1.2	2.9	3.5	-9.8***	-4.8***	-16.2***
*Motivation to "make it"	1.7	3.5	4.0	-1.3***	-5.4***	-16.0***
*Ability to change	1.5	3.2	4.1	-13.7***	-7.3***	-17.8***
*Energy to change	1.6	3.3	4.4	-11.6***	-9.8***	-22.6***
*Feeling trapped	1.3	3.2	4.1	-12.0***	-5.5***	-18.2***
Someone to talk to	1.8	1.1	1.2	7.8***	-0.4(N.S.)	6.8***
Number of people	0.3	4.1	7.0	-3.1(.001)	-2.2(.036)	-4.7***
Someone to turn to	1.7	1.1	1.0	6.9***	1.0(N.S.)	8.9***
Number of people	1.3	2.8	4.3	-2.0(.057)	-2.2(.036)	-3.2(.003)

*** = p = .000.

The intervention also had a significant effect on their support network. At the final interview they reported having significantly more people to talk to and to turn to when in trouble.

It is clear then from these experiences that despite the fact that services are now generally not offered specifically for prostitutes, and that the majority of prostitutes are not utilizing general services for victims of sexual assault, sufficient outreach work can bring in large numbers of prostitutes in need of counseling, and can be effective in mediating problems revolving around sexual assault.

2. ROLE CLARIFICATION

The second major problem in providing treatment for prostitute victims of sexual assault revolves around the dichotomy of their roles. On the one hand the women are seeking treatment with assigned victim status, while on the other the illegal nature of their work assigns a stigma and criminal role to them.

Carol was a 26-year-old prostitute at the time she came for counseling. She had been working on the streets as a prostitute since she was 17. She had just been raped for the second time since working the streets. She was suffering serious physical injuries, including multiple lacerations throughout her body, and was psychologically traumatized. Despite the fact that she called the hotline for help, Carol vacillated between being able to accept any kind of support for her victimization and lashing out at the conventional world.

Howard Becker, in his book *Outsiders*,[4] points out that some statuses override all others, and in that case, identification with the master status takes priority over all others. For Carol there is no question that the labeling process was critical to her. She felt completely cut off from conventional society, and her behavior and self-image in counseling were the consequence of her negative perception of public reaction to her as a prostitute. She felt that she was seen as a prostitute as a life-style, and not only when she was working; no matter what else she did she would be rejected because of this status. Whenever a counselor began to talk to her of her victimization, of gaining some sort of support for herself, Carol would begin screaming that no support was possible for her because she was a prostitute. She would then erupt into a defense of her prostitution activities and a fury at its being a criminal offense. Before helping Carol deal with the sexual abuse trauma the counselor had to explore and clarify Carol's attitudes toward prostitution, and her perceptions of the response of others to her prostitution status.

Carol's overriding feeling that most people have little sympathy for prostitute victims of sexual assault is reflected in the responses of the 200 women prostitutes

---

[4] Becker, Howard, *Outsiders,* Free Press, New York, 1963.

in the study who were asked how they saw the social system responding to their victimization. When asked how doctors are apt to respond to the rape of prostitutes, as opposed to women who are not prostitutes, over 90% of the subjects responded by saying that the reaction is likely to be much more negative toward the prostitutes. "Doctors are the worst. They were pigs about treating me. A doctor would say, 'Well, she's out there selling her body. She got what she deserved.'" "The cops would think that a prostitute can't be raped anyway. The D.A. wouldn't prosecute at all 'cause he couldn't see any reason for it 'cause he would think she would go out there and sell it to a stranger, so who cares? What's the difference?" "The jury probably thinks, 'Poor guy; he shouldn't be blamed for it; she provoked it; it's her job.'" "Everybody thinks prostitutes are asking to be raped; they have little sympathy for that life-style."

In dealing with the client's defined role as a prostitute, the counselor must determine whether prostitution itself is or is not a problem for the client. Insofar as the woman hates what she does and feels unable to leave, insofar as she feels she is trapped into prostitution, then prostitution is a problem for her. If, however, the prostitute feels that she has made a decision to prostitute as a matter of survival, or if she enjoys prostitution, then the fact of prostitution should not be seen as a problem for her. Insofar as prostitution generally is considered a problem, we ought not to blame or treat the individual engaging in the work, but as a society we must remediate the institutions by directly confronting our values and changing the social conditions that underlie the problem.

All of these are value-laden issues that the counselor must clarify in her own mind, as well as with her client. Despite our training in objectivity and "professional detachment," professional helpers, like all people, harbor personal values and attitudes. Given the role and status confusion of the prostitute victim of sexual assault who comes for treatment, it is critical that the counselor clarify his or her own values before asking what the problems are that the client is bringing to counseling. If the problem is only sexual assault victimization, then status as a prostitute becomes irrelevant, except insofar as the counselor's perceptions of how others will treat her client affect her own personal responses. If, however, prostitution itself is a problem for the client, insofar as she feels trapped in it, then the counselor has a second series of issues around which therapy sessions should center.

3. PSYCHOLOGICAL PARALYSIS

The third area that poses the greatest problem for counselors is a syndrome I have labeled *psychological paralysis*. When people come to believe that they cannot change a situation they become psychologically paralyzed to act, even — indeed especially — in their own interest. They turn away from offers of assistance even though they cry out, often desperately, for help.

For example, Dorothy came to Delancey Street for help at the age of 21; she had been prostituting on the streets since she was 15. Dorothy grew up in a middle class area in a small urban city in the east and attended parochial school until she was 14, when she ran away from home. Up to that time she had lived at home with her mother, stepfather, a sister, and a stepbrother. Her stepfather drank excessively while she was growing up; her mother took a lot of doctor-prescribed pills.

She saw her stepfather hit her mother violently on numerous occasions, and she herself was beaten by the stepfather randomly throughout the years she lived at home. She had no recollection of her real father, assuming he must have left the home early since the only father she ever remembered was the stepfather.

When she tried to describe why she was beaten, Dorothy had no idea. She said there were some times when her stepfather was drunk or had a fight with her mother that she thought he would physically abuse her. However, there were other times when the beatings came for absolutely no reason Dorothy was able to ascertain. "He just did it whenever he wanted. I don't know why. It wasn't like things I would do. Sometimes I would come home from school with a bad report card when I was real young and think, 'Oh, God, I'm really going to get it for this one.' But then I showed it to them and no one seemed to care. So it wasn't really for things I'd do when I'd be bad or something. He'd just do it when he felt like it."

In her early years in school, Dorothy described herself as feeling really lonely and rejected by the "popular kids I wanted to belong to." As she moved through grammar school, she began to move slowly out of isolation and found friends among a group of "tough kids." "You know, we were always getting in trouble in school: drinking, cutting school a lot, starting fights and stuff like that. I didn't much care what we did as long as I had some friends to belong to."

Dorothy was sexually abused by her stepfather from the time she was 10 until she was 14. "I was ten years old when my stepfather first raped me. He was drunk and cried . . . said my mom was mean to him and wouldn't love him or do what he said. He asked me if I loved him and when I said that I guessed so, he said, 'Then you'll do as I say and never ask questions and never tell Mom.' I did it, but it made me to sick. I felt sick and disgusted . . . I wanted to die; I thought everyone could tell what he did to me by looking at me. . . . I stayed by myself a lot at school. . . . Once I cut myself all up with my father's razor. I guess I wanted to get back at him or show him how much he was hurting me or something. I'm not really sure why I did it. . . . Finally I ran away from home. At first I tried to get a straight job, but I looked real young and I didn't have no skills or no education or nothing. . . . At first when they tried to talk me into prostituting, I said, 'No.' Finally I got scared and hungry and lonely enough. I hate myself and I really hate sex. I despise it. I'll never enjoy it. I hate the way they look and the way they smell. But as long as I can make money off these tricks, who cares?"

From the age of 15 to 21, Dorothy had prostituted on the streets of major cities from the east to the west coast. She was working for a pimp when she came for counseling, although she said there was really no advantage in having one. Victimization as part of her work is high. She has been beaten many times by customers and has been beaten regularly by her pimp. When asked about being beaten by her pimp, Dorothy replied, "It made him feel like more of a man and I felt it was my duty . . . I'm used to it by now. They can't really hurt me no more."

Dorothy listed seven major disadvantages of prostitution, including the fact that she thought it was absolutely disgusting and hated to do it. The only advantage she cited was that it provided money for her survival. Despite the fact that Dorothy described herself as detesting prostitution, she saw no real option for herself. No matter what possibilities the counselor brought forth, Dorothy's response was always, "Yes, but. . . ." She initially called Delancey Street because her pimp had beaten her up, and for the first time, had injected her with heroin. When she called the Crisis Line, she was desperate, sobbing, and begging for help and protection. When some shelter was found, along with offers of social support, Dorothy turned them all down. She stated that she had overreacted, and that she had now come to an understanding with her pimp. Much to the exasperation of the counselor, Dorothy made four more crisis calls, and each time, when assistance, support, and options were offered, Dorothy turned them down.

Her responses are typical of many prostitutes who call for help, and provide the basis for the professional response cited at the outset of this chapter; they are simply unamenable to treatment and do not want to change. However, I would like to underscore the fact that Dorothy desperately wants to change and is a fine candidate for treatment, as long as we recognize that the underlying problem here is a sense of hopelessness and learned helplessness so intense that it has indeed turned into psychological paralysis.

Those people who are subjected to continuous abuse and victimization about which they have no understanding and over which they have no control, as represented by the life experiences of Dorothy, develop a psychological paralysis that prohibits their ability to do anything at all about further victimization. As learned helplessness grows into psychological paralysis, people become totally passive, debilitated, unable to change destructive behavior, self-deprecating, and entrapped in helplessness and hopelessness.

A growing body of literature in social science has shown that when people (and animals) undergo a series of negative events over which they have no control, the result is learned helplessness. Experimental psychologist Martin Seligman[5] and other researchers have shown through controlled experiments

---

[5] Seligman, Martin, *Helplessness: On Depression, Development and Death,* Freeman Press, San Francisco, 1979.

that when punishment is administered randomly and at varied intervals, subjects quickly learn that there is no response they can make to control the punishment. Both with animals and with people it was shown that when there was nothing they could do to stop unpredictable aversive events, subjects simply ceased any voluntary activity. They remained passive, became severely depressed, and did nothing to avoid the punishment. The earlier in life subjects received this treatment the longer it took to overcome the effects of learned helplessness. Learned helplessness has been found to be related to depression, to ineffective ways of dealing with events, even positive ones. After people have developed learned helplessness they are less likely to believe that they have control over the success or failure of their experiences, assuming that all things that happen will happen randomly. The belief is that action is futile and that one cannot control the elements in life that would relieve suffering or bring gratification.

Psychological paralysis, as I define it, seems to occur as an outgrowth of extended and repeated situations of learned helplessness. The final lessons serve as one more advancement of the psychological paralysis syndrome, characterized by immobility, acceptance of victimization, feelings of being trapped and hopeless, and the inability to take the opportunity to change. It is this sense of psychological paralysis that pervades that segment of the prostitution population who claim to hate what they are doing, who feel they did not choose to be prostitutes, yet who seem to be completely unable to do anything about their situation even when other opportunities are offered. They maintain the belief that bad consequences would occur to them no matter what new steps they may take. They have lost any sense of control over their lives and have accepted feeling trapped and victimized.

In those situations where such a syndrome exists it becomes critical to first treat the sense of psychological paralysis. Until this is done, other modes of treatment cannot help the woman, because she will not believe that any help will be effective. It is imperative to understand that the inability to take the opportunity to change does not reflect an innate quality of enjoyment of victimization inherent in the client. Rather it is a socially learned behavior that must be unlearned through a systematic process designed to return to the woman an understanding that consequences are indeed related to her own actions, and that therefore control over her life is possible. Reversing psychological paralysis involves empowerment training, role modeling, and controlled situations in which the client can directly see the outcomes, both positive and negative, as being directly related to her own performance.

The basis of the Delancey Street model is to provide a series of structured and tangible realistic situations, along with emotional support. Women learn to take responsibility for their actions, until they begin to glimpse the possibility that the situations of their lives that they do not want can be changed, and that, indeed, they can be the agents of change. Accordingly, one of the primary focal points of the Delancey Street services, in addition to those mitigating the negative impact of sexual assault, has been the attempt to reverse the sense of psychological paralysis. This is accomplished through a number of interventions guiding the victims toward recognizing and effectively coping with the positive and negative outcomes of their performance in a conscious effort to develop a sense of control over their lives.

A cluster of questions was designed in the counseling questionnaire to measure the components of psychological paralysis. These items are included in the section on self-concept (See Appendix A_3.) In accordance with my hypothesis, subjects' scores on the measure of psychological paralysis showed a sense of complete lack of control over their lives upon entering counseling. The effects of the intervention model on the psychological paralysis of the women were striking upon termination of counseling. According to both their own reports and their counselors' after completing services, they felt mostly in control of their lives; they thought they could probably "make it" in society; they felt mostly able to change the things in their lives that were problems for them; they felt they had the energy to change those things in their lives that are problems; and they mostly felt not trapped. (See Table 14-1 for the specific changes on those scales starred in the self-concept section.)

4. LEARNING LIFE SKILLS

The fourth area of concern in dealing with prostitutes who are victims of sexual assault revolves around those women who need and want to work in great depth with many of the problems interwoven with sexual abuse in their lives. That is, after reversing some of the negative impacts of sexual assault on prostitute victims, and after helping women overcome the motivational deficit to change attendant to psychological paralysis by gaining a sense of control over their lives, there may be some very serious real-life needs for these women to relearn a way to live legitimately and successfully in society. Women may require not only psychological strength and the development of a positive self-concept to live their lives as they choose, they may equally require retraining in vocational skills, education, interpersonal relationships, and a myriad of practical social survival skills.

It is important to recognize among those coming for help those who would like to go beyond dealing only with the presenting problem of sexual abuse. As in other aspects of treating prostitutes there is little available on their treatment in the research literature from which to develop a model. What does exist is primarily based on single-case studies, or often only theoretical overviews of the problem. Since there are a number coming for treatment who want a full range of services, it becomes important to set up a large-scale network with a range of support services and practical skills. In the last 12 years, Delancey Street has treated over 1000 women prostitutes in an intensive residential program of complete reeducation.

Dolores was a 20-year-old Latina who came to Delancey Street immediately following a suicide attempt off the ledge of a high-rise condominium. She entered Delancey Street in complete despair. "I knew of only two choices available to me at that moment. I was going to try to get into Delancey Street, but I didn't know if they would take me. I was in pretty bad shape at the time, physically and every other way. If they wouldn't take me, I was heading directly for the Golden Gate Bridge."

From the time she was 13 until she was 20, Dolores essentially lived on the streets prostituting. She had attempted suicide several times, and had been in and out of ten different rehabilitation programs. She had left school in the eighth grade, was unskilled and unschooled. Her first suicide attempt, at the age of 11, followed several years of sexual exploitation by her father. Because suicide was considered by her mother's church as the ultimate act against God, her mother had her committed to a state mental hospital while the rest of the family left the United States and returned to Puerto Rico.

When Dolores entered Delancey Street, she promised (as all residents must) to stay two years; and she intended (as we believe all residents do) to stay only a few months, clean up, and then leave. The residents of the Delancey Street Foundation,[6] like Dolores, are the hard-core helpless. These are traditionally considered by society to be unamenable to treatment and considered by themselves to be beyond help and beneath hope.

Begun in 1971 with a $1000 loan, and a commitment to receive no government funds but rather to earn its own way in society, Delancey Street currently has 350 residents earning their own way, living in several buildings in San Francisco at no cost to the taxpayers. A rural facility in northern New Mexico, started in 1977, houses an additional 100 residents. About an hour out of New York City is the newest Delancey Street, acquired in 1980, with about 20 residents. The population averages about one-third black, one-third Latin, and one-third Anglo, with occasional small percentages of American Indian, Asian, and other racial and ethnic groups. Residents range in age from 13 to 73, with about one-fourth to one-third being women prostitutes the others are male offenders, drug addicts, alcoholics, and children.

The treatment program is a unique combination of residential rehabilitation and community work designed to change customary patterns of interaction with society. In order to break the cycle of poverty–prostitution–self-destruction–

---

[6] For a description of the Delancey Street Foundation, see Silbert, "Delancey Street Foundation: A-Process of Mutual Restitution," written for Gartner & Reissman, eds., *Mental Health & the Self-Help Revolution,* Human Science Press, 1980; and Hampden-Turner, Charles, *Sane Asylum: Inside the Delancey Street Foundation,* San Francisco Book Company, San Francisco, 1976.

victimization, it is not enough that the prostitute's personality be treated in isolation, nor that she be kept as a marginally functional member of society. Such interruptions of her life-style are tenuous at best and leave untouched the prostitute's need to develop her strengths, her abilities, and her role in society neither as a victim nor as someone trapped in a life-style she did not choose.

Delancey Street's program begins with a total break in the woman's current pattern. She moves from a street subculture into a tightly structured community where she begins a process of complete reeducation. This process involves leaderless group encounter sessions three times a week, in-house education consisting of vocational training in eight training school/businesses whose student workers prepare for careers in accounting, managing of restaurants and catering services, automotive maintenance and antique car restoration, advertising specialty sales, handcrafts, terrariums, woodwork production and sales, and moving and long-distance hauling operations.

All the women are tutored, and acquire an education equivalent to that represented by a high school diploma. Those who elect to go on to college may do so. To date, women who came in as high school dropouts have gone on to complete numerous advanced business programs, and to receive a law degree, a master's degree, nursing credentials, and numerous other more practical degrees and certificates.

Women are also trained in social survival skills. Every morning and every noon at a daily seminar they study vocabulary words and concepts (for example, Emerson's essay on self-reliance). They learn the basics of money management and of our economic system; civics; archaeology and anthropology; etiquette, fashion, clothing, style; sources of energy; consumer awareness; ecology; all the concepts and ideas that provide us with the tools to lead a well-rounded life. These sessions are presented in seminar fashion where each participant speaks for a few minutes on the subject being discussed. This way they learn not only the content of subject matter but also the process of group speaking, of presenting an idea, and connecting a theory to a personal experience.

Training in interpersonal relations is one of the central areas of education in Delancey Street. The majority of residents have a very difficult time interacting with others, have no trust in other people, and have never really maintained a close relationship with anyone. The formal method for learning interpersonal skills is the group process in which residents must participate three times weekly for three to four hours each session. Here residents explore their feelings for another and their actions and behavior toward one another. They learn how the impact of what they say and do can be brought into greater congruence with what they hope to communicate to others.

Perhaps one of the most difficult areas of education in Delancey Street has to do with educating the self. It stresses the fact that the positive self-concept that each of these women lacks upon entry must be earned, not talked into existence.

Rather than simply enshroud the negative self-concept with responses of support from others, residents replace self-hate with self-respect by acting in such a way as to earn it and also earn positive reinforcement from others. In the tightly structured environment of Delancey Street residents who follow the rules cannot help but succeed.

Because there is no formal staff at Delancey Street, there is no we-they division. Everyone works. Every resident is also a staff of some sort to newer residents. The rules apply equally to everyone. Therefore everyone is both a giver and a receiver. Everyone has a role model to look up to and everyone struggles to be a role model to the newer residents. This process of people working *with* one another, rather than *for* one another, is critical to the integrity of the program and to the treatment process itself. It is a program in which people with no sense of self-worth feel needed, useful, and important to others, and can develop a sense of dignity about themselves and the work they are doing, not only in their own lives but in helping those around them to change.

The big change that takes place here is that the women are finally able to reverse the sense of helplessness and hopelessness, the sense that the consequences of life are random and have nothing to do with one's behavior, so that it is useless to try. The Delancey Street process is geared to teach the women that they do in fact have some control over the successes and failures of their experiences. They begin to gain control over their lives and lose the feeling that they are trapped and victimized.

Dolores has been at Delancey Street for three years now. She originally remained out of fascination and manipulation. Now she sees people she knew as losers on the street living in San Francisco's most exclusive residential area, well groomed, and well dressed. She believed, "There must be some game going on at Delancey Street," and planned to stay to get in on it. Before she realized it, she had internalized enough of the processes that she had been imitating that she began to rethink her old attitudes. She had worked long enough and hard enough to see herself gaining skills and work habits and being successful in the different jobs she had held. She had been confronted about herself often enough by her peers during group therapy to come to take responsibility both for the problems she had created and for the successes she was achieving. In short, Dolores experienced something new; she saw a small hope for herself. Instead of playing the "cure game" while knowing secretly that she would always stay a failure, Dolores began to believe that she could and would change. And then she stayed at Delancey Street for the right reason: to redo her life.

Dolores is currently working as secretary to the president's office. She has been licensed to drive a truck; she has learned bookkeeping. She is attending college, and serves as a counselor and role model for women who are new to the foundation. She was an interviewer on the prostitution study, and was recently appointed by the President of the United States to serve on the National Juvenile

Justice Commission. Perhaps more important, Dolores is beginning to be free of the debilitating impact of the past and her psychological paralysis. She is beginning to trust, and she is beginning to learn to be close to people.

Along with learning business and legal skills Dolores is particularly excited by the fact that she heads the Crisis Outreach Service for prostitute victims of sexual assault. "When Mimi picked me to do this, I can't remember being more excited. I know that when you're out there on the streets, you can't let yourself believe anything else is possible, because you don't believe you could make it any other way. But if I could reach just one of them to let them see. I know I'm like a living proof that anything and everything is possible. If someone as messed up as I was could get out of that gutter, truly anybody could with the right support and the right environment. I know there's no way of undoing the years of abuse and molestation, of guilt and hatred, and all the things I did to people as well. But Delancey Street has taught me how to take control of my life and not to let the past cripple me ever again. I have turned myself into someone I want to be, and never again will I have to be trapped by what I used to be. If I can show that to one girl — just one girl — out there on the street. . . ."

Appendix A

INITIAL CLIENT QUESTIONNAIRE

(1): 1

(2-4) Service recipient number: _____

(5) Service utilized:
1. Individual counseling
2. Group counseling
3. Individual and group counseling
4. Other: _____

(6) Counselor:
1. Teri
2. Auristela
3. Charlotte
4. Alice
5. Mimi
6. Other: _____

(7-12) Date of interview: _____

(13-16) Total time of interview (in minutes): _____

Background Information

(17-18) Age: _____

(19) Race:
1. Black
2. White
3. Latina
4. Asian
5. American Indian
6. Other: _____

(20) Current financial situation:
1. Very poor
2. Just making it
3. Average
4. Comfortable
5. Very wealthy

(21) Present marital status:
1. Married
2. Common law
3. Separated
4. Widowed
5. Divorced
6. Single; never married
7. Gay relationship
8. Other relationship
9. Other: _____

(22) Number of children: _____

(23) Present living arrangement:
   1. Living with husband/common law/boyfriend
   2. Living with pimp/madam
   3. Living with parents
   4. Living with relatives
   5. Living with friends
   6. Living in a residential facility
   7. In transit
   8. No place to live
   9. Other: _____

(24) Sexual preference:
   1. Heterosexual (prefer man)
   2. Homosexual (prefer women)
   3. Bisexual (like both)
   4. Asexual (neither)
   5. Other: _____

(25) Do you use drugs?

1	2	3	4	5
Never	Very rarely	Occasionally	Quite often	All the time

(26) What drugs?
   1. Heroin
   2. LSD/mescaline/hallucinogens
   3. Methadone
   4. Dust/THC/PCP
   5. Cocaine
   6. Stimulants/amphetamines/uppers/speed
   7. Sedatives/barbiturates/Valium/downers
   8. Marijuana or derivatives
   9. Other: _____

(27–29) For how long? _____ (months)

(30) Have you been:
   1. Raped
   2. Sexually assaulted (juvenile)
   3. Both
   4. Neither

(31) If neither, did you experience other situations in your background that cause you problems now?
   1. Yes
   2. No

General description of rape/juvenile assault or other problem:

_____

_____

_____

(For problem other than rape/assault, go to Question No. 44.)

(32) If rape or assault, who was the assailant?
    1. Father   4. Family friend
    2. Brother   5. Acquaintance
    3. Other relative   6. Stranger

(33) Was more than one person involved?
    1. Yes
    2. No

(34) If yes, how many? _____

(35–36) How old were you at the time? _____

(37–38) For juvenile assault only:
How many times did he assault you?
(1 = once, 2 = twice, etc.) _____
Over what period of time? _____ (Months)

(39–41) Acts of violence involved (e.g., held down, locked up, threatened, promised, implied it was your duty, beaten)
    1. _____   6. _____
    2. _____   7. _____
    3. _____   8. _____
    4. _____   9. _____
    5. _____   10. _____

(42–43) Total number of acts of violence: _____

(44) Were you injured?
    1. Yes
    2. No

(45) If yes, how seriously?
    1. Broken bones
    2. Cuts requiring medical attention
    3. Cuts not requiring medical attention
    4. Bruises requiring medical attention
    5. Injuries to genital area
    6. Injuries on face or body
    7. Bruises not requiring medical attention
    8. Shock
    9. Other: _____

Do you have, as a result of the rape/assault or other problem:

(46) Menstrual difficulties: 1. Yes _____   2. No _____

(47) Sleep problems: 1. Yes _____   2. No _____

(48) Aches and pains: 1. Yes _____   2. No _____

(49) Some other problem: 1. Yes _____   2. No _____

If yes, please describe: _____

_____

_____

(50) Total number of other problems mentioned: _____

Rape/Assault Impact (Emotional)

To what extent are you experiencing any of the following emotions? Indicate the number that best describes the degree to which the rape/assault or other problem made you experience:

1	2	3	4	5
Not at all	A little	Average	Rather strongly	Very strongly

(51) Fear _____

(52) Helplessness _____

(53) Hopelessness _____

(54) Anger (toward the rapist); thoughts about killing him _____

(55) Shock; disbelief _____

(56) Unhappiness; depression _____

(57) Relief to be alive _____

(58) Hatred (toward men in general) _____

(59) Numbness; nothing _____

(60) Shame; embarrassment _____

(61) Guilt; self-blame _____

Other emotional reactions to the rape/assault or other problem:

_____

_____

_____

_____

Rape/Assault Impact (Mental)

To what extent is the rape/assault or other problem affecting your mental attitudes? Indicate the number that best describes the degree to which it is affecting your attitudes toward:

1	2	3	4	5
Strong negative effect	Moderate negative	No effect	Moderate positive	Strong positive effect

(62) Yourself _____

(63) Men _____

(64) Sex _____

(65) Emotional relationships _____

(66) Friendships _____

(67) Your life _____

(68) Your future _____

Explain "strong negative effects": _____

_____

_____

Other mental impacts of the rape/assault or other problem:

_____

_____

_____

_____

(69) To what extent did the rape/assault affect your decision to enter prostitution? _____

1	2	3	4	5
Not at all	Not much	Neither yes nor no	Moderately	Very strongly

(70) Tranquilizers _____

(71) Alcohol _____

(72) Cigarettes _____

(73) Illegal drugs (marijuana, cocaine, uppers, downers, heroin) _____

(74) Sleeping pills _____

What behavioral changes occurred in your life as a result of the rape/assault (e.g., stopped going to certain places, ran away, obtained a weapon?

1. _____

2. _____

3. _____

4. _____

5. _____

(75–76) Total number of behavioral changes mentioned:

(77) How do you feel about yourself *in general*?

1	2	3	4	5
Very negative	Slightly negative	Mixed	Slightly positive	Very positive

(78) How do you feel about yourself *right now*?

1	2	3	4	5
Very negative	Slightly negative	Mixed	Slightly positive	Very positive

(79) How do you feel about *people* around you?

1	2	3	4	5
Very negative	Slightly negative	Mixed	Slightly positive	Very positive

(80) How do you feel about your *life*?

1	2	3	4	5
Very negative	Slightly negative	Mixed	Slightly positive	Very positive

(1): 2

(2–4) Subject number: _____

(5) Do you feel in *control* of your life?

1	2	3	4	5
Not at all	Mostly no	Not sure	Mostly yes	Very much

(6) Do you think you can *"make it"* in society?

1	2	3	4	5
Definitely not	Probably not	Not sure	Probably yes	Definitely yes

(7) Do you think you have the *skills* to "make it"?

1	2	3	4	5
Definitely not	Probably not	Not sure	Probably yes	Definitely yes

(8) What do you think your *future* will be like?

1	2	3	4	5
Very bad	Not so good	Not sure	Not so bad	Very good

(9) Do you feel self-*confident*?

1	2	3	4	5
Not at all	Not very	Not sure	Quite	Very much

(10) Do you feel *proud* of yourself?

1	2	3	4	5
Not at all	Not very	Not sure	Quite	Very much

(11) Do you think you have the *motivation* and will power to make it in society?

1	2	3	4	5
Definitely not	Not much	Not sure	Yes; sure	Definitely yes

(12) Are you able to *communicate* well with people?

1	2	3	4	5
Definitely not	Not very well	Not sure	Yes; somewhat	Definitely yes

(13) How *able* do you feel to change the things in your life that are problems to you?

1	2	3	4	5
Totally unable to change my problems	Mostly unable to change my problems	Neither able nor unable to change problems	Mostly able to change my problems	Totally able to change my problems

(14) How much *energy* do you think you have to change the things in your life that are problems for you?

1	2	3	4	5
No energy at all; feel paralyzed to change problems	Not much energy; feel somewhat paralyzed to change	Feel neither energized nor paralyzed to change	Some energy to change problems	Extremely energized to change

(15) How *trapped* do you feel in your problems?

1	2	3	4	5
Totally trapped	Somewhat trapped	Neither yes nor no	Mostly not trapped	Not trapped at all

(16) Is there *someone* you can *talk to* about everything?

    1. Yes _____

    2. No _____

(17) If yes, who? _____

(18) Total number of people mentioned: _____

(19) Is there someone you can *turn to* when you are in trouble?

    1. Yes _____

    2. No _____

(20) If yes, who? _____

(21-22) Total number of people mentioned: _____

Appendix B

MIDPOINT CLIENT QUESTIONNAIRE

(1): 4

(2-4) Service recipient number: _____

(5) Service utilized:
   1. Individual counseling
   2. Group counseling
   3. Individual and group counseling
   4. Other: _____

(6) Counselor:
   1. Teri
   2. Auristela
   3. Charlotte
   4. Alice
   5. Mimi
   6. Other: _____

(7-12) Date of interview: _____

(13-16) Total time in counseling (in hours): _____

(17) Are you still experiencing any physical impacts of the rape/assault or other problem (e.g., bruises, sleep problems, menstrual difficulties)? If yes, what?
   1. _____
   2. _____
   3. _____
   4. _____
   5. _____
   6. _____

(18-19) Total number of problems mentioned: _____

To what extent are you experiencing any of the following emotions?

1	2	3	4	5
Not at all	A little	Average	Rather strongly	Very strongly

(20) Fear _____

(21) Helplessness _____

(22) Hopelessness _____

(23) Anger (toward the rapist) _____

(24) Shock; disbelief _____

(25) Unhappiness; depression _____

(26) Relief to be alive _____

(27) Hatred toward men in general _____

(28) Numbness; nothing _____

(29) Shame; embarrassment _____

(30) Guilt; self-blame _____

Other emotional reactions to the rape/assault or other problem still remaining:

_____

_____

_____

_____

To what extent is the rape/assault or problem still affecting your mental attitudes toward the following:

1	2	3	4	5
Strong negative effect	Moderate negative	No effect	Moderate positive	Strong positive effect

(31) Yourself _____

(32) Men _____

(33) Sex _____

(34) Emotional relationships _____

(35) Friendships _____

(36) Your life _____

(37) Your future _____

(38) Prostitution _____

Other mental impacts:

_____

_____

_____

_____

Explain "strong negative effects":

_____

_____

_____

_____

Are you still experiencing a change in your use of the following substances, since the rape?

1	2	3	4	5
Much less	Slightly less	No change	Slightly more	Much more

(39) Tranquilizers, sleeping pills _____

(40) Alcohol _____

(41) Cigarettes _____

(42) Drugs (marijuana, cocaine, uppers, downers, heroin) _____

(43) Are you still noting the behavioral changes that occurred in your life as a result of the rape/assault or other problem?

1. Yes _____ 2. No. _____ 3. Some, but not as much _____

What changes?

1. _____

2. _____

3. _____

4. _____

(44) Total number of behavioral changes mentioned _____

Self-concept

(45) How do you feel about yourself *in general*?

1	2	3	4	5
Very negative	Slightly negative	Mixed	Slightly positive	Very positive

(46) How do you feel about yourself *right now*;

1	2	3	4	5
Very negative	Slightly negative	Mixed	Slightly positive	Very positive

(47) How do you feel about the *people* around you?

1	2	3	4	5
Very negative	Slightly negative	Mixed	Slightly positive	Very positive

(48) How do you feel about your *life*?

1	2	3	4	5
Very negative	Slightly negative	Mixed	Slightly positive	Very positive

(49) Do you feel in *control* of your life?

1	2	3	4	5
Not at all	Mostly no	Not sure	Mostly yes	Very much

(50) Do you think you *can "make it"* in society?

1	2	3	4	5
Definitely not	Probably not	Not sure	Probably yes	Definitely yes

(51) Do you think you have the *skills* to "make it?

1	2	3	4	5
Definitely not	Probably not	Not sure	Probably yes	Definitely yes

(52) What do you think your *future* will be like?

1	2	3	4	5
Very bad	Not so good	Not sure	Not so bad	Very good

(53) Do you feel self-*confident*?

1	2	3	4	5
Not at all	Not very	Not sure	Quite	Very much

(54) Do you feel *proud* of yourself?

1	2	3	4	5
Not at all	Not very	Not sure	Quite	Very much

(55) Do you think you have the *motivation* and will power to make it in society?

1	2	3	4	5
Definitely not	Not much	Not sure	Yes; sure	Definitely yes

(56) Are you able to *communicate* well with people?

1	2	3	4	5
Definitely not	Not very well	Not sure	Yes; somewhat	Definitely yes

(57) How *able* do you feel to change the things in your life that are problems for you?

1	2	3	4	5
Totally unable to change my problems	Mostly unable to change my problems	Neither able nor unable to change problems	Mostly able to change my problems	Totally able to change my problems

(58) How much *energy* do you think you have to change the things in your life that are problems for you?

1	2	3	4	5
No energy at all; feel paralyzed to change problems	Not much energy; feel somewhat paralyzed to change	Feel neither energized nor paralyzed to change	Some energy to change problems	Extremely energized to change

(59) How *trapped* do you feel in your problems?

1	2	3	4	5
Totally trapped	Somewhat trapped	Neither yes nor no	Mostly not trapped	Not trapped at all

(60) Is there *someone* you can *talk to* about everything?
1. Yes _____ 2. No _____

(61) If yes, who? _____

(62–63) Total number of people mentioned: _____

(64) Is there someone you can *turn to* when you are in trouble?
1. Yes _____ 2. No _____

(65) If yes, who? _____

(66–67) Total number of people mentioned: _____

(68) Did you notice any changes in yourself as a result of these meetings?

1	2	3
Yes	No	Not sure

(69) If yes, were they
1. Positive changes   2. Negative changes

(70) Did you experience changes in your emotional state (e.g., more or less helpless, hopeless)?

1	2	3	4	5
Very negative change	Slight negative change	No change	Slight positive change	Very positive change

Explain response in detail: _____

_____

_____

(71) Did you experience changes in your behavior (doing more/less or different things)?

1	2	3	4	5
Very negative change	Slight negative change	No change	Slight positive change	Very positive change

Did you experience changes in your mental state (attitudes toward yourself, other people, sex, etc.)?

1	2	3	4	5
Very negative change	Slight negative change	No change	Slight positive change	Very positive change

Explain response in detail: _____

_____

_____

Any other changes? _____

_____

Index